ONE
—— FOR ——
ALL!

ONE
— FOR —
ALL!

**FAVOURITE DISHES
ADAPTED
FOR SPECIAL DIETS**

Pam Dotter

Columbus Books
London

Acknowledgements The author would like to thank Jill
Metcalfe, Chief Dietician of the British Diabetic Association
for her help in compiling the diabetic adaptations, Dilys
Wells for her assistance with the dietary calculations and
also Rita Greer for her help with the gluten/wheat-free
adaptations.

Note The dietary symbols used in this book
were devised by Rita Greer, and some of them
can be found on commercial food products.

First published in Great Britain in 1987 by
Columbus Books Limited
19-23 Ludgate Hill, London EC4M 7PD

Design concept by Gwyn Lewis
Typography by Pat Craddock

British Library Cataloguing in Publication Data
Dotter, Pam
    One for all!: favourite dishes adapted for special diets.
    1. Cookery for dietary problems
    I. Title
    641.5'63   RM219

ISBN 0-86287-298-7

Phototypeset by Falcon Graphic Art Ltd
Wallington, Surrey

Printed and bound by
R.J. Acford, Chichester, Sussex.

Contents

Introduction

Food habits are established early in life. Many of us have fond memories of childhood meals and rate Mum as the best cook ever, so we tend to stick to the tastes, eating habits and types of food that we grew up with. But lifestyles and the pace of life have changed. Far fewer women are now at home all day producing wholesome cooked meals from basic, raw ingredients, so supermarkets sell an inviting selection of attractively packaged foods that need the minimum of preparation. There is more choice, but sometimes we do not choose wisely and we are guilty of eating unbalanced meals that are high in sugar and saturated fat, which can be detrimental to our health. And because we now eat so many more processed foods, which often have a high artificial-additive content, the incidence of food allergies has been very much on the increase in recent years. Also very common, and showing no signs of a decline, are diabetes and coeliac disease (intolerance of gluten and wheat), which are treated to a large extent by carefully regulated diets. Heart disease is one of the many medical conditions that can benefit from a diet low in saturated fat – from which we would all benefit. Other conditions require diets that are higher in fibre than usual, while the answer to food allergies caused by artificial additives lies in the provision of a diet as free of such additives as one can humanly make it. Then there is the vegetarian diet: whether chosen on health or on ideological grounds, this is a regime that requires careful attention to protein intake and replacement of the nutrients that would otherwise be part of a diet incorporating meat.

These, then, are some of the most common 'special diets', followed by thousands upon thousands of us either permanently or for a period in our lives. Probably the individual on the special diet is just one member of a family or household: how does the meal-provider of that household cope? Does she produce two different meals, or version of the meal, every day? Or is there some way of avoiding that double-the-effort treadmill and keeping both the odd-man-out and the rest of the family happy?

The answer is yes: you can produce delicious meals for the whole family that are also suitable for your 'special diet' diner because you have, in this book, the key to the adaptation. The recipes chosen cover all meals, including snacks and suppers and the 'cakes and bakes' that we all like, regardless of our diet, to indulge in from time to time – after all, what would life be like if we could never have the occasional treat? So you will find here a great many of your old favourites, the dishes you grew up with, including some seasonal 'musts' such as pancakes, Christmas cake and pudding, mince pies and hot cross buns. You will also find some exciting not-so-familiar recipes to try out. And alongside each basic recipe you will find these symbols:

d	diabetic
	gluten/wheat-free
	saturated fat-free
	non-essential additive-free
	higher-fibre
	vegetarian

together with instructions on how to adapt for each of these special diets – which often boils down

7

simply to making it 'healthier' and more in line with modern nutritional guidelines.

What this means is that instead of finding that your gastronomic horizons have been substantially curtailed by the necessity to follow a special diet, you may well find them widened beyond all imagining.

All the adapted recipes produce just as delicious a result as the standard dish, and if you are simply looking for a generally healthier diet, with less emphasis, perhaps, on meat, more on fibre and as little saturated fat as possible, you will find the adaptations in this book a useful guide. Slimmers will probably wish to opt for a combination of the higher-fibre and saturated-fat-free modifications.

Otherwise, the featured dietary modifications are as follows.

Diabetic Diet

The recipes are calculated in terms of grams of carbohydrate (CHO) and calorie content, and follow the recommendations of the Nutrition Sub-committee of the British Diabetic Association (see page 9).

Diabetics are unable to change sugar into energy within their bodies. Whether or not they are insulin-dependent, they need to follow a carefully regulated diet aimed at keeping the level of sugar in the blood as near normal as possible. There is no one diet, because diabetics vary in age, weight, activity levels and in the type of medication they need. Each diabetic will have received dietary guidelines from his or her doctor, but generally the advice is to cut out sugar and sugary foods as far as possible and to include starchy foods such as bread (particularly wholemeal) and potatoes, because these foods break down into sugar in the body more slowly than refined foods. High-calorie fatty foods are discouraged. All in all, a diabetic diet is simply a healthy diet – one which the whole family would benefit from following.

The aim of a diabetic diet is to balance the amount of insulin available with the diet and activities of the sufferer and thus keep the blood sugar at the normal level. While it is the carbohydrates that have the quickest and most direct effect on the glucose content of the blood, all aspects of the diet must be considered. It is important for diabetics not to become – or continue to be – overweight, because insulin, whether taken by tablet or by injection, becomes less effective if the sufferer is obese, and obesity makes it more difficult to get the balance right.

The British Diabetic Association's general guidelines are as follows:

(1) Cut down on sugar and sugary foods.
(2) Include reasonable quantities of carbohydrate foods, particularly those high in fibre, for fibre slows down the absorption of carbohydrates, helping to control the rate at which glucose enters the bloodstream.
(3) Cut down on fats and fatty foods. As well as being high in calories, too much fat in the diet is known to be bad for the heart and the circulation.
(4) If alcohol is permitted, take it only in moderation. Avoid sugary drinks such as liqueurs, sweet wines, including sweet sherries, port and sweet vermouths. Choose dry wine, dry aperitifs, ordinary beer, lager or cider. If drinking spirits, such as whisky, rum or gin, dilute with sugar-free mixers or water. Never have more than three drinks in any one day and never drink and drive.

A selection of these foods should form the basis of all meals: wholemeal bread, wholewheat pasta, brown rice; fresh or frozen fruits and vegetables; canned fruits in natural juice; lean meat and poultry with the fat removed; fish; reduced-fat spreads and low- or reduced-fat cheeses; skimmed or semi-skimmed milk; low-fat yoghurts.

The following foods should be eaten only occasionally: white bread and other white-flour products; prepared pies, pasties and savoury flans; fatty meats and sausages, pâtés and spreads; full-fat dairy foods such as full-fat milk, cheese, yoghurt and cream cheese; spreads such as margarine; butter; nuts; fruit juices and alcoholic drinks.

Certain foods are best avoided as far as possible: sugar, glucose, sugary foods, including sweets and chocolate; canned fruits in syrup, sweetened drinks; cakes and pastries; prepared sweetened puddings and instant desserts.

Diabetics are usually given a list of foods with

their carbohydrate content. For convenience, 10 g of carbohydrate (CHO) is normally counted as a unit for exchanging one carbohydrate food for another. Thus, the diet can be varied and the daily ration of carbohydrate kept constant. If weight loss is essential a calorie allowance may be recommended as well or instead of a CHO plan. Each diabetic recipe in the book has its total carbohydrate (CHO) and calorie content listed so that they may be included in the individual daily meal plan.

Fitting in with family meals should be no problem, because the diabetic diet is good for the whole family, especially if there are weight problems. High fibre, low fat and low sugar are the requirements of a slimming diet, too, and slimmers can follow the diabetic modifications with success.

Special foods for diabetics

Many chemists' shops and healthfood stores sell special foods for diabetics. Apart from artificial sweeteners to replace sugar, these special foods are by no means necessary for a diabetic diet. In fact, many of them are high in fat and offer no calorie saving – which makes them unsuitable for those who must lose weight. This is particularly true of the confectionery items. The British Diabetic Association has successfully campaigned for new legislation and labelling. Now products must state that they are not suitable for the overweight diabetic if they do not offer at least a 50 per cent saving in calories when compared with the standard product.

Sugar substitutes Fructose (fruit sugar) is the most natural and flavoursome substitute for sugar. It contains the same number of calories as ordinary sugar, but as it is almost twice as sweet, less is required. The British Diabetic Association recommends that no more than 1 oz/25 g is eaten in any one day because in larger quantities it may affect control.

Sorbitol This can also be used for baking and jam-making. It has the same number of calories but is less sweet than sugar and is a powerful laxative. Just as with fructose it must be limited to 1 oz/25 g per day.

Note The limit of 1 oz/25 g applies to one or other or a combination of both. It does not mean 1 oz/25 g of one *and* 1 oz/25 g of the other.

Intense or artificial sweeteners These are available in tablet and liquid form and are useful for hot and cold drinks. Powders are available for sprinkling on breakfast cereals and adding to uncooked desserts. As they contain bulking agents it is recommended that they are only used in small quantities. Saccharin breaks down during cooking; it loses its sweetness and becomes bitter when heated. A recently introduced sweetener, acesulfame K, has zero calories, leaves no bitter taste and remains sweet during cooking. Aspartame is another powerful sweetener that leaves no bitter aftertaste. Though it breaks down on heating it is satisfactory if stirred into hot dishes just before serving. These sweeteners are available under various brand names.

Further information on diabetic diets

Contact the British Diabetic Association, 10 Queen Anne Street, London W1M 0BD for information on progress in medical care for diabetics, basic dietary information and recipe booklets. Members receive a regular bi-monthly newspaper (*Balance*), which publishes the latest news and practical hints on day-to-day problems.

The British Diabetic Association also publishes a range of useful books, available from the above address: *Simple Diabetic Cookery; Better Cookery for Diabetics; Cooking the New Diabetic Way: the high-fibre calorie-conscious book;* and *Countdown* (information on ready-prepared foods). *The Diabetics' Cookbook* (Martin Dunitz) by Roberta Longstaff and Jim Mann will also be found helpful.

Gluten/Wheat-free Diet

Wheat, rye, barley and oats are basic ingredients of a normal diet, yet many people are allergic to them, including sufferers from coeliac disease (often children) and, so some doctors claim, multiple sclerosis.

Another disorder is simply called wheat and gluten insensitivity, symptoms of which are muscle stiffness, aches, swelling of the joints, sneezing, eye-watering, a stuffed-up or running nose, chest pains, nausea, stomach pains and cramps, a swollen stomach, bloated feeling, sweating, tiredness, skin rashes and itches, throat troubles, swallowing difficulties and swollen throat. The sufferer may also be irritable, apathetic, depressed, moody and confused. In coeliac disease, the small intestine becomes damaged by gluten and the patient becomes malnourished and fails to thrive. Children fail to grow and are thin, weak and listless.

There is no drug treatment or cure but these symptoms disappear when wheat and gluten are removed from the diet. It is usually a diet for life. Dietary advice and meal plans will be provided by the doctor on diagnosis, but the diet is not an easy one to follow since so many of our foods are based on wheat flour, and so many manufactured food products contain wheat or gluten elements.

Gluten itself is part of the protein found only in wheat, rye, barley and oats. It is the rubbery binder that stretches to hold the bubbles of air as in bread-making. Most breads, cakes and pastries, the batter on fried fish, sausages, gravy powder, soups and soup mixes, pastes, spreads, sweets and breakfast cereals are just some of the many foods that contain gluten. Some pills and toothpaste do too. It is essential to read the labels on food products very carefully if you are trying to avoid gluten. A full list of gluten-containing foods and products will be provided by your doctor. (The Coeliac Society will also supply such a list, but only to those with a certificate to prove coeliac disease.)

Foods which are free of gluten include sago, rice, rice flour, maize flour (sometimes called cornflour, but not always wheat-free), soya flour, potato flour, split peas and split pea flour, nuts, fresh and dried fruit, vegetables, fats (but not packet shredded suet), eggs, meat, fish and cheese.

Special flour is available for baking bread, cakes, scones and biscuits. The method of preparation is very different because of the composition of the flour and special recipes must be followed.

These foods lack vitamins of the B complex and bran and may need to be supplemented in tablet form. Soya bran and rice bran can be used instead of wheat bran.

The main problem for the meal-provider who has to fit a gluten/wheat-free diet into normal family meals is that all bread, baked foods, pasta and stuffings need to be free of wheat and gluten, either just for the individual with the intolerance or for everyone.

Cakes and biscuits made with gluten/wheat-free flour are very good and can be enjoyed by all the family.

For breakfast, rice-based cereal and gluten/wheat-free bread can provide the answer. Otherwise, keep main meals simple, and replace wheat-flour thickenings or coatings with potato or rice flour. Serve a good portion of vegetables and fresh fruit or stewed fruit with cream or ground rice pudding or egg custard. (Use eggs sparingly, however.) Such meals should fit happily into the family's standard eating pattern.

When eating out, those with a gluten/wheat intolerance should take gluten-free bread with them and be careful to avoid all thickened sauces and gravies. If eating out privately, it is always wise to warn the hostess of the problem and to suggest suitable foods in advance. No one on such a diet should ever eat wheat-based food in the interests of 'good manners'.

All the gluten/wheat-free recipes in this book have been tested using Trufree special dietary flour, the composition of which is very different from ordinary wheat flour. The method of use is different, too, so for this reason some basic recipes (pages 214-23) have been reproduced from *The Gluten-free and Wheat-free Bumper Bake Book* (Bunterbird, see below) by kind permission of the author, Rita Greer.

Further information on gluten/wheat-free diets

Contact the Coeliac Society of Great Britain and Northern Ireland, PO Box 181, London NW2 2QY; the Energen Foods Company Ltd, 10 Victoria Road, London NW10 6NU; Rite-Diet Foods Ltd, Welfare Foods, Stockport, Cheshire; or, for information on Trufree and Jubilee flours, the Cantassium Company, 225 Putney Bridge Road, London SW15 2PY (this is also the address of the publisher Bunterbird Ltd).

Other useful books, besides Rita Greer's *Bumper Bake Book* (see above), include *Diets to Help Coeliacs and Wheat Sensitivity*, (Thorsons), also by Rita Greer, and Sainsbury's Food Guide *Modified Diets*, by Jill Leslie for the British Nutrition Foundation.

Saturated Fat-free Diet

Fat supplies more than twice as much energy weight for weight than other foods. One gram of fat releases 9 kilocalories and the same quantity of either protein or carbohydrate releases only 4 kilocalories. It therefore makes sense not only for those on slimming diets but for all of us to eat less fat.

The Committee on Medical Aspects of Food Policy (COMA) has recommended a reduction of 17 per cent in our fat intake, particularly our intake of saturated fats, which encourage cholesterol build-up in the blood. The accumulation of cholesterol is dangerous because it clogs up the arteries, which can cause coronary heart disease, one of the commonest causes of death in the Western world. Other factors which have been shown to contribute to this disease are smoking, lack of exercise and stress. Research shows that eating unsaturated rather than saturated fats can help to lower the cholesterol level of the blood.

To avoid such problems, choose low-fat foods wherever possible.

Fats Polyunsaturated fats can help to lower blood cholesterol. The main sources are oils from plant seeds – safflower, sunflower, corn oil and soya. Choose margarines that contain a high proportion of unsaturated fats. (Check the labels carefully: these are usually the soft margarines.) Eat bread either without butter or with a minimal amount of low-fat spread.

Dairy foods Choose low-fat polyunsaturated dairy foods to replace the saturated fats. Use skimmed milk instead of whole milk, and either low-fat yoghurt, skimmed milk, quark or fromage frais to replace cream and full-cream evaporated milk. Substitute low-calorie hard cheese such as Edam or curd cheese for the regular hard cheeses, or look for low-fat Cheddar. Cottage cheese, which is infinitely versatile as well as being low in fat (and calories), has the advantage of containing protein, calcium and vitamins too. Choose Camembert in preference to full-fat soft cheese.

Meat and poultry Cut all visible fat off meat and look out for low-fat joints and mince at the butchers. They may appear expensive, but remember you are not buying fat that you will only have to cut off. Poultry and rabbit are lower in fat than red meats. The fat is usually just under the skin, so remove it before cooking. Buy low-fat sausages, or make your own and grill them rather than frying. Make your own hamburgers, using lean mince.

Fish The fat in fish is relatively rich in polyunsaturates. Choose herrings, mackerel, or smoked fish such as kippers. Cook white fish by grilling, not frying.

Grocery products Choose low-calorie salad dressings or make your own with low-fat yoghurt and a squeeze of lemon juice, flavoured with fresh herbs or garlic. Chocolate contains cocoa butter – saturated fat – so use only small quantities of cocoa for flavouring; alternatively, replace with carob, obtainable from healthfood stores. Canned fish is now available in brine without added oil.

Foods to avoid These include whole milk, cream, flavoured milks, coffee creamer products, cream substitutes, butter, lard, suet, nuts, hard margarine, coconut, liver, kidney, luncheon meat, continental sausages, full-fat sausages, corned beef, duck, goose, rich butter sauces such as hollandaise and bearnaise, butter icings, pastry, cakes, hard cheese and cheese spreads. Eggs and egg yolks should be limited to three per week.

Cooking methods Grill instead of frying; spit-roast or roast meat on a rack to let the fat drain away. If you must have chips, use frozen oven chips and drain them on absorbent kitchen paper. Stir-fry instead of shallow frying: if you cut meat into thin pieces it will cook quickly in its own juice without needing more than a teaspoonful of oil to stop it sticking. For vegetables that need longer cooking, cover after stir-frying and steam. Steam food to keep it moist instead of roasting and basting with fat.

When eating out, those on a low-saturated-fat diet should, in restaurants, choose simple grilled food without sauces, ask for vegetables without butter and avoid chips. Have fresh fruit for dessert instead of cheese. For packed meals, use low-fat spread on the bread and pack a small carton of salad to add moisture. When eating with friends, avoid butter, gravy and sauces. Cut off all visible fat from meat and the skin from poultry. Choose fruit or, if on offer, a fresh fruit salad instead of rich, creamy desserts.

Further information on saturated fat-free diets
Contact the British Heart Foundation, 57 Gloucester Place, London W1H 4DH; the Chest, Heart and Stroke Association, Tavistock House North, Tavistock Square, London WC1H 9JE; or the Flora Project, 24-28 Bloomsbury Way, London WC1A 2PX. A useful book of recipes is *Low-fat Cookery* (Sainsbury's) by Wendy Godfrey.

Non-essential Additive-free Diet

Artificial and other non-essential food additives have been found to be the culprits for many health disorders. Some additives are used to maintain freshness and prevent spoilage. Preservatives kill the micro-organisms which cause decay and endanger health. They extend the shelf-life of products and preserve the natural colour of some foods. Sugar and salt are the traditional preservatives, but both are recognized to be bad for health, and some manufacturers have begun to look for alternative methods of preserving their products. Anti-oxidants (vitamin C, for example) prevent fat becoming rancid and fruit juice going brown.

Other additives are used to assist the processing and preparation of food. Emulsifiers and stabilizers, for example, are used when two ingredients in a product do not mix easily (oil and vinegar in salad cream are one instance). They are also added to ice cream and cakes to avoid the necessity for extra fat. Gelling agents, made from a natural base (for example, pectin made from apples), are added to improve the texture of food and to help jams set. There are also raising agents such as baking powder and anti-caking agents such as magnesium carbonate (which keeps salt running smoothly), bleaching agents, bulking agents, firming agents, flour improvers, freezants and glazing agents.

Additives that improve the flavour and appearance of food include natural sweeteners such as sucrose (ordinary sugar), dextrose, fructose (fruit sugar) and lactose (milk sugar), and artificial sweeteners which are used in low-calorie products. Then there are colours, flavours and flavour enhancers. Concentrated natural flavours are usually present as extracts or essential oils. Flavour enhancers such as monosodium glutamate intensify existing flavours.

Yet other additives actually improve the nutritional value of food: nutrients, usually vitamins, are added to replace those lost in processing or to fortify foods with nutrients that could be lacking in the diet. White flour is fortified (by law) to be equivalent in nutritive value to wholemeal bread, and margarine has vitamins A and D added to make it equivalent nutritionally to butter.

All additives used in the UK have been tested and those permitted within the EC have been given an 'E' number; by referring to published lists of E numbers (various books, some of them available free from supermarkets, explain what they mean), you can find out exactly what the food you are buying contains and can reject any that you prefer not to eat.

Children who are hyperactive are advised to avoid certain food additives, particularly food colourings and flavours, glutamates, nitrites and nitrates, BHA, BHT and benzoic acid, because these are likely to produce adverse reactions. Hyperactive children sleep for only a few hours at a time and may suffer from eczema, asthma, excessive thirst and respiratory difficulties.

The Hyperactive Children's Support Group recommends that the following E-numbered additives are avoided:

E102	Tartrazine	E110	Sunset yellow FCF
E104	Quinoline yellow	E120	Cochineal
107	Yellow 2G	E122	Carmoisine
E123	Amaranth	155	Brown HT
E124	Ponceau 4R	E210	Benzoic acid
E127	Erythrosine	E211	Sodium benzoate
128	Red 2G	E220	Sulphur dioxide
E132	Indigo carmine	E250	Sodium nitrite
E133	Brilliant blue FCF	E251	Sodium nitrate
E150	Caramel	E320	Butylated hydroxyanisole
E151	Black PN	E321	Butylated hydroxytoluene
154	Brown FK		

Asthmatics and aspirin-sensitive people may also be allergic to certain additives, and the following substances are generally agreed to be undesirable in the diets of babies and young children.

E212	Potassium benzoate
E213	Calcium benzoate
E214	Ethyl 4-hydroxybenzoate
E215	Ethyl 4-hydroxybenzoate, sodium salt
E216	Propyl 4-hydroxybenzoate
E217	Propyl 4-hydroxybenzoate, sodium salt
E218	Methyl 4-hydroxybenzoate
E219	Methyl 4-hydroxybenzoate, sodium salt
E310	Propyl gallate
E311	Octyl gallate
E312	Dodecyl gallate
621	Sodium hydrogen L-glutamate
622	Potassium hydrogen L-glutamate
623	Calcium dihydrogen di-L-glutamate
627	Guanosine 5^1 (disodium phosphate)
631	Inosine 5^1 (disodium phosphate)
635	Sodium 5^1 ribonucleotide

The easiest way to avoid non-essential additives is to avoid packaged and some canned products, prepared meat products (including sausages), 'fast foods', substitute foods such as packet desserts and artificial creams. Avoid flavour enhancers in stock cubes. Look out for products without added colouring. Shop at supermarkets that advertise additive-free own-brand products and read the labels of other products carefully. Wholemeal bread has fewer additives than white bread.

Home cooking enables you to do without most manufactured foods. You need not spend all day in the kitchen if you make your kitchen equipment work for you. For example, make bone stock in 10 minutes in a pressure cooker and store it in the refrigerator for up to two days or in the freezer for up to 3 months. Make cakes using the quick-mix method and a mixer (incidentally, if you paint food colourings on to iced cakes rather than adding the colouring to the icing, you will use only an insignificant amount). Make sauces by whisking all the ingredients together in a saucepan.

The recipes in this book will show you how to avoid additives and make your own 'fast food'.

Further information on avoiding additives

Contact the Secretary of the Hyperactive Children's Support Group, 59 Meadowside, Angmering, Sussex BN16 4BW, enclosing a s.a.e. An informative book to consult is *E for Additives* (Thorsons) by Maurice Hanssen.

Higher-fibre Diet

Fibre is the least digestible part of cereal grains and fruit and vegetables. It takes a bit more chewing than refined foods but has more satiety value. Bran is the fibre from wheat, oats, rice and rye that is often removed during milling.

A high-fibre diet adds bulk, makes you feel full for longer and is consequently good for slimmers. Fibre also slows down the rate of absorption of sugar, and is therefore recommended for diabetics. Current nutritional advice is that we should all eat more fibre. It can help us to avoid constipation, one of the most common complaints of Western society, and other disorders caused by eating too high a proportion of refined foods: diverticular disease, cancer of the colon, appendicitis, varicose veins and haemorrhoids, for example.

To include more fibre in the diet:

(1) Eat wholegrain bread, bread with added bran, pasta, breakfast cereals, rice.

(2) Adapt home-baked dishes to use wholemeal flour instead of white. (A little extra liquid will usually be required because the bran absorbs a high proportion of water. The recipes in this book show how to do this.)

(3) Add cereal bran to breakfast cereals and home-cooked dishes such as mince, stews and hamburgers.

(4) Eat more fresh fruit and vegetables. Include at least one green vegetable and one root vegetable with every meal. Eat some vegetables raw and serve plenty of salads mixing fruits, vegetables and nuts. High-fibre green vegetables include spinach.

(5) Include dried vegetables such as peas, beans, lentils, split peas, barley and brown rice in the diet.

(6) Make more use of dried fruit. Apricots, figs and prunes are particularly high in fibre. Serve them cooked together or use them in cakes instead of the more usual dried fruits.

(7) Serve baked beans on wholemeal toast for a high-fibre snack.

(8) Eat the peel or skin of potatoes, tomatoes, apples, pears and so on.

Many of the recipes in this book have a naturally high fibre content, but for those needing extra fibre follow the special modifications suggested.

Further information on fibre in the diet
Contact the Kellogg Company of Great Britain Ltd,
P.O. Box 278, Stretford, Manchester M32 8RA; or the
Flour Advisory Bureau, 21 Arlington Street, London
SW1A 1RN. Among many useful books containing
high-fibre recipes are *The F-plan Diet* (Penguin) by
Audrey Ayton, *The Wholemeal Kitchen* (Heinemann
for Booker Health Foods) by Miriam Polunin, *The
Beans and Lentil Cookbook* (Thorsons) by Pamela
Dixon and *Wholefood Cookery for Everyone* (Sains-
bury's) by Gail Duff.

Vegetarian Diet

Many people like to serve a non-meat meal at least
once a week in the interests of economy, good
nutrition and variety of flavour and texture. Others
decide to cut out meat altogether. Whatever the
reason for choosing to follow a meatless diet –
economy, aversion to eating flesh, preference for a
lighter, low-fat diet or for natural wholefoods – a
vegetarian diet is a very healthy one. The vegetarian
adaptations and recipes in this book concentrate on
fresh natural ingredients, whole grains, vegetable
proteins and dairy products. Some of the main
courses and snacks include fish, too (this and the
presence of dairy foods make the recipes unsuitable
for vegans). The diet represented by these recipes is
high in fibre and low in fat – particularly saturated
fat.

Meat is one of the main sources of protein in a
normal diet. Those who do not eat meat must ensure
that they take in enough protein from other sources.
The only foods which contain complete protein are
meat, fish, dairy products, eggs, tofu (beancurd) and
soya beans. Any one of these foods could provide
enough protein on its own for one meal. Vegetables
of the peas and beans family and grains all contain
proteins, but because these proteins are not complete
the two types of foods must be eaten together to
complement each other. A combination of proteins
will provide a balanced and interesting diet: for
example, either grains or peas and beans can be
served with dairy foods; baked beans on toast com-
bines beans and grain; bread can be served with a

bean casserole, perhaps as a topping with cheese or
garlic butter to add texture and flavour.

When time is short use canned beans, but it is
more economical to soak and cook a large quantity
and store the cooked beans, either in the refrigerator
or the freezer, until required. A pressure cooker is
useful for cooking beans, especially soya beans and
chick peas, which can take a long time to boil. An
easy way to cook a small quantity of dried peas or
beans is to leave them to soak overnight in a wide-
necked vacuum jar. Boil the soaked beans for 10
minutes, drain, then re-boil with fresh water, pour
into the warmed flask, seal and leave overnight.

Among the best foods for a vegetarian diet are:
Whole grains such as wholewheat flour and bread,
brown rice, ground brown rice and semolina, oats,
wholewheat pasta, bulgar (cracked wheat), barley,
oatmeal and wheatgerm.
Beans and peas All soya products, including tofu
(see below); also aduki beans, black beans, black
eyed peas, cannelini, chick peas or garbanzos, kidney beans, lentils, pintos, mung beans, split peas.
Some of these are delicious and very nutritious when
sprouted. As well as the familiar bean sprouts from
mung beans, try soya sprouts, lentils and chick peas.
Nuts and seeds Almonds, pecans, sesame seeds,
sunflower seeds, walnuts, hazelnuts, brazil nuts.
Dairy foods Rennet-free hard cheese is available, as
is low-fat hard cheese. Low-fat soft cheeses include
quark (skimmed-milk soft cheese), cottage cheese,
curd cheese, fromage frais and ricotta cheese.
Grocery products Vegetable bouillon cubes and
pastes can replace meat-based stock cubes. Vegetable
oils such as olive oil and safflower oil can be used for
salad dressings and peanut (groundnut) oil for
frying. Vegetable oil margarines: read the labels
carefully. Any that are polyunsaturated are made
from vegetable oils.
Tofu (soya beancurd) is an important food for
vegetarians, especially those who choose to avoid
dairy products. High in protein and low in fat, it can
be made at home or bought fresh from the dairy
section of a supermarket, healthfood store or oriental
food store. Tofu is bland and it takes up flavours
easily. It can be cooked in many different forms –
grilled or fried like a cutlet, or coated and deep

fat-fried like fish, for example; it can be marinated and eaten with a mixture of stir-fried vegetables; made into a sauce for serving on pasta, crumbled into salads, flavoured and used as a sandwich spread, or used as a base for low-fat desserts to replace cream. Its uses are almost endless.

It is not difficult to incorporate vegetarian meals into the family's normal regime, and everyone will benefit from eating vegetable fats and wholefoods and lots of vegetables and salads. The meat portion of the meal can be replaced with tofu, fish, cheese, eggs or beans.

Further information on vegetarian diets

Contact the Vegetarian Society of the United Kingdom Ltd, Parkdale, Dunham Road, Altrincham, Cheshire. Among the many books available that contain good vegetarian recipes are *First Steps in Vegetarian Cooking* by Kathy Silk, *The Vegetarian on a Diet* by Margaret Cousins and Jill Metcalfe, *The Magic of Tofu* by Jane O'Brien and *Pulse Cookery* by Pamela Dixon. All of these titles are published by Thorsons.

Notes on the recipes

(1) All weights are for items before preparation and cooking *unless* specifically stated otherwise in the recipe.
(2) Standard eggs, size 3, are used throughout.
(3) Though semi-skimmed milk is specified in all the recipes, if skimmed milk is used instead the calorie savings will be:

for each tablespoonful:	.75
per ¼ pint (125 ml):	6.25
per ½ pint (250 ml):	12.5
per 1 pint (500 ml):	25

(4) If whole milk is used, additional calories will be:

for each tablespoonful:	3.30
per ¼ pint (125 ml):	22.5
per ½ pint (250 ml):	55
per 1 pint (500 ml):	110

The weights of ingredients are listed in both imperial and metric measures. Please follow one or the other, otherwise the recipes will not work.

'Vecon' is a trade name for concentrated vegetable extract. Any brand may be used.

'Trufree' and 'Jubilee' are trade names for the particular brand of gluten-free flour on which the gluten/wheat-free recipes in this book have been based. No two types of gluten-free flour behave in exactly the same way, so you may find that you need to adapt if you use a different brand.

Soups

Make a meal more satisfying by serving soup as a first course. Alternatively, serve a large, steaming bowl of soup with bread for a snack. These soups are quick to make and easy to adapt to the special diets featured.

Bacon and bean soup   26
Chicken and vegetable soup   24
Country kitchen soup   23
Lentil, orange and carrot soup   22
Minestrone soup   21
Quick cream of mushroom soup   27
Quick leek and potato soup   25
Scotch broth   18
Tomato soup   20
Vegetable and bean soup   24
Vegetable and lentil soup   19

Scotch Broth

Special Diets

Serves 4: 215 calories per portion

- 1 lb/500 g middle neck of lamb
- 1 oz/25 g pearl barley
- 2 level teaspoons salt
- ¼ level teaspoon pepper
- 2 medium-sized carrots
- 1 medium-sized onion
- 1 small turnip
- 1 lb/500 g leeks
- 1 tablespoon chopped parsley

1. Ask the butcher to cut the meat into even-sized pieces. Remove all the fat from the meat. Wash the barley.

2. Place the meat, barley, 2 pints/1 litre water, salt and pepper in a large saucepan. Bring to the boil; skim. Cover and simmer for 1 hour.

3. Peel and slice the carrots and onion. Wash and peel the turnip; cut into small dice. Trim the roots, tops and any tough outside leaves from the leeks. Cut the leeks in half lengthwise; open out and wash thoroughly to remove any soil; cut into small rings.

4. Add the vegetables to the saucepan; bring back to the boil. Cover and simmer for a further 45-60 minutes or until the vegetables and barley are cooked.

5. Remove the lamb from the saucepan. Remove the meat from the bones; cut into small pieces. Return the meat to the saucepan. Re-heat the broth, taste and add more salt and pepper, if necessary. Add the chopped parsley and serve immediately.

Note If possible, cool quickly, chill and remove any surface fat. Re-heat as required.

Increase the barley to 2 oz/50 g. CHO: 25 g Calories: 240

Replace the pearl barley with brown rice.

Δ
No change necessary. Chill the soup and remove the fat as in note.

No change necessary.

As for diabetic.

Omit the lamb and replace with a large can of red kidney beans and 1 teaspoon mixed dried herbs. Serve sprinked with parmesan cheese.

Vegetable and Lentil Soup

Special Diets

Serves 4: 165 calories per portion

 1 medium-sized onion
 2 medium-sized carrots
 1 medium-sized parsnip
 1 small turnip
 2 sticks of celery
 3 rashers streaky bacon
 4 oz/100 g lentils
 1 oz/25 g margarine
 2 pints/1 litre boiling water
 2 level teaspoons salt
 pepper

1. Peel and thinly slice the onion, carrots and parsnip. Peel the turnip and cut into small dice. Wash and slice the celery.
2. Remove the rind and bone from the bacon; cut the bacon into strips.
3. Place the lentils in a colander and wash under cold running water.
4. Melt the margarine in a large saucepan. Add the bacon and cook for 1 minute. Add the vegetables and lentils; cook for about 5 minutes, stirring occasionally.
5. Add the boiling water, salt and a shake of pepper. Bring to the boil; cover and simmer for 1-1¼ hours or cook at high pressure for 20 minutes, until the vegetables are tender. Serve piping hot for a substantial first course with crusty rolls, or with cooked, sliced sausages for a snack meal.

No change necessary. Serve with wholemeal bread.
CHO: 20 g Calories: 165

No change necessary.

Use lean bacon and polyunsaturated margarine. Serve with low-fat cheese, not sausages, for a snack meal.

No change necessary.

No change necessary.

Omit the bacon and use vegetable margarine. Sprinkle with vegetarian cheese and serve with wholemeal bread.

Tomato Soup

Serves 4: 290 calories per portion

1 onion
1 stick of celery
2 oz/50 g margarine
3 bacon rinds
1½ lb/750 g tomatoes
salt and pepper
2 teaspoons sugar
1 chicken stock cube
¾ pint/375 ml boiling water
1 tablespoon cornflour
2 tablespoons top of the milk
2 thick slices bread
oil for frying

1. Peel and slice the onion. Wash and chop the celery. Melt the margarine in a saucepan; add the onion, celery and bacon rinds. Cook for 2-3 minutes.
2. Wash the tomatoes and cut into quarters; place in the saucepan with some salt and pepper and the sugar. Bring to the boil, cover and simmer until soft (about 10-15 minutes). Sieve the tomato mixture into another saucepan.
3. Dissolve the stock cube in boiling water; blend a little with the cornflour and mix all together. Pour into the saucepan with the tomato purée and bring to the boil, stirring. Taste and add more salt and pepper, if necessary. Stir in the milk.
4. Remove the crust from the bread; cut into small cubes.
5. Fry the bread in oil until golden brown all over; remove from the pan and drain on kitchen paper.
6. Serve the fried bread cubes with the soup.

Increase the fibre by chopping all the ingredients in a food processor or liquidizer and omit the sieving. Use wholemeal bread and toast instead of frying it. Replace the sugar with a drop of liquid sweetener. Replace the top of the milk with skimmed milk. CHO: 20 g Calories: 215

Omit the bread cubes or use gluten-free bread. Check that the stock cube does not contain starch. Replace if necessary.

Omit the bacon rinds. Use polyunsaturated margarine. Replace the stock cube with yeast extract or concentrated vegetable extract. Replace the top of the milk with skimmed milk. Toast the bread instead of frying.

Use bone stock and omit the stock cube.

Increase fibre as for diabetic. Use wholemeal bread.

Omit the bacon rinds and replace the stock cube with concentrated vegetable extract.

Minestrone Soup

Serves 6: 190 calories per portion

4 rashers streaky bacon
1 medium-sized onion
salt
2 sticks celery
1 tablespoon oil
1 clove garlic, crushed
14-oz/398-g can tomatoes
1 chicken extract cube
pepper
3 oz/75 g short-cut macaroni
2 carrots
chopped parsley
2 oz/50 g grated parmesan cheese

1. Remove the rind and bone from the bacon; cut the bacon into thin strips. Peel and slice the onion. Scrub the celery and cut into slices.
2. Heat the oil in a large saucepan; add the bacon, onion, celery and garlic and cook gently for 5 minutes, stirring occasionally. Remove the saucepan from the heat.
3. Add the canned tomatoes to the saucepan; add 1½ pints/825 ml water, the crumbled extract cube, 1 level teaspoon salt and a shake of pepper. Bring to the boil, stir in the macaroni and simmer for 15-20 minutes.
4. Peel and grate the carrots; add the grated carrot and 1 rounded tablespoon chopped parsley to the saucepan; stir until evenly mixed. Taste and add more seasoning if necessary. Pour the soup into a warmed tureen. Serve with parmesan cheese and crusty bread.

Special Diets

Use wholemeal macaroni. Serve with wholemeal bread.
CHO: 18 g Calories: 190

Replace the macaroni with brown rice and check that the stock cube does not contain starch or MSG.

Use very lean bacon and cut off all the fat. Use polyunsaturated oil. Replace the parmesan cheese with 1 oz/25 g roasted crushed sesame seeds.

Use wholemeal macaroni and serve with wholemeal bread.

Omit the chicken stock cube.

Replace the bacon with 4 oz/100 g sliced green beans added 5 minutes before the end of the cooking time. Replace the chicken extract cube with vegetable extract.

Lentil, Orange and Carrot Soup

Special Diets

Serves 4: 185 calories per portion

- 1 onion
- 4 medium carrots
- 4 oz/100 g lentils
- 1 chicken stock cube
- 1 pint/500 ml boiling water
- 1 pint/500 ml tomato juice
- rind and juice of one orange
- salt and pepper
- milk
- natural low-fat yoghurt

1. Chop the onion; wash and slice the carrots; place in a saucepan with the lentils, stock cube dissolved in boiling water, tomato juice and the pared rind of the orange. Bring to the boil, cover and simmer for ½ hour.

2. Liquidize the soup, add the orange juice and seasonings to taste. Adjust the thickness with milk. Re-heat and serve each bowl with a swirl of yoghurt.

No change necessary.
CHO: 38 g Calories: 185

No change necessary, but check that the stock cube does not contain starch or MSG.

No change necessary.

Replace the stock made from a cube with bone stock or yeast extract.

No change necessary.

Use yeast or vegetable extract instead of the chicken stock cube.

Country Kitchen Soup

Special Diets

Serves 6: 175 calories per portion

3 medium-sized leeks
4 oz/100 g button mushrooms
2 large potatoes
2 oz/50 g butter
2 oz/50 g plain flour
1½ pints/1 litre well-flavoured meat stock
½ pint/250 ml semi-skimmed milk
1½ level teaspoons salt
pepper
1 level tablespoon chopped parsley

1. Trim the roots, tops and any tough outside leaves from the leeks. Cut in half lengthwise, then open out and wash thoroughly to remove any soil; cut into rings. Wash and finely slice the mushrooms.
2. Peel and thinly slice the potatoes. Melt the butter in a large saucepan, add the potato slices and leeks and fry gently for 2-3 minutes without browning. Add flour and continue cooking for 2 minutes.
3. Add the stock, milk, salt and a shake of pepper. Bring to the boil, stirring; cover and simmer for 20 minutes. Add the mushrooms and continue cooking for a further 5 minutes. Taste and add more salt and pepper, if necessary.
4. To serve, pour the soup into a warmed tureen and sprinkle with chopped parsley.
Note If stock is not available, dissolve 2 chicken stock cubes in 1½ pints/1 litre boiling water and omit the seasonings.

Leave the potatoes unpeeled; use wholemeal flour and skimmed milk. Replace the butter with low-fat margarine.
CHO: 28 g Calories: 125

Replace the flour with maize flour.

Replace the butter with polyunsaturated margarine and use skimmed milk.

Use bone stock.

Leave the potatoes unpeeled. Add 4 oz/100 g frozen peas in step 3 with the mushrooms.

Use vegetable or yeast extract to make stock.

23

Chicken and Vegetable Soup

Serves 4: 170 calories per portion

    1 small onion, chopped
    1 stick celery, sliced
    1 carrot, sliced
    1 tablespoon oil or chicken dripping
    1½ pints/1 litre chicken stock
    1 potato, grated
    salt and pepper
    2 tablespoons plain flour
    1 oz/25 g polyunsaturated margarine

1. Cook the onion, celery and carrot in oil or dripping in a covered pan for 5 minutes, shaking the pan occasionally.
2. Add the stock, potato, 1 teaspoon salt and a generous shake of pepper. Cover and cook for 10-30 minutes (for the best flavour, cook for the maximum time). Mash the flour with the butter or margarine on a plate, then whisk into the boiling soup. Cook for 2 minutes taste and add more seasonings, if necessary. Serve with crisp bread rolls.

Use wholemeal flour for thickening.
CHO: 13 g Calories: 170

Use a large potato for thickening and omit the flour: whisk in the butter or margarine on its own. Alternatively, add 2 oz/50 g red lentils with the stock and cook for 30 minutes. If using a stock cube check that it does not contain starch or MSG.

Reduce the oil to 1 teaspoon. Omit the butter or margarine and blend the flour with water or skimmed milk.

Use home-made chicken stock.

Use wholemeal flour instead of plain. Add lentils as for gluten-free.

Vegetable and Bean Soup
Replace the chicken stock with vegetable stock made from vegetable or yeast extract. Add a small can of baked beans for extra flavour.

Quick Leek and Potato Soup

Serves 6: 110 calories per portion

    1 lb/450 g leeks
    1 oz/25 g polyunsaturated margarine
    2 chicken stock cubes
    5 rashers streaky bacon
    1 (2-3-serving) packet instant mashed potato

1. Trim off the roots, some of the green tops and any tough outside leaves from the leeks. Cut the leeks halfway through lengthwise. Open out and wash thoroughly to remove any soil; close up and cut into rings.
2. Melt the margarine in a medium-sized saucepan; fry the leeks for 3 minutes. Add 2 pints/1 litre cold water and the crumbled stock cubes. Bring to the boil, cover and simmer for 20 minutes.
3. Remove the rind and bone from the bacon. Press the rashers flat with the back of a knife; cut into thin strips. Fry the bacon until crisp and well browned; drain on kitchen paper.
4. Remove the soup from the heat and stir in the instant mashed potato (to thicken the soup). Serve the soup, sprinkled with crisply fried bacon. For a supper dish, serve with additional crispy fried bacon and crusty bread.

Special Diets

Use 4 oz/100 g lean bacon.
CHO: 14 g Calories: 90

No change necessary, but check that the stock cube does not contain starch or MSG.

Replace the streaky bacon with very lean bacon.

Replace the chicken stock cubes and water with 2 pints/1 litre well-flavoured bone stock. Replace the instant potatoes with 8 oz/225 g pre-pared potatoes cooked with the leeks. Mash or liquidize before serving.

Add a can of butter beans before serving.

Use vegetable margarine and replace the chicken stock cubes with vegetable stock or cubes or 2 tablespoons Vecon.

Bacon and Bean Soup

Special Diets

Serves 6 as a snack, 4 as main course: 95-140 calories per portion

    4 oz/100 g haricot beans
    1 knuckle of bacon (about 8 oz/225 g meat)
    1 large onion, chopped
    1 large carrot, chopped
    3 sticks celery, sliced
    1 sachet bouquet garni herbs
    salt and pepper

1. Place the beans and bacon separately in bowls, cover with cold water and leave overnight; drain.
2. Place in a large saucepan or pressure cooker with the onion, carrot, celery and bouquet garni. Add 4 pints/2 litres water to the saucepan, or 3 pints/1½ litres to the pressure cooker. Cover and simmer for 2 hours or cook at high pressure for 40 minutes.
3. Remove the bacon and bouquet garni. Peel the skin off the bacon, cut the meat into small cubes and return to the pan. Add salt and pepper to taste and serve with crisp rolls as a snack. For a main meal, double the quantity of root vegetables, add 2 potatoes at the start; add 8 oz/225 g shredded cabbage and cook for 5 minutes at the end.

No change necessary.
CHO: snack 13 g; main course 20 g
Calories: snack 95; main course 140 g

No change necessary.

Cut all the fat off the bacon knuckle before cooking. Blot the surface of the soup with kitchen paper before serving.

No change necessary.

No change necessary, but use more (6 oz/150 g) haricot beans if desired.

Omit the bacon knuckle. Double the quantity of beans and add vegetables as for a main course. Add 1 rounded tablespoon yeast extract or vegetable stock paste and flavour with 1 tablespoon tomato paste, ½ teaspoon chilli powder and 1 tablespoon Worcestershire sauce. For a quick soup, replace the haricot beans with 15 oz/425 g canned beans in chilli sauce and cook for 20-30 minutes.

Quick Cream of Mushroom Soup

Serves 4: 165 calories per portion

> 4 oz/100 g mushrooms, wiped and finely chopped
> 1 medium onion, finely chopped
> 2 oz/50 g butter
> 1 oz/25 g plain wholemeal flour
> ½ pint/250 ml semi-skimmed milk
> 1 chicken stock cube
> ½ pint/275 ml boiling water
> 2 tablespoons cream or top of the milk
> freshly chopped parsley

1. Place the mushrooms, onion and butter in a saucepan, cover and cook over a low heat for 5 minutes, shaking the pan occasionally.
2. Stir in the flour, milk, stock cube dissolved in boiling water and some salt and pepper. Bring to the boil, stirring, cover and cook for 5 minutes. For a smooth soup, liquidize or sieve.
3. Pour into bowls, swirl some cream or top of the milk in each and sprinkle with parsley.

Special Diets

Replace the butter with polyunsaturated margarine.
CHO: 10 g Calories: 165

Replace the wholemeal flour with Trufree flour.

Replace the butter with 1 teaspoon polyunsaturated oil and cook in a non-stick saucepan; use skimmed milk and omit the cream.

Replace the chicken stock cube with 2 teaspoons yeast extract, or additive-free stock cube or stock from boiling meat or vegetables.

Add 2 tablespoons natural bran and liquidize with the soup.

Replace the butter with vegetable margarine or 2 tablespoons oil; replace the milk with water and add 1 tablespoon soya flour; replace the chicken stock cube with vegetable stock or extract or yeast extract. Omit the cream.

Salads

Serve a simple green salad with every meal and add one or two of these vegetable or fish salads to make a main meal. Very few changes are necessary for the special diets.

Apple and avocado salad   47
Beetroot and apple salad   43
Belgian salad   32
Celery and walnut salad   36
Cucumber salad   49
French dressing   53
Mayonnaise   52
Mexican-style potato salad   34
Mushroom salad   40
Orange salad   50
Oriental salad   42
Potato salad   38
Quick Russian salad   35
Red apple salad   37
Rice and corn salad   39
Rice medley salad   45
Salad with blue-cheese dressing   46
Seafood dressing   52
Shredded salad   44
Smoked mackerel and orange salad   31
Spanish salad   48
Tartare sauce   52
Three-bean salad   51
Thousand Island potato salad   41
Tuna salad   33
Winter salad   30

Winter Salad

Serves 8: 405 calories per portion

  1½ lb/625 g white cabbage
  1 large carrot
  2 oz/50 g shelled walnuts (optional)
  1 red-skinned eating apple
  1 tablespoon lemon juice
  ½ pint/275 ml mayonnaise or salad cream
  salt and pepper

1. Cut off the excess stalk and coarse leaves from the cabbage; wash the cabbage thoroughly and shred finely.
2. Peel and grate the carrot. Chop the walnuts, if using. Cut the apple and remove the core; cut into small pieces.
3. Mix the apple with lemon juice in a large bowl. Add the cabbage, carrot and walnuts; mix together.
4. Add the mayonnaise and stir the salad until well coated; add some salt and pepper. Serve cold with meats and savoury flans.

Special Diets

Use low-calorie mayonnaise or salad cream mixed with an equal quantity of natural yoghurt.
CHO: 6 g Calories: 235

Use home-made mayonnaise; otherwise, make sure that the mayonnaise does not contain starch.

Use polyunsaturated mayonnaise or oil for home-made mayonnaise.

Use home-made mayonnaise.

Mix in 8 oz/225 g cooked frozen peas.

No change necessary.

Smoked Mackerel and Orange Salad

Serves 4: 445 calories per portion

12½-oz/360-g packet smoked mackerel
2 tablespoons vinegar
3 peppercorns
1 bay leaf
6 oz/175 g long-grain rice
4 medium tomatoes
2 small oranges
2 tablespoons sunflower oil
salt and pepper
1 bunch watercress

1. Wash and trim the mackerel, if necessary. Place in a frying-pan and add ½ pint/275 ml cold water. Add 1 tablespoon vinegar, the peppercorns and bay leaf. Bring to the boil and cook gently for 2 minutes; remove the pan from the heat and leave the mackerel in its liquor until cold. Remove, drain and cut into neat pieces.
2. Cook the rice in a large saucepan of boiling, salted water for about 12 minutes. Test by pressing a grain between thumb and finger. Drain in a sieve or colander and rinse in cold water; leave until cold.
3. Place the tomatoes in a bowl and cover with boiling water. Leave for 1 minute; drain, peel and cut into quarters.
4. Scrub the oranges; cut the skin and pith from one with a sharp or serrated knife. Hold the orange over a plate and cut out segments.
5. Mix the orange rind and juice, 1 tablespoon vinegar, oil and some salt and pepper together in a large bowl. Stir in the cold rice, mackerel, tomatoes and orange segments; mix together gently. Pile on to a serving dish and arrange sprigs of watercress round the edge of the dish.

Special Diets

Use brown rice and polyunsaturated oil.
CHO: 44 g Calories: 445

No change necessary.

Use polyunsaturated oil.

Make sure the mackerel is natural and not coloured.

Use brown rice and add 3 oz/75 g chopped walnuts.

No change necessary.

Belgian Salad

Serves 4: 100 calories per portion

    1 large carrot
    2 heads chicory
    6 radishes
    1 eating apple
    2 oz/50 g shelled walnuts
    juice of ½ lemon
    ½ level teaspoon salt
    pepper

1. Scrape, wash and grate the carrot. Wash the chicory, radishes and apple. Arrange some chicory leaves on a round serving dish, radiating out from the centre; slice the remainder. Trim and slice the radishes. Cut the walnuts into quarters.
2. Cut the apple into quarters, then into eighths. Remove the core and cut the apple across, into slices; place in a bowl. Pour the lemon juice over. Add the carrot, sliced chicory, radishes, walnuts, salt and a shake of pepper.
3. Mix together carefully and pile on the chicory leaves in a serving dish. Serve with cold meat or grilled pork chops.

No change necessary.
CHO: 6 g Calories: 100

No change necessary.

No change necessary.

No change necessary.

No change necessary.

No change necessary. Serve with other salads.

Tuna Salad

Serves 4: 380 calories per portion

> 5 oz/150 g spaghetti rings
> 2 medium red-skinned eating apples
> 1 tablespoon lemon juice
> 2 sticks celery
> 2 rounded tablespoons seedless raisins
> 7-oz/198-g can tuna fish in brine
> 1 level tablespoon parsley
> 2 level tablespoons mayonnaise
> 5 fl oz/150 ml natural yoghurt

1. Bring a large saucepan of salted water to the boil; add the pasta and cook for 10 minutes or as directed on the packet. Drain in a sieve; rinse with cold water.
2. Wash the apples, cut into quarters, remove the cores and cut into small dice; place in a large bowl with the lemon juice and stir until well coated (to prevent browning).
3. Scrub the celery and slice finely; add to the bowl with the raisins.
4. Empty the can of tuna fish into the basin and mix thoroughly with the other ingredients. Stir in the parsley and pasta.
5. To make the dressing, place the mayonnaise in a small basin, gradually add the yoghurt and stir until smooth; add to the ingredients in the basin; carefully stir the mixture until evenly coated with the dressing. Place the salad in a serving dish and serve with a crisp green salad.

Special Diets

d
Use wholemeal pasta. Replace the raisins with canned sweetcorn. Use low-calorie mayonnaise.
CHO: 45 g Calories: 335

Use gluten-free pasta (see recipe, page 216).

No change necessary, but use polyunsaturated oil for the mayonnaise, and low-fat yoghurt.

No change necessary, but use home-made mayonnaise.

Use wholemeal pasta.

No change necessary.

Mexican-style Potato Salad

Serves 4: 230 calories per portion

> 1 lb/450 g new potatoes
> 2 tablespoons French dressing
> 2 oz/50 g streaky bacon
> 11½-oz/300-g can sweetcorn
>   with red and green peppers
> watercress
> 5 fl oz/150 ml natural yoghurt
> ½ level teaspoon salt
> pepper

1. Wash and scrape the potatoes; cut into ½-inch/1.25-cm dice. Cook in boiling, salted water until tender. Drain, rinse in cold water and dry on kitchen paper. Place the French dressing in a bowl, add the potatoes and stir lightly to coat; leave until cold.
2. Remove the rind and bone from the bacon; cut the bacon into thin strips. Fry slowly until crisp; drain on kitchen paper and leave to cool.
3. Drain the sweetcorn; wash and trim the watercress.
4. Just before serving, stir the sweetcorn, yoghurt, salt and a shake of pepper into the potato mixture; mix well. Pile on to a serving dish and surround with sprigs of watercress. Crumble the bacon over and serve with cold beef, sausages or meat pie.

Special Diets

Leave the skin on the potatoes; use lean bacon, grill and drain well.
CHO: 28 g Calories: 230

No change necessary.

Remove all the fat from the bacon and drain thoroughly. Use low-fat yoghurt.

Use natural-set yoghurt.

Leave the skin on the potatoes.

Replace the bacon with 1 oz/25 g chopped salted peanuts.

Quick Russian Salad

Serves 4: 135 calories per portion

       8 oz/225 g new potatoes
       salt
       8-oz/225-g pack frozen mixed vegetables
       4 tablespoons salad cream
       pepper

1. Wash and scrape the potatoes, cut into ½-inch/1.25-cm dice. Fill a saucepan about 2 inches/5 cm deep with water, bring to the boil, add some salt, the potatoes and mixed vegetables. Bring back to the boil, cover and simmer for 8 minutes, or until tender; drain.

2. Place the salad cream, ½ level teaspoon salt and a shake of pepper in a bowl; add the vegetables, mix gently and leave until cold. Pile on to a serving dish and serve with cold meat, sausages or pies.

Special Diets

Leave the skins on the potatoes, use low-calorie salad cream.
CHO: 16 g Calories: 100

Make sure the salad cream does not contain starch.

Use salad cream made from sunflower oil.

Use home-made mayonnaise instead of salad cream.

Leave the skins on the potatoes.

No change necessary.

Celery and Walnut Salad

Celery and Walnut Salad

Serves 4: 365 calories per portion

> 4 oz/100 g long-grain rice
> 1 large head celery
> 2 oz/50 g shelled walnuts

Dressing:

> 6 tablespoons French dressing (see recipe)
> 1-2 cloves garlic (optional)
> 2 level tablespoons French mustard
> 1 level teaspoon dried oregano
> 2 level teaspoons chopped parsley
> 2 teaspoons lemon juice

1. Cook the rice in boiling, salted water for about 12 minutes. Test by pressing a grain between thumb and finger. Drain in a sieve and rinse with cold water. Place in a large bowl.

2. Wash the celery; chop finely and add to the bowl. Chop the walnuts and add.

3. Pour the French dressing into a bowl. Peel the garlic (if using) and crush the cloves; add to the French dressing with the remaining dressing ingredients. Beat together with a fork.

4. Add the dressing to the bowl and mix to coat thoroughly. Pile into a salad bowl. Chill until ready to serve.

Use brown rice.
CHO: 28 g Calories: 365

Check that the mustard does not contain starch.

Use polyunsaturated oil for the dressing.

No change necessary.

Use brown rice.

No change necessary.

Red Apple Salad

Serves 6: 75 calories per portion

    3 medium red-skinned eating apples
    2 tablespoons lemon juice
    3 sticks celery
    2 oz/50 g sultanas
    1 small lettuce
    1 oz/25 g walnut pieces

1. Quarter and core the apples; cut into cubes. Toss the apple in lemon juice (to prevent browning).
2. Scrub and slice the celery; add to the apples with the sultanas.
3. Wash the lettuce; arrange the leaves on 6 small plates.
4. Pile the apple mixture on to the plates. Coarsely chop the walnuts and sprinkle over the salad.

No change necessary.
CHO: 14 g Calories: 75

No change necessary.

No change necessary.

No change necessary.

No change necessary.

No change necessary.

37

Potato Salad

Serves 6: 215 calories per portion

> 2 lb/1 kg potatoes
> 2 tablespoons French dressing (see recipe)
> 3 rashers lean streaky bacon
> 2 small spring onions
> 2 rounded tablespoons mayonnaise (see recipe)

1. Peel the potatoes and cook in boiling, salted water for 20 minutes. Drain and cut into ½-inch/1-cm cubes; place in a bowl. Add the French dressing and turn gently until evenly coated.
2. Pre-heat a moderate grill. Remove the rind and bone from the bacon and grill until crisp. Chop the bacon finely.
3. Slice the onions and add to the potatoes. Add the mayonnaise and mix well together. Place on a serving dish and sprinkle the bacon in a line down the centre.

Special Diets

Leave the peel on the potatoes. Use lean bacon and drain well.
CHO: 27 g Calories: 215

No change necessary.

Use very lean bacon and drain well.

No change necessary.

Leave the peel on the potatoes.

Omit the bacon and replace with 1 oz/25 g toasted sesame seeds.

Rice and Corn Salad

Serves 8: 253 calories per portion

8 oz/225 g long-grain rice
12-oz/350-g can sweetcorn with peppers
2 oz/50 g seedless raisins
2 sticks celery, sliced
2 oz/50 g broken walnuts
6 tablespoons olive oil
3 tablespoons wine or cider vinegar
1 teaspoon made mustard
1 crushed clove of garlic (optional)

1. Cook the rice in plenty of boiling, salted water for 10 minutes until a grain pressed between the fingers is clear throughout. Drain in a sieve or colander and rinse with cold water. Spread out on oiled greaseproof paper to dry for ½ hour, then place in a large basin.
2. Drain the sweetcorn into a bowl, reserving the liquor, and add the sweetcorn to the rice with the raisins, celery and walnuts.
3. Add the oil, vinegar, mustard and garlic (if using) to the bowl containing the sweetcorn liquor. Whisk together with a fork until thick, then stir into the salad. Chill and leave for the flavours to blend for at least ½ hour, if possible. Serve with cold meats or fish or with other salads.

Special Diets

As for high-fibre. Reduce raisins to 1 oz/25 g.
CHO: 17 g Calories: 245

No change necessary, but check that the mustard does not contain starch.

No change necessary.

No change necessary.

Replace the white rice with brown rice and cook for 30-35 minutes.

No change necessary.

Mushroom Salad

Serves 4: 165 calories per portion

> 2 oz/50 g lean streaky bacon
> 1 slice white bread from a large loaf
> 2 tablespoons groundnut oil for frying
> 4 oz/100 g button mushrooms
> 1 tablespoon lemon juice
> 2 tablespoons soya oil
> salt and pepper
> pinch dry mustard
> pinch caster sugar
> chopped parsley

1. Remove the rind and bone from the bacon; cut the bacon into small pieces. Remove the crusts from the bread; cut the bread into ½-inch/1.25-cm cubes.
2. Place the bacon in a small saucepan over a low heat and fry slowly until crisp and golden. Remove from the saucepan and drain on crumpled kitchen paper.
3. Add a little oil or fat to the saucepan; add the bread cubes and fry until golden brown and crisp. Drain on crumpled kitchen paper. Wash and slice the mushrooms.
4. Place the lemon juice, oil, some salt, pepper, the dry mustard and sugar in a serving bowl and beat with a fork.
5. Add the mushrooms and fried bread. Stir the mixture carefully, until coated with dressing. Crumble the bacon over and sprinkle with parsley. Serve with cold meat, pork pie, tuna or grilled fish.

Use very lean bacon. Use wholemeal bread and toast the bread.
CHO: 3 g Calories: 100

Use gluten-free bread or replace with 1 oz/25 g sunflower seeds but do not fry them. Check that the mustard contains no starch.

Use very lean bacon and grill it. Toast the bread instead of frying, if desired, to further decrease the fat content.

No change necessary.

Use wholemeal bread and add 4 oz/ 100 g high-fibre vegetables such as peas or sweetcorn.

Replace the bacon with 1 oz/25 g sunflower seeds.

Thousand Island Potato Salad

Serves 4: 195 calories per portion

> 1½ lb/725 g new potatoes
> endive or lettuce
> 1 lb/500 g tomatoes
> 3 tablespoons bottled Thousand Island dressing
> ¼ level teaspoon salt
> 1 level teaspoon chopped chives

1. Wash and scrape the potatoes, cut into ½-inch/1.25-cm dice and cook in boiling, salted water until tender. Drain well and leave to cool.
2. Wash the endive or lettuce; drain well, then break the endive into sprigs or shred the lettuce.
3. Place the tomatoes in a bowl and cover with boiling water; leave for 1 minute, drain, then peel. Chop the tomatoes and place in bowl.
4. Stir in the potatoes, dressing and salt. Place on a serving dish, arrange the endive or lettuce round the salad and sprinkle with chives.

Special Diets

Leave the skins on the potatoes and tomatoes. Replace the Thousand Island dressing with 3 tablespoons thick low-fat yoghurt mixed with ½ teaspoon chopped olives, ½ hard-boiled egg (chopped) and 1 tablespoon tomato ketchup.
CHO: 45 g Calories: 155

Check that the dressing does not contain starch. If it does, replace with home-made mayonnaise mixed with ½ teaspoon chopped olives, ½ hard-boiled egg (chopped) and 1 tablespoon tomato ketchup.

Use dressing made with polyunsaturated oil or make as for gluten-free using polyunsaturated mayonnaise or low-fat yoghurt.

Use home-made mayonnaise flavoured as for gluten-free.

Leave the skins on the potatoes and tomatoes. Add 4 oz/100 g cooked or canned broad beans.

No change necessary.

Oriental Salad

Serves 4: 90 calories per portion

      8 oz/225 g Chinese leaves
      4 oz/100 g beansprouts
      8 oz/225 g tomatoes
      ½ small cucumber
      4 gherkins
      2 tablespoons bottled Catalina or French dressing

1. Wash the Chinese leaves and shred finely.
2. Wash the beansprouts and drain.
3. Place the tomatoes in a bowl and cover with boiling water. Leave for 1 minute, drain, then peel. Chop and place in a bowl.
4. Wash the cucumber; cut into small dice. Slice the gherkins.
5. Add the Chinese leaves, cucumber, gherkins, beansprouts and dressing to the tomatoes and mix well.
6. Pile into a shallow serving dish.

Use French dressing made from polyunsaturated oil. Leave the skins on the tomatoes.
CHO: 5 g Calories: 90

Check that the dressing does not contain starch.

Use French dressing made with polyunsaturated oil.

Use home-made dressing.

Leave the skins on the tomatoes. Add 2 oz/50 g toasted split almonds.

No change necessary.

Beetroot and Apple Salad

Serves 3: 70 calories per portion

> 3 oz/75 g cooked beetroot
> 1 large cooking apple
> 1 tablespoon low-fat thick yoghurt
> 1 tablespoon mayonnaise
> 1 teaspoon creamed horseradish
> watercress

1. Peel and cut the beetroot into ¼-inch/6-mm dice. Peel, core and roughly chop the apple.
2. Mix the yoghurt, mayonnaise and horseradish in a bowl. Add the beetroot and apple and stir the mixture carefully until coated with dressing.
3. Pile on to a serving dish and garnish with watercress.

Special Diets

Leave the skin on the apple. Use low-calorie mayonnaise.
CHO: 10 g Calories: 70

Check that the mayonnaise and horseradish do not contain starch.

Use polyunsaturated oil mayonnaise.

Use home-made mayonnaise and horseradish sauce.

Leave the skin on the apple.

No change necessary.

Shredded Salad

Special Diets

Serves 4: 95 calories per portion

> 1 large carrot
> 8 oz/225 g tomatoes
> 6 spring onions (optional)
> 1 lettuce
> 3 tablespoons French dressing

1. Wash, scrape and grate the carrot. Place the tomatoes in a bowl and cover with boiling water. Leave for 1 minute, drain, then peel.
2. Wash and finely slice the spring onions, if using. Place the tomatoes on a plate and cut into thin wedges. Wash, dry and shred the lettuce.
3. Just before serving, place the French dressing in a bowl and add the other ingredients. Stir the salad carefully until coated with dressing. Serve with cold meat, canned fish or grilled meat.

No change necessary.
CHO: 5 g Calories: 95

No change necessary.

Use polyunsaturated oil for the French dressing.

Use home-made French dressing.

Add 4 oz/100 g shredded raw cabbage.

No change necessary. Serve with other fresh salads.

Rice Medley Salad

Serves 4: 370 calories per portion

4 oz/100 g long-grain rice
3 large sticks celery
3-inch/7.5-cm piece cucumber
6 oz/175 g Cheddar cheese
2 tablespoons oil
1 tablespoon lemon juice
½ teaspoon Worcestershire sauce
½ level teaspoon salt
pepper
2 oz/50 g seedless raisins
1 tomato

1. Cook the rice in a large saucepan of boling, salted water for about 12 minutes. Test by pressing a grain between thumb and finger; drain and rinse with cold water. Leave to cool.
2. Wash and slice the celery. Cut the cucumber and cheese into ¼-inch/6-mm dice.
3. Place the oil, lemon juice, Worcestershire sauce, salt and a shake of pepper in a small basin and beat with a fork.
4. Place the rice, celery, cucumber, cheese and raisins in a bowl, add the dressing and stir the mixture carefully, until coated with dressing.
5. Pile on to a serving dish. Cut the tomato into 6 wedges and arrange round the salad. Serve with cold meat.

Special Diets

Use brown rice and cook as directed on the packet (about ½ hour). Use polyunsaturated oil and replace the Cheddar cheese with 4 oz/100 g low-fat hard cheese.
CHO: 37 g Calories: 315

No change necessary.

Replace the Cheddar cheese with cottage cheese and use polyunsaturated oil.

No change necessary.

Use brown rice and cook as directed on the packet (about ½ hour).

Use vegetable oil and vegetarian cheese.

Salad with Blue-cheese Dressing

Serves 4: 715 calories per main course portion

1 lb/500 g new potatoes
4 tablespoons wine or cider vinegar
8 tablespoons sunflower oil
1 level teaspoon garlic salt
1 level teaspoon made English mustard
salt and pepper
1 oz/25 g walnuts
8 oz/225 g uncooked beetroot
1 oz/25 g sultanas
2 medium-sized carrots
2 small or 1 medium-sized turnip
3 sticks celery
4 eggs
4 tomatoes
4 oz/100 g Danish blue cheese
5 fl oz/142 ml soured cream

1. Wash the potatoes; cut into pieces if large. Cook in boiling salted water for 10 minutes; drain.
2. To make the French dressing, place the vinegar, oil, garlic salt, mustard and a good shake of salt and pepper in a screw-top jar; shake well. Pour a little dressing over the warm potatoes. Roughly chop the walnuts and stir into the potatoes. Leave to cool.
3. Peel and finely dice or grate the beetroot. Place in a bowl with the sultanas and a little French dressing; mix well.
4. Peel the carrots and turnips; grate into a bowl. Wash and slice the celery and add. Mix in the remaining dressing.
5. Hard-boil the eggs for 10 minutes; crack and cool in cold water. Wipe the tomatoes and cut each into eight segments. Shell the eggs and cut into quarters; mix with the tomatoes.
6. Grate the Danish blue cheese into a bowl. Mix in the soured cream and a good shake of salt and pepper.
7. Arrange the vegetables in rows in a large dish. Pour the Danish blue dressing along the centre; serve immediately.

For extra low fat replace the soured cream with low-fat natural yoghurt. CHO: 40 g Calories: 385

Check that the mustard does not contain starch or replace with French mustard.

Use polyunsaturated oil. Replace the Danish blue cheese and soured cream with 4 oz/100 g low-fat soft cheese blended with 2 level tablespoons anchovy purée or essence and 2 tablespoons skimmed milk.

Use organically grown vegetables, if available.

Add 4 oz/100 g butter beans, broad beans or sweetcorn.

Use vegetable oil.

Apple and Avocado Salad

Serves 4: 125 calories per portion

>1 10-oz/175-g ripe avocado
>2 tablespoons lemon juice
>1 medium red dessert apple
>1 medium (4-oz/100-g) green dessert apple
>2-inch/5-cm piece cucumber
>4 spring onions

Dressing:

>2 tablespoons lemon juice
>2 tablespoons olive oil
>1 teaspoon French mustard
>salt and pepper

1. Peel the avocado, cut in half, remove the stone and slice. Toss in lemon juice to prevent discoloration.
2. Core and slice the apples and toss in the lemon juice.
3. Arrange the avocado and apples on a plate with the cucumber slices.
4. Trim the spring onions, slice the tops to within 2 inches/5 cm of their base and add to the salad. Cut the tops lengthwise into shreds to within 1 inch/2.5 cm of their base, place in cold water and leave until the tops have curled. Use to garnish the salad.
5. Mix all the dressing ingredients together and pour over the salad just before serving.

No change necessary.
CHO: 9 g Calories: 125

No change necessary. Check that the mustard does not contain starch.

Replace half the olive oil with safflower oil.

Use fresh lemon juice.

No change necessary.

No change necessary.

Spanish Salad

Serves 6: 125 calories per portion

> 2 green, yellow or red peppers
> 8 oz/225 g white cabbage
> 2 oz/50 g green olives
> 2 tablespoons French dressing (see recipe)
> 2 oz/50 g cocktail onions or Spanish onions, chopped
> 4 oz/100 g cold cooked peas or beans
> 3 rounded dessertspoons thick mild mayonnaise

1. Discard the seeds, core and remove the white pith from the peppers and slice into strips. Place in a small saucepan, cover with cold water; bring to the boil, then drain.
2. Wash the cabbage, discard any stalk and shred very finely. Cut the olives into quarters, removing the stones. Place the French dressing in a bowl and add the pepper, cabbage, olives, onions and peas or beans. Stir the mixture carefully until coated with dressing. Leave for 2 hours for the flavours to blend.
3. Add the mayonnaise to the bowl; stir the mixture carefully until coated with dressing. Place in a salad bowl and serve with cold meat.
Note This salad will keep in a closed container in a refrigerator for 3-4 days. If fresh peppers are unavailable, use canned peppers, but do not cook.

Use low-calorie mayonnaise and halve the quantity of French dressing.
CHO: 5 g Calories: 100

No change necessary, but check the mayonnaise label for starch.

Use sunflower-oil mayonnaise.

No change necessary. Use only naturally coloured mayonnaise (see recipe) and peas.

Increase the quantity of peas or beans.

No change necessary. Serve with other vegetable salads.

Cucumber Salad

Serves 6: 16 calories per portion

> 1 cucumber (about 12 oz/225 g)
> salt
> 5 fl oz/150 ml natural yoghurt
> 1 spring onion
> ½ teaspoon tabasco sauce
> 1 tablespoon chopped fresh mint

1. Wash the cucumber. Cut sufficient slices of cucumber to arrange in halves round the edge of the serving dish. Dice the remainder, place in a bowl and sprinkle with a little salt.
2. Place the yoghurt in a small basin; chop the onion finely and add to the yoghurt with the tabasco sauce. Mix well together.
3. Drain any liquid from the diced cucumber; pile in the centre of the serving dish and coat with the dressing.
4. Sprinkle the mint over the salad.

| d |
No change necessary.
CHO: 2 g Calories: 16

| ♨ |
No change necessary.

| ♦ |
No change necessary.

| ✐ |
No change necessary.

| ☻ |
No change necessary.

| ↳ |
No change necessary.

Orange Salad

Serves 6: 60 calories per portion

> 1 small lettuce
> 3 medium-sized oranges
> 2 tablespoons vinegar
> 2 tablespoons sunflower oil
> ¼ level teaspoon salt
> pinch of pepper
> 1 level tablespoon mixed fresh herbs

1. Wash, dry and shred the lettuce. Divide between 6 small plates.
2. Cut the peel and pith from the oranges with a sharp or serrated knife, then cut into very thin slices; arrange on the lettuce.
3. Mix the vinegar, oil, salt and pepper together and pour over the orange. Chop the herbs and sprinkle over the salad.

No change necessary.
CHO: 4 g Calories: 60

Use cider or wine vinegar.

No change necessary.

No change necessary.

Use thin-skinned oranges and do not remove the skin. Slice the oranges very finely.

No change necessary.

Three-bean Salad

Serves 6: 262 calories per portion

If you have the dressing ready in advance, this salad will take only a few minutes to finish. Alternatively, make it up two days ahead and store in the refrigerator, covered with clingfilm.

1 clove garlic (optional)
4 tablespoons corn oil
2 tablespoons vinegar
2 tablespoons lemon juice
1 teaspoon brown sugar
½ teaspoon mustard
2 tablespoons chopped fresh parsley
pepper
6 spring onions
14-oz/396-g can cannelini beans
15-oz/425-g can red kidney beans
15-oz/425-g can butter beans

1. Crush the garlic, if using, and place in a mixing bowl. Add the oil, vinegar, lemon juice, sugar, mustard, parsley and a good shake of pepper. Beat together.
2. Finely slice the spring onions, add to the mixing bowl with the drained beans, mix well and turn in the dressing to coat.

Replace the sugar with a drop of liquid sweetener.
CHO: 16 g Calories: 255

Use cider or wine vinegar. Check that the mustard contains no wheat flour.

No change necessary.

No change necessary.

No change necessary.

No change necessary.

Mayonnaise

420 calories per 2 oz/50 g

> 1 egg yolk
> ½ level teaspoon salt
> ¼ level teaspoon dry mustard
> ¼ level teaspoon caster sugar
> ½ pint/250 ml oil (see note)
> 1 tablespoon cider or wine vinegar or lemon juice

1. Place the egg yolk, salt, mustard and sugar in a small basin; beat with a wooden spoon, whisk or electric mixer until well blended.
2. Add the oil, a drop at a time, beating well after each addition. When the mixture begins to thicken, add the oil a teaspoonful at a time.
3. When the mixture becomes very thick, or when all the oil has been added, beat in the vinegar or lemon juice.
4. Store the mayonnaise in an airtight container in a refrigerator for up to 3 weeks.
Note If using a liquidizer use 1 whole egg and place all the ingredients except the oil in a liquidizer goblet. Blend well. Remove the small cap in the lid, then switch on and pour the oil through the hole in a steady stream. If the mixture becomes very thick, add 1 tablespoon boiling water.
First-pressing olive oil gives a very good rich flavour but it can be mixed with a blander-flavoured oil such as sunflower or corn oil. Add crushed garlic and herbs, if liked.

Tartare Sauce
Add 2 tablespoons each chopped gherkins, chopped capers and chopped fresh parsley.

Seafood Dressing
Add 2 tablespoons tomato ketchup.

Replace the sugar with a drop of sweetener. Just before serving, mix with an equal quantity of low-fat thick natural yoghurt.
CHO: 1 g per 2 oz/50 g Calories: 110 per 2 oz/50 g

Use Dijon mustard and check that it does not contain starch.

Use half olive oil and half safflower seed oil.

No change necessary.

Serve with high-fibre raw vegetable salads.

No change necessary.

French Dressing

100 calories per tablespoon

> 6 tablespoons olive oil
> 2 tablespoons wine, cider or herb vinegar
> ½ level teaspoon salt
> a good shake or grind of pepper
> ½ level teaspoon dry mustard
> ½ level teaspoon sugar
> 1 clove garlic, crushed (optional)

1. Place all the ingredients in a small basin and whisk with a fork. Alternatively, place in a small screw-top jar or firmly closed plastic container and shake vigorously, or place in a liquidizer goblet and blend well. Store in a bottle or covered plastic container. Shake before using.

Note Wine or tarragon vinegar gives a particularly good flavour.

Special Diets

Replace the sugar with a shake of low-calorie powdered sweetener or a drop of liquid sweetener.
CHO: 1 g per tablespoon Calories: 90 per tablespoon

Omit the mustard.

Replace the olive oil with sunflower oil and use a herb vinegar for extra flavour.

No change necessary.

Serve with a raw vegetable salad.

No change necessary.

Main Courses

These traditional home-cooked dishes can be adapted without much extra work to make them acceptable for a variety of diets, as demonstrated. They all taste delicious, and the family is likely to find the adaptation just as enjoyable as the basic recipe.

Southern-style Baked Cod

Serves 4: 215 calories per portion

butter
4 cod steaks

Stuffing:

1 7-oz/200-g can sweetcorn kernels
1 level tablespoon chopped parsley
4 rounded tablespoons fresh white breadcrumbs
½ small onion, finely chopped (optional)
salt and pepper

small tomato wedges

1. Pre-heat a moderate oven (375°F/190°C/Gas 5).
2. Thickly butter a shallow ovenproof dish. Wash and trim the cod steaks, dry on kitchen paper and place in the dish.
3. Place all the stuffing ingredients together in a bowl and stir thoroughly until well mixed. Spread over the cod steaks.
4. Bake in the oven for 25 minutes. Arrange the tomato wedges in the centre of the dish and return to the oven for a further 5 minutes.

Lightly grease the dish with oil. Use wholemeal breadcrumbs.
CHO: 15 g Calories: 195

Use crumbs of gluten-free bread (see recipe, page 214).

Lightly grease the dish with oil.

No change necessary.

Use wholemeal breadcrumbs.

Lightly grease the dish with oil.

Herrings in Oatmeal

Special Diets

Serves 4: 320 calories per portion

 4 medium-sized herrings
 5 level tablespoons oatmeal or rolled (porridge) oats
 1 level teaspoon salt
 knob of margarine
 lemon wedges

1. Cut the heads off the herrings, using a sharp knife. Scrape the skin with a round-ended knife from tail to head to remove the scales. Wash under running water. Cut along the underside of each fish from head to tail. Remove the roe and reserve for serving separately. Gently scrape away the gut and discard.

2. Open each fish and place, skin side uppermost, on a board. Press firmly along the back of the fish to loosen the backbone. Turn the fish over and ease away the backbone from the fish, starting at the head end. Cut off the fins.

3. If using rolled oats, place in a plastic bag and crush with a rolling-pin.

4. Mix the oatmeal or crushed oats with salt on a plate and press each side of the fish into the oats to coat thoroughly.

5. Melt the margarine in a large frying-pan; fry the herrings, two at a time, for 5-8 minutes, turning each carefully with a fish slice during cooking.

6. Arrange the herrings on a warmed serving dish and garnish with lemon wedges. Serve immediately.

No change necessary.
CHO: 11 g Calories: 320

Replace the oatmeal with millet flakes.

Use polyunsaturated margarine.

No change necessary.

Mix some oat bran with the oatmeal.

Use safflower margarine.

Plaice with Tangy Tartare Sauce

Serves 4: 290 calories per portion

>   1 packet (4) plaice fillets
>   4 level tablespoons plain flour
>   1 level teaspoon paprika
>   salt
>   2 oz/50 g butter
> *Dressing:*
>   4 gherkins
>   2 level teaspoons capers
>   1 11-oz/300-g can sweetcorn with red and green peppers
>   4 tablespoons salad cream
>
>   lemon wedges and parsley to garnish

1. Remove the grill rack and pre-heat a moderate grill. Warm a flat serving dish and a small glass bowl.

2. Wash the plaice fillets and dry on kitchen paper; trim if necessary. Mix the flour, paprika and a shake of salt together on a plate. Coat the plaice fillets in the seasoned flour. Reserve any remaining seasoned flour for the dressing.

3. Melt the butter in a grill pan. Dip the plaice fillets in butter, then turn over. Grill for 10-12 minutes until golden brown. Arrange the plaice on a warmed serving dish and keep warm.

4. Chop the gherkins and capers. Stir the remaining seasoned flour into the butter in the grill pan. Add the chopped gherkins and capers, corn and salad cream. Heat the mixture through under the grill, stirring occasionally.

5. Pour the dressing into a warmed glass bowl and place on the serving dish with the fish. Garnish with lemon wedges and a sprig of parsley. Serve immediately with chipped potatoes.

Use wholemeal flour for coating. Replace the butter with 1 oz/25 g polyunsaturated margarine. Use low-calorie salad cream. Serve with jacket potatoes or brown rice.
CHO: 10 g Calories: 220

Replace the plain flour with potato flour or maize flour. Check that the salad cream contains no starch.

Replace the butter with polyunsaturated margarine. Use salad cream made from sunflower oil. Serve with jacket potatoes topped with low-fat soft cheese and chives.

Use home-made mayonnaise instead of bottled salad cream.

Use wholemeal flour for coating and serve with jacket potatoes.

Replace the butter with vegetable margarine.

Serves 4: 225 calories per portion

> 4 plaice fillets
> 1⅞-oz/48-g jar crab spread
> 1 oz/25 g butter
> 8-oz/225-g carton frozen whole-leaf spinach

Topping:
> 1 egg, separated
> 1 level tablespoon chopped parsley
> 4 level tablespoons salad cream

1. Remove the rack from the grill pan and pre-heat a moderate grill. Warm a shallow 1-pint/500-ml ovenproof dish.
2. Wash the plaice fillets and remove the dark skin, if desired. Place the fillets, skin (or skinned side) uppermost on a board. Spread each with the crab spread and roll up from the tail end.
3. Melt the butter in grill pan. Dip the plaice fillets in butter and grill for 10-12 minutes, turning once.
4. Cook the spinach as directed on the carton; drain, add a knob of butter and seasoning to taste; spread in an ovenproof dish. Arrange the plaice fillets on the spinach; keep warm.
5. Place the egg yolk in a basin. Add the parsley and salad cream and mix well. Whisk the egg white until stiff, then fold into the mixture. Pile over the plaice fillets and spinach. Return to the grill and cook until risen and golden brown. Serve at once with lemon wedges and buttered new potatoes.

Omit the butter and lightly brush the plaice with oil. Omit the butter from the spinach. Use low-calorie salad cream.
CHO: 1 g Calories: 180

Check that the crab spread does not contain starch. Replace with canned crabmeat or low-fat soft cheese and fresh herbs. Check that the salad cream does not contain starch.

Replace the butter with polyunsaturated margarine. Replace the salad cream with fromage frais mixed with 1 tablespoon lemon juice.

Replace the crab spread with fresh or frozen crab meat. Replace the salad cream with home-made mayonnaise.

No change necessary.

Replace the butter with vegetable margarine.

Curried Haddock Platter

Serves 4: 525 calories per portion

1 large onion
8 oz/225 g young carrots
1 clove garlic
salt and pepper
12 oz/350 g haddock fillet
2 tablespoons groundnut oil
2 level teaspoons curry paste
2 level teaspoons curry powder
1 level tablespoon plain flour
15½-oz/425-g can butter beans
7-oz/198-g can tuna steak in brine
1 tablespoon lemon juice
8 oz/225 g long-grain rice

1. Peel and thinly slice the onion and carrots. Peel the garlic and crush with a little salt. Wash the haddock, remove the skin and cut the fish into small pieces.
2. Place the onion, carrots, garlic, oil, curry paste and curry powder in a saucepan and fry for 5 minutes, stirring occasionally. Add the flour and cook for 1 minute. Add the haddock, the contents of the cans of butter beans and tuna, ¼ pint/150 ml water and the lemon juice. Bring slowly to the boil, stirring gently; cover and simmer for 10 minutes, until the fish is tender.
3. Cook the rice in a large saucepan of boiling, salted water for about 12 minutes. Test by pressing a grain between thumb and finger. Drain and rinse with boiling water. Turn into a warmed serving dish.
4. Taste the curry and season with salt and pepper if necessary; pour over the rice.

Thicken the sauce with wholemeal flour and serve on brown rice. Cut the oil for frying by half.
CHO: 72 g Calories: 490

Replace the flour with potato flour. Check that the curry powder and paste do not contain starch.

Use polyunsaturated oil.

Use curry powder and paste without added colourings.

Thicken the sauce with wholemeal flour and serve with brown rice.

No change necessary.

Salmon Pasties with Parsley Sauce

Special Diets

Serves 4: 820 calories per portion

Cheese shortcrust pastry:
- 2 oz/50 g lard
- 2 oz/50 g polyunsaturated margarine
- 8 oz/200 g plain flour
- 4 oz/100 g grated Cheddar cheese
- 1 teaspoon English mustard powder
- cold water to mix

Filling:
- 7½-oz/212-g can pink salmon
- 8 oz/200 g peeled and diced potato
- 2 hard-boiled eggs, chopped
- 4 oz/100 g frozen peas, thawed
- 1 teaspoon salt
- pepper

Sauce:
- 4-5 sprigs fresh parsley, chopped
- 1 oz/25 g polyunsaturated margarine
- 1 oz/25 g plain flour
- ½ pint/250 ml semi-skimmed milk
- salt and pepper

1. Pre-heat a moderately hot oven (400°F/200°C/Gas 6).
2. Rub the lard and margarine into the flour with the fingertips or in a food processor or mixer. Add the cheese and mustard and mix to a firm dough with water.
3. Drain the liquor from the salmon and reserve. Discard the skin and bone and flake the fish. Mix with the potato, egg, peas, salt and a good shake of pepper.
4. Roll the pastry out into 4 8-inch/20-cm circles; brush round the edges with water, divide the salmon mixture into four and place a portion in the centre of each circle. Seal the edges to the tops of the pasties. Flute with the fingers and place on a baking sheet. Brush with beaten egg or milk and bake for 40-45 minutes.
5. Meanwhile, to make the sauce, place all the ingredients in a saucepan and whisk or beat over a low heat until the sauce thickens. Serve with the hot pasties.
Note Alternatively, serve the pasties cold with salad.

As for higher fibre and saturated fat-free.
CHO: 64 g Calories: 820

Use gluten-free pastry (see recipe, page 217). Use French mustard. In the filling, replace the flour with rice flour (preferably whole-grain).

Replace the lard with polyunsaturated margarine; omit the cheese; use skimmed milk.

Use uncoloured cheese.

Use wheatmeal (80% extraction) flour for the pastry or replace half with wholemeal flour. Leave the peel on the potatoes.

Use vegetable fat instead of lard.

Salmon Pasties with Parsley Sauce

Special Diets

Serves 4: 820 calories per portion

Cheese shortcrust pastry:
    2 oz/50 g lard
    2 oz/50 g polyunsaturated margarine
    8 oz/200 g plain flour
    4 oz/100 g grated Cheddar cheese
    1 teaspoon English mustard powder
    cold water to mix

Filling:
    7½-oz/212-g can pink salmon
    8 oz/200 g peeled and diced potato
    2 hard-boiled eggs, chopped
    4 oz/100 g frozen peas, thawed
    1 teaspoon salt
    pepper

Sauce:
    4-5 sprigs fresh parsley, chopped
    1 oz/25 g polyunsaturated margarine
    1 oz/25 g plain flour
    ½ pint/250 ml semi-skimmed milk
    salt and pepper

1. Pre-heat a moderately hot oven (400°F/200°C/Gas 6).
2. Rub the lard and margarine into the flour with the fingertips or in a food processor or mixer. Add the cheese and mustard and mix to a firm dough with water.
3. Drain the liquor from the salmon and reserve. Discard the skin and bone and flake the fish. Mix with the potato, egg, peas, salt and a good shake of pepper.
4. Roll the pastry out into 4 8-inch/20-cm circles; brush round the edges with water, divide the salmon mixture into four and place a portion in the centre of each circle. Seal the edges to the tops of the pasties. Flute with the fingers and place on a baking sheet. Brush with beaten egg or milk and bake for 40-45 minutes.
5. Meanwhile, to make the sauce, place all the ingredients in a saucepan and whisk or beat over a low heat until the sauce thickens. Serve with the hot pasties.
Note Alternatively, serve the pasties cold with salad.

As for higher fibre and saturated fat-free.
CHO: 64 g Calories: 820

Use gluten-free pastry (see recipe, page 217). Use French mustard. In the filling, replace the flour with rice flour (preferably whole-grain).

Replace the lard with polyunsaturated margarine; omit the cheese; use skimmed milk.

Use uncoloured cheese.

Use wheatmeal (80% extraction) flour for the pastry or replace half with wholemeal flour. Leave the peel on the potatoes.

Use vegetable fat instead of lard.

Southern-style Baked Cod

Serves 4: 215 calories per portion

butter
4 cod steaks

Stuffing:

1 7-oz/200-g can sweetcorn kernels
1 level tablespoon chopped parsley
4 rounded tablespoons fresh white breadcrumbs
½ small onion, finely chopped (optional)
salt and pepper

small tomato wedges

1. Pre-heat a moderate oven (375°F/190°C/Gas 5).
2. Thickly butter a shallow ovenproof dish. Wash and trim the cod steaks, dry on kitchen paper and place in the dish.
3. Place all the stuffing ingredients together in a bowl and stir thoroughly until well mixed. Spread over the cod steaks.
4. Bake in the oven for 25 minutes. Arrange the tomato wedges in the centre of the dish and return to the oven for a further 5 minutes.

Lightly grease the dish with oil. Use wholemeal breadcrumbs.
CHO: 15 g Calories: 195

Use crumbs of gluten-free bread (see recipe, page 214).

Lightly grease the dish with oil.

No change necessary.

Use wholemeal breadcrumbs.

Lightly grease the dish with oil.

Herrings in Oatmeal

Serves 4: 320 calories per portion

    4 medium-sized herrings
    5 level tablespoons oatmeal or rolled (porridge) oats
    1 level teaspoon salt
    knob of margarine
    lemon wedges

1. Cut the heads off the herrings, using a sharp knife. Scrape the skin with a round-ended knife from tail to head to remove the scales. Wash under running water. Cut along the underside of each fish from head to tail. Remove the roe and reserve for serving separately. Gently scrape away the gut and discard.
2. Open each fish and place, skin side uppermost, on a board. Press firmly along the back of the fish to loosen the backbone. Turn the fish over and ease away the backbone from the fish, starting at the head end. Cut off the fins.
3. If using rolled oats, place in a plastic bag and crush with a rolling-pin.
4. Mix the oatmeal or crushed oats with salt on a plate and press each side of the fish into the oats to coat thoroughly.
5. Melt the margarine in a large frying-pan; fry the herrings, two at a time, for 5-8 minutes, turning each carefully with a fish slice during cooking.
6. Arrange the herrings on a warmed serving dish and garnish with lemon wedges. Serve immediately.

No change necessary.
CHO: 11 g Calories: 320

Replace the oatmeal with millet flakes.

Use polyunsaturated margarine.

No change necessary.

Mix some oat bran with the oatmeal.

Use safflower margarine.

Plaice with Tangy Tartare Sauce

Serves 4: 290 calories per portion

    1 packet (4) plaice fillets
    4 level tablespoons plain flour
    1 level teaspoon paprika
    salt
    2 oz/50 g butter

Dressing:

    4 gherkins
    2 level teaspoons capers
    1 11-oz/300-g can sweetcorn with red and green peppers
    4 tablespoons salad cream

    lemon wedges and parsley to garnish

1. Remove the grill rack and pre-heat a moderate grill. Warm a flat serving dish and a small glass bowl.
2. Wash the plaice fillets and dry on kitchen paper; trim if necessary. Mix the flour, paprika and a shake of salt together on a plate. Coat the plaice fillets in the seasoned flour. Reserve any remaining seasoned flour for the dressing.
3. Melt the butter in a grill pan. Dip the plaice fillets in butter, then turn over. Grill for 10-12 minutes until golden brown. Arrange the plaice on a warmed serving dish and keep warm.
4. Chop the gherkins and capers. Stir the remaining seasoned flour into the butter in the grill pan. Add the chopped gherkins and capers, corn and salad cream. Heat the mixture through under the grill, stirring occasionally.
5. Pour the dressing into a warmed glass bowl and place on the serving dish with the fish. Garnish with lemon wedges and a sprig of parsley. Serve immediately with chipped potatoes.

Use wholemeal flour for coating. Replace the butter with 1 oz/25 g polyunsaturated margarine. Use low-calorie salad cream. Serve with jacket potatoes or brown rice. CHO: 10 g Calories: 220

Replace the plain flour with potato flour or maize flour. Check that the salad cream contains no starch.

Replace the butter with polyunsaturated margarine. Use salad cream made from sunflower oil. Serve with jacket potatoes topped with low-fat soft cheese and chives.

Use home-made mayonnaise instead of bottled salad cream.

Use wholemeal flour for coating and serve with jacket potatoes.

Replace the butter with vegetable margarine.

Fluffy Fish Florentine

Serves 4: 225 calories per portion

> 4 plaice fillets
> 1⅞-oz/48-g jar crab spread
> 1 oz/25 g butter
> 8-oz/225-g carton frozen whole-leaf spinach

Topping:
> 1 egg, separated
> 1 level tablespoon chopped parsley
> 4 level tablespoons salad cream

1. Remove the rack from the grill pan and pre-heat a moderate grill. Warm a shallow 1-pint/500-ml ovenproof dish.
2. Wash the plaice fillets and remove the dark skin, if desired. Place the fillets, skin (or skinned side) uppermost on a board. Spread each with the crab spread and roll up from the tail end.
3. Melt the butter in grill pan. Dip the plaice fillets in butter and grill for 10-12 minutes, turning once.
4. Cook the spinach as directed on the carton; drain, add a knob of butter and seasoning to taste; spread in an ovenproof dish. Arrange the plaice fillets on the spinach; keep warm.
5. Place the egg yolk in a basin. Add the parsley and salad cream and mix well. Whisk the egg white until stiff, then fold into the mixture. Pile over the plaice fillets and spinach. Return to the grill and cook until risen and golden brown. Serve at once with lemon wedges and buttered new potatoes.

Omit the butter and lightly brush the plaice with oil. Omit the butter from the spinach. Use low-calorie salad cream.
CHO: 1 g Calories: 180

Check that the crab spread does not contain starch. Replace with canned crabmeat or low-fat soft cheese and fresh herbs. Check that the salad cream does not contain starch.

Replace the butter with polyunsaturated margarine. Replace the salad cream with fromage frais mixed with 1 tablespoon lemon juice.

Replace the crab spread with fresh or frozen crab meat. Replace the salad cream with home-made mayonnaise.

No change necessary.

Replace the butter with vegetable margarine.

Curried Haddock Platter

Special Diets

Serves 4: 525 calories per portion

- 1 large onion
- 8 oz/225 g young carrots
- 1 clove garlic
- salt and pepper
- 12 oz/350 g haddock fillet
- 2 tablespoons groundnut oil
- 2 level teaspoons curry paste
- 2 level teaspoons curry powder
- 1 level tablespoon plain flour
- 15½-oz/425-g can butter beans
- 7-oz/198-g can tuna steak in brine
- 1 tablespoon lemon juice
- 8 oz/225 g long-grain rice

1. Peel and thinly slice the onion and carrots. Peel the garlic and crush with a little salt. Wash the haddock, remove the skin and cut the fish into small pieces.

2. Place the onion, carrots, garlic, oil, curry paste and curry powder in a saucepan and fry for 5 minutes, stirring occasionally. Add the flour and cook for 1 minute. Add the haddock, the contents of the cans of butter beans and tuna, ¼ pint/150 ml water and the lemon juice. Bring slowly to the boil, stirring gently; cover and simmer for 10 minutes, until the fish is tender.

3. Cook the rice in a large saucepan of boiling, salted water for about 12 minutes. Test by pressing a grain between thumb and finger. Drain and rinse with boiling water. Turn into a warmed serving dish.

4. Taste the curry and season with salt and pepper if necessary; pour over the rice.

Thicken the sauce with wholemeal flour and serve on brown rice. Cut the oil for frying by half.
CHO: 72 g Calories: 490

Replace the flour with potato flour. Check that the curry powder and paste do not contain starch.

Use polyunsaturated oil.

Use curry powder and paste without added colourings.

Thicken the sauce with wholemeal flour and serve with brown rice.

Use polyunsaturated oil.

No change necessary.

Tangy-topped Cod

Serves 4: 200 calories per portion

½ oz/15 g butter
1¼ lb/550 g cod fillet
½ packet apple and lemon stuffing mix
2 rashers streaky lean bacon
2 tomatoes
salt and pepper

1. Pre-heat a moderate oven (375°F/190°C/Gas 5). Butter a 2-pint/1-litre shallow ovenproof dish.
2. Wash the cod; remove the skin, if desired, and cut into 4 equal portions; place in the dish.
3. Make up the stuffing as directed on the packet; spread evenly on top of the cod portions. Remove the rind and bone from the bacon; cut each rasher across in half, then cut each half into 2 strips. Place 2 bacon strips in a cross on top of the stuffing on each cod portion.
4. Cut the tomatoes in halves; arrange, cut sides uppermost, around the fish. Sprinkle the tomatoes with salt and pepper and dot with butter.
5. Bake in the centre of the oven for 20-25 minutes, until the fish is tender. Serve immediately with creamed potatoes and buttered sweet corn.

Replace the stuffing mixture with a home-made one: 2 oz/50 g wholemeal breadcrumbs, 1 small unpeeled apple, the grated rind and juice of half a lemon, ½ teaspoon chopped fresh mint, salt and pepper, bound together with a little beaten egg. Omit the butter and lightly brush the dish of tomatoes with oil.
CHO: 8 g Calories: 175

Replace the stuffing mix as for diabetic but use crumbs from gluten-free bread (see recipe, page 214).

Omit the butter and lightly brush the dish of tomatoes with oil. Omit the bacon and replace with a gherkin fan on each.

Replace the stuffing mix as for diabetic, using white breadcrumbs if preferred.

Replace stuffing mix as for diabetic.

Replace the bacon with strips of vegetarian cheese, added 5 minutes before the end of the cooking time.

Somerset Cod Pie

Serves 4: 350 calories per portion

> 1 small onion
> 4 tomatoes
> 1¼ lb/550 g cod fillet
> 1 oz/25 g polyunsaturated margarine
> 2 level tablespoons plain flour
> ¼ pint/150 ml cider
> salt and pepper
> 1 packet (5-6 servings) instant mashed potato
> ½ oz/15 g butter

1. Pre-heat a moderately hot oven (400°F/200°C/Gas 6).
2. Peel and chop the onion. Place the tomatoes in a bowl and cover with boiling water. Leave for 1 minute; drain, peel and cut into quarters. Wash the cod and remove the skin; cut into 1-inch/25-cm cubes.
3. Melt the margarine in a frying-pan. Add the onion and cook for 3 minutes. Stir in the flour and cook for 1 minute. Make the cider up to ½ pint/275 ml with cold water. Add to the pan and bring to the boil, stirring continuously; simmer for 2 minutes. Add the fish, tomatoes and some salt and pepper. Cook for 1 minute, then pour into a 3-pint/1.5-litre ovenproof dish.
4. Make up the instant potato as directed on the packet. Spread evenly over the fish mixture and dot with butter. Place on a baking sheet.
5. Bake in the centre of the oven for 30-35 minutes, until the potato is golden brown. Serve the pie hot with a green vegetable.

Replace the plain flour with wholemeal flour. Use dry cider. Omit the butter from the top of the potato. CHO: 9 g Calories: 320

Replace the plain flour with potato flour.

Omit the butter.

Replace the instant mashed potato with 1½ lb/650 g potatoes, peeled and mashed.

Replace the plain flour with wholemeal flour.

Use vegetable margarine.

Cod and Tuna Pie

Serves 4: 420 calories per portion

    8 oz/225 g cod fillet
    2 rashers streaky bacon

Sauce:

    ½ oz/15 g polyunsaturated margarine
    1 level tablespoon plain flour
    ¼ pint/150 ml semi-skimmed milk
    salt and pepper
    ¼ level teaspoon mixed dried herbs
    7-oz/200-g can tuna steak in brine
    7½-oz/212-g packet frozen puff pastry, just thawed

    beaten egg or milk to glaze

1. Pre-heat a hot oven (425°F/220°C/Gas 7).
2. Wash the cod and remove the skin; cut into small pieces. Remove the rind and bone from the bacon and cut into strips.
3. Melt the margarine in a small saucepan; add the bacon and cook for 2 minutes. Add the flour and cook gently for 2 minutes. Add the milk, bring to the boil, stirring continuously, and simmer for 2 minutes. Add salt and pepper and mixed dried herbs. Remove the fat from the heat and stir in the contents of the can of tuna and the cod. Turn the mixture into an 8½-inch/21-cm ovenproof pie-plate.
4. Roll out the pastry and trim to a round 1 inch/2.5 cm larger than the top of the pie-plate. Cut a ½-inch/1.25-cm-wide pastry strip from the edge. Dampen the edge of the pie-plate; place the strip of pastry on the edge; brush with water. Place the remaining pastry on top and press the edges together firmly.
5. Using the back of a knife, cut the edge to form 'flakes', flute the edge. Roll out the pastry trimmings and make 'leaves' to decorate the top of the pie. Make a hole in the centre of the pie; arrange the leaves around it. Brush the pie with beaten egg or milk.
6. Place the pie on a baking sheet and bake in the centre of the oven for 20-25 minutes, until the pastry is golden brown. Serve hot with creamed potatoes and peas.

Use wholemeal flour instead of plain. Cut all fat off the bacon. Use skimmed milk.
CHO: 25 g Calories: 410

Replace the flour with maize flour. Replace the puff pastry with gluten-free shortcrust (see recipe, page 217).

Omit the bacon. Use polyunsaturated margarine and skimmed milk. Replace the pastry topping with mashed potato.

No change necessary.

Use wholemeal flour instead of plain and wholemeal puff pastry.

Omit the bacon: use vegetable-fat puff pastry.

Caribbean Fish Platter

Serves 2: 505 calories per portion

    1 level tablespoon plain flour
    salt and pepper
    12 oz/325 g (2) plaice fillets
    2 oz/50 g butter
    4 oz/100 g (1) banana
    1 10-oz/275-g can potatoes
    2 tomatoes
    1 lemon
    1 rounded teaspoon chopped fresh parsley
    ¼ level teaspoon dried thyme

1. Mix the flour, ¼ level teaspoon salt and a shake of pepper together on a plate. Place the fillets, skin-side down, on a board and cut the fish off the skin, starting at the tail end of each, by holding the tail firmly and cutting off the flesh with a pushing movement. Cut each fillet into two lengthwise and coat in seasoned flour.
2. Melt 1 oz/25 g butter in a frying-pan; fry the fish for 2-3 minutes on each side until golden brown. Place on a warmed serving dish; keep warm.
3. Peel and cut the banana into two lengthwise; coat in seasoned flour and fry for 1-2 minutes on each side, or until slightly browned. Place on a serving dish with the fish.
4. Wipe out the pan with kitchen paper. Drain the liquid from the potatoes. Melt ½ oz/12 g butter in a frying-pan, add the potatoes and fry until golden brown; place on the serving dish.
5. Cut the tomatoes in halves; fry for 2-3 minutes on each side until just soft, then place on the serving dish.
6. Cut the lemon in half lengthwise, cut one half into wedges and squeeze the juice from the remainder.
7. Heat the remaining butter in a frying-pan until golden brown, stir in the lemon juice, parsley, thyme, ¼ level teaspoon salt and a shake of pepper. Pour over the fish and garnish with lemon wedges. Serve immediately.

Use wholemeal flour for coating. Replace the canned potatoes with tiny unskinned new potatoes. Use polyunsaturated margarine instead of butter.
CHO: 38 g Calories: 505

Replace the flour with rice flour.

Replace the butter with polyunsaturated margarine.

No change necessary.

As for diabetic.

Replace the butter with vegetable margarine.

Sicilian Casserole

Serves 4: 208 calories per portion

1½-lb/225-g pack frozen sliced green beans
1¼ lb/550 g cod fillet
10-oz/275-g can condensed tomato and rice soup
a few drops Worcestershire sauce

1. Pre-heat a moderate oven (375°F/190°C/Gas 5).
2. Cook the beans as directed on the pack; drain and place in a 2-pint/1-litre casserole.
3. Wash the cod; remove the skin and any bones. Cut into 1-inch/2.5-cm pieces. Carefully mix with the beans in the casserole.
4. Place the soup, 3 tablespoons cold water and the Worcestershire sauce in a saucepan. Bring to the boil, stirring, and pour into the casserole. Cover with a lid or foil.
5. Place the casserole on a baking sheet. Bake in the centre of the oven for 30-35 minutes, until the fish is tender. Serve hot with creamed potatoes.
Note For this dish, you could replace the cod with haddock fillet.

Special Diets

Replace the tomato soup with tomato juice and add some cooked brown rice.
CHO: 4 g Calories: 150

As diabetic. Replace the Worcestershire sauce with a pinch of chilli powder.

No change necessary.

As diabetic.

No change necessary. Serve with spinach and jacket potatoes.

No change necessary.

Savoury Fish Envelope

Serves 4: 475 calories per portion

1 lb/450 g smoked cod fillet
2 eggs
4 oz/100 g frozen peas
1 oz/25 g polyunsaturated margarine
1 oz/25 g plain flour
½ pint/250 ml semi-skimmed milk
1-2 teaspoons lemon juice
salt and pepper
7½-oz/212-g packet frozen puff pastry, just thawed
beaten egg to glaze
parsley to garnish

1. Pre-heat a hot oven (450°F/230°C/Gas 8).
2. Wash the cod; place in a large saucepan or frying-pan and cover with water. Bring to the boil, then simmer until the cod is cooked (about 4-5 minutes, depending on the thickness of the fish); drain. Remove the bones and flake the fish.
3. Hard-boil the eggs for 10 minutes, crack and leave to cool in cold water. Shell and dry on kitchen paper, then chop. Cook the peas in a little boiling salted water for 3 minutes, then drain.
4. Place the margarine in a saucepan, with the flour. Add the milk and bring to the boil, stirring continuously. Simmer for 2 minutes. Add the lemon juice and some salt and pepper. Stir in the flaked cod, peas and chopped hard-boiled egg. Leave the fish mixture to cool.
5. Roll out the pastry on a floured board and trim to an 11-inch/28-cm square. Pile the fish mixture in the centre. Brush the edges of the pastry with water. Bring the 4 corners of the pastry over the fish mixture to the centre, forming an envelope; seal the edges firmly. Place on a baking sheet and brush with beaten egg.
6. Bake in the centre of the oven for 20-25 minutes until golden brown. Remove from the oven and carefully lift on to a serving dish or board. Garnish with a sprig of parsley. Serve hot with baby carrots and new potatoes.

Replace the plain flour with wholemeal flour. Use wholemeal puff pastry.
CHO: 28 g Calories: 465

Replace the flour with maize flour. Replace the puff pastry with gluten-free shortcrust (see recipe, page 217).

Replace the puff pastry with shortcrust made from polyunsaturated margarine.

Replace the smoked cod fillet with fresh cod fillet and use home-made flaky pastry.

Replace the plain flour with wholemeal. Use wholemeal puff pastry.

Use vegetable-fat puff pastry.

Halibut in Seafood Sauce

Serves 4: 325 calories per portion

> 4 halibut steaks, each about 6 oz/175 g in weight
> ½ pint/275 ml semi-skimmed milk
> 1 oz/25 g butter
> 1 oz/25 g flour
> 2 hard-boiled eggs
> 3¼-oz/100-g can Norwegian shrimps
> salt and pepper

1. Place the halibut steaks in a frying-pan and cover with the milk. Bring to the boil and simmer for 10-12 minutes until cooked. Remove from the pan and place on a warm serving dish.
2. Cream the butter and flour together in a small basin. Add the milk from the pan and whisk until blended. Return to the pan, bring to the boil and simmer for 3-4 minutes.
3. Chop the eggs and drain the shrimps. Add to the sauce, season to taste, re-heat and pour over the fish.

Special Diets

Use polyunsaturated margarine instead of butter; use skimmed milk. Serve with spinach to increase the fibre content of the meal.
CHO: 9 g Calories: 325

Thicken the sauce with maize flour instead of wheat flour.

Use polyunsaturated margarine instead of butter; use skimmed milk.

No change necessary.

Serve with spinach to increase the fibre content of the meal.

Use vegetable margarine instead of butter.

Chicken with Cucumber Sauce

Serves 4: 315 calories per portion

>   4 small chicken joints,
>   each about 5 oz/125 g in weight
>   2 oz/50 g polyunsaturated margarine
>   1 chicken stock cube
>   ¾ pint/375 ml boiling water
>   2 tablespoons soured cream
>   salt and pepper
>   ½ cucumber

1. Coat the chicken joints in flour.
2. Melt the margarine in a large frying-pan. Fry the chicken joints slowly for 20-25 minutes, turning occasionally, until golden brown and tender.
3. Remove the joints and place on a warm serving dish.
4. Add the remaining flour to the fat in the pan and cook for 2 minutes. Dissolve the stock cube in boiling water and add to the pan. Bring to the boil, stirring, and cook for 2 minutes; add salt and pepper to taste.
5. Peel the cucumber, cut into small dice and add to the sauce; re-heat lightly, stir in the soured cream and pour over the chicken. Serve with grilled, halved tomatoes.

Remove the skin from the chicken before coating. Replace the soured cream with low-fat natural yoghurt. CHO: 12 g Calories: 290

Replace the plain flour with maize flour.

Skin the chicken and remove any fat. Replace the soured cream with low-fat natural yoghurt.

Omit the stock cube and add bone stock. Wash the cucumber well.

Use wholemeal flour. Add 2 heaped tablespoons sweetcorn to the cucumber.

Onion with Cucumber Sauce
Omit the chicken. Fry 2 large halved onions in margarine, add 2 teaspoons coriander, then cover and cook slowly for 20 minutes. Place in a serving dish. Add 1 oz/25 g flour, 1 tablespoon yeast extract, ½ pint/ 250 ml water, the cucumber and the contents of a small can of sweetcorn to the pan. Add the soured cream, pour over the onions and sprinkle with 1 oz/25 g toasted flaked almonds.

Chicken Paprika

Special Diets

Serves 4: 105 calories per portion

    1 large onion
    1 oz/25 g plain flour
    2 level teaspoons paprika
    1 oz/25 g polyunsaturated margarine
    4 chicken joints, about 5 oz/125 g each
    2 level tablespoons tomato purée
    ¾ pint/375 ml stock or water
    salt and pepper
    2-3 tablespoons natural yoghurt

1. Peel and chop the onion. Mix the flour and paprika together. Melt the margarine in a large frying-pan.
2. Coat the chicken joints in flour and fry with the onion, turning, for 2-3 minutes, until lightly browned; remove and keep warm. Add the remaining flour to the fat in the pan; cook for 2 minutes. Stir in the tomato purée and stock or water; bring to the boil, stirring. Add some salt and pepper.
3. Return the chicken joints to the pan, cover with a lid or large piece of foil and simmer for 25-30 minutes, until tender.
4. Remove the joints and place on a warm serving dish.
5. Stir the yoghurt into the sauce and spoon over the chicken. Serve with plain boiled rice or noodles.

Remove the skin from the chicken.
CHO: 10 g Calories: 105

Replace the plain flour with maize flour. Serve on boiled rice.

Remove the skin from the chicken.

Use a free-range fresh chicken, if possible. Use bone stock or water instead of the stock cube.

Use wholemeal flour. Add a small (5.29-oz/150-g) can butter beans.

Mushroom Paprika

Replace the chicken with ¾ lb/400 g mushrooms, trimmed, wiped and dippped in milk before coating. Cook for 10 minutes in the sauce, then add 4 oz/100 g frozen peas and bring to the boil. Serve on brown rice.

Lemony Chicken Roast

Special Diets

Serves 4: 540 calories per portion

1 chicken, about 3 lb/1.4 kg drawn weight

Stuffing:

1 large onion
2 lemons
1 oz/25 g butter
3 level tablespoons chopped parsley
2 level teaspoons dried tarragon
6 oz/175 g fresh breadcrumbs
½ level teaspoon salt
pepper
1 egg

Glaze:

1 level tablespoon moist brown sugar
1 teaspoon Worcestershire sauce
1 oz/25 g polyunsaturated margarine

parsley
lemon slices (optional)

1. Pre-heat a moderately hot oven (400°F/200°C/Gas 6).
2. Remove the giblets, rinse the chicken, then dry with kitchen paper. Cover the giblets with water and simmer for 30 minutes to make stock for gravy, if desired.
3. Peel and finely chop the onion. Scrub the lemons, grate the rind and squeeze the juice.
4. Melt the butter in a pan and gently fry the onions until softened but not browned (about 5 minutes). Add the lemon rind, parsley, tarragon, breadcrumbs and seasoning and beaten egg. Mix well.
5. Form half the mixture into balls and use the rest to stuff the neck end of the chicken. Place the lemon juice, sugar and Worcestershire sauce in a pan and heat together until the sugar has dissolved.
6. Melt the margarine in a roasting tin; place the chicken in the tin. Baste well and roast in the oven for about 1 hour. After 30 minutes' cooking time, place the stuffing balls round the chicken and pour the glaze over the chicken. Return to the oven, basting occasionally.
7. To serve, place the chicken on a warmed serving dish and arrange the stuffing balls around. Pour the pan juices over the chicken and garnish with parsley sprigs and lemon slices, if desired.

Replace the butter with low-fat spread. Use wholemeal breadcrumbs. Replace the brown sugar with liquid sweetener.
CHO: 22 g Calories: 470

Use crumbs from gluten-free bread (see recipe, page 214).

Replace the butter with polyunsaturated margarine.

Use a free-range chicken. Scrub the lemon thoroughly.

Use wholemeal breadcrumbs and add 2 oz/50 g walnuts to the stuffing.

Not suitable. Serve fish, cheese or lentil loaf instead.

Braised Chicken with Vegetables

Special Diets

Serves 4: 280 calories per portion

3-lb/1.4-kg chicken
8 oz/225 g button onions
8 oz/225 g carrots
4 sticks celery
1 chicken stock cube
1 oz/25 g polyunsaturated margarine
1 tablespoon sunflower oil
1 rounded tablespoon plain flour
pepper
gravy browning
salt

1. Pre-heat a moderate oven (375°F/190°C/Gas 5).
2. Remove the giblets from the chicken; place in a saucepan, cover with water, bring to the boil and simmer for 30 minutes.
3. Peel the onions and carrots; cut the carrots into quarters lengthwise. Wash the celery and cut into 1-inch/2.5-cm lengths.
4. Strain the giblet stock into a measuring jug and make up to ¼ pint/125 ml with water if necessary. Add a chicken stock cube; stir until dissolved.
5. Heat the margarine and oil in a large frying-pan. Add the chicken and fry until browned all over, turning frequently. Place the chicken in a large 4-pint/2-litre casserole. Add the vegetables to the remaining fat in the pan and fry for 5 minutes. Stir in the flour, add the stock and a shake of pepper. Bring to the boil, stirring, and pour over the chicken. Cover the casserole and place in the centre of the oven. Cook for 1 hour until the chicken and vegetables are tender.
6. Lift the chicken on to a warmed serving dish. Remove the trussing string. Stir a little gravy browning into the sauce, if desired. Taste and season with salt and pepper. Serve the vegetables and gravy with chicken and boiled potatoes.

Remove all fat from the chicken and giblets.
CHO: 8 g Calories: 280

Replace the chicken stock cube with yeast extract. Check that the gravy browning contains no starch. Replace the flour with maize flour.

Remove all the fat and skin from the chicken. Replace the stock cube with ½ teaspoon dried thyme or a sprig of fresh thyme.

Replace the chicken stock cube with 1 sprig fresh thyme or ½ teaspoon dried thyme. Omit the gravy browning.

Use wholemeal flour.

Braised Cauliflower with Vegetables
Replace the chicken with 1 large lightly cooked cauliflower. Omit the frying and pour the vegetable sauce over. Serve with grated parmesan cheese.

Roast Turkey

Special Diets

136 calories per 5 oz/150 g turkey

 1 oven-ready turkey
 chestnut or forcemeat stuffing (see recipes)
 cooking fat
 bacon rolls (see recipe) and chipolata sausages
 2 level tablespoons plain flour
 salt and pepper
 watercress
 bread sauce (see recipe)

1. Pre-heat a moderate oven (375°F/190°C/Gas 5).
2. Remove the giblets, rinse the inside of the bird with cold water and dry with kitchen paper. Place the giblets in a saucepan with 1½ pints/750 ml water. Bring to the boil, cover and simmer for 1 hour; strain.
3. Calculate the cooking time of the turkey by adding the weight of the stuffing ingredients to the drawn weight of the bird, to find total weight; allow 15 minutes per lb/500 g up to 14 lb/6.4 kg and 10 minutes per lb/500 g for every lb/500 g over 14 lb/6.4 kg.
4. Stuff the neck end of the bird with chestnut or half of the forcemeat stuffing. Use the remainder to make stuffing balls (see recipe). Truss the turkey with fine string. Cover the breast with cooking fat. Wrap in a double thickness of greaseproof paper and tie securely with string or place in a roasting bag.
5. Place in the centre of the oven and place a meat tin underneath to catch the drips. Potatoes may be roasted in the tin under the turkey; place in the oven 1 hour before the end of the calculated cooking time.
6. About 25 minutes before the end of the cooking time, place the bacon rolls and chipolata sausages in a roasting tin on the floor of the oven.
7. When cooked, remove the potatoes from the tin. Slit the paper underneath the turkey to allow the fat to run into the tin below, before removing the turkey from the oven.
8. Place the turkey on a warmed serving dish; remove the paper and string and the trussing string. Place the turkey in the oven, with the

No change necessary. Use low-fat sausages.
CHO: – Calories: 136 per 5 oz/150 g

Use home-made sausages (see recipe, page 89). Replace the flour for thickening the gravy with maize meal.

Remove as much fat as possible from the carcass and prick the skin. Pour off all the fat and make gravy from the drippings. Use low-fat sausages.

No change necessary.

No change necessary.

Not suitable. Replace with a special vegetarian dish such as vol-au-vents filled with vegetables and nuts or seafood or poached salmon.

heat turned off and the door ajar, while making the gravy.

9. Pour off most of the fat from the roasting tin; stir the flour into the tin. Add 1 pint/500 ml giblet stock, salt and pepper. Bring to the boil, stirring, then simmer for 3 minutes. Strain into a warmed gravy boat.

10. Just before serving, arrange the bacon rolls, chipolata sausages and stuffing balls around the turkey. Place a small bunch of watercress at the tip of the breastbone of the turkey. Serve with bread sauce (see recipe).

Bread Sauce

Serves 6: 78 calories per portion

> 1 small onion
> 2 cloves
> 6 peppercorns
> ½ pint/250 ml semi-skimmed milk
> 2 oz/50 g fresh white breadcrumbs
> 1 oz/25 g butter
> ½ level teaspoon salt

1. Peel and slice the onion. Place in a small saucepan with the cloves, peppercorns and milk. Cover and leave to infuse over a very low heat for 20-30 minutes. Strain into an ovenproof bowl or gravy boat.

2. Stir in the breadcrumbs, 1 oz/25 g butter and salt; leave in a warm place until the bread has swollen. Place in the oven to re-heat just before serving.

Chestnut Stuffing

Serves 6: 170 calories per portion

> 1 small onion
> 8 oz/225 g lean streaky bacon or bacon pieces
> 15¾-oz/153-g can chestnut purée (unsweetened) or chestnut
>   purée made from 1½ lb/675 g chestnuts
> 1 level teaspoon sugar
> salt and pepper

1. Peel and finely chop the onion. Remove the rind and bone from the bacon; cut the bacon into small dice.

2. Place all the ingredients in a bowl; mix well together. Use to stuff the neck end of the turkey.

Use wholemeal breadcrumbs, and low-fat margarine instead of butter. CHO: 7 g Calories: 76

Use crumbs made from gluten-free bread (see recipe, page 214).

Use skimmed milk and polyunsaturated margarine instead of butter.

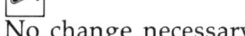
No change necessary.

Use wholemeal breadcrumbs.

Use vegetable margarine instead of butter.

Omit the sugar. CHO: 23 g Calories: 164

No change necessary.

Cut all visible fat off the bacon.

No change necessary.

No change necessary.

Omit the bacon and replace with an egg and 1 rounded tablespoon chopped fresh herbs.

Forcemeat Stuffing

Serves 6: 320 calories per portion

> 8 oz/225 g fresh white breadcrumbs
> 4 oz/100 g shredded suet
> 1 rounded tablespoon chopped parsley
> grated rind of 1 lemon
> salt and pepper
> 1 egg
> milk to bind (about 2 tablespoons)
> breadcrumbs for coating
> groundnut oil for frying (about 1 oz/25 g)

1. Mix all the dry ingredients together.
2. Beat and add the egg and sufficient milk to bind. Use half of the stuffing to stuff the neck end of the turkey. Use the remainder to make stuffing balls.
3. To make stuffing balls, shape the stuffing into balls about the size of a walnut and coat with breadcrumbs; press the crumbs firmly on to the balls.
4. Heat some fat in a frying-pan, add the stuffing balls and fry until golden brown all over; drain on kitchen paper. Alternatively, cook in the tin with the bacon rolls and sausages in the oven.

Use wholemeal breadcrumbs, and 3 oz/75 g vegetable suet or melted polyunsaturated margarine.
CHO: 19 g Calories: 312

Use crumbs made from gluten-free bread (see recipe, page 214). Replace the suet with melted margarine.

Use skimmed milk and vegetable suet or melted polyunsaturated margarine.

No change necessary.

Use wholemeal breadcrumbs.

As for diabetic.

Bacon Rolls

Remove the rind and bone from 4 oz/100 g streaky bacon; stretch the bacon rashers with the back of a knife. Cut in halves, horizontally. Roll up and place in a small roasting tin. Place on the floor of the oven for about 20 minutes before the end of the cooking time.
Note Use lean bacon and drain well after cooking.

Chicken Mayonnaise

Serves 4: 320 calories per portion

> 1 tablespoon lemon juice
> ½ level teaspoon dried rosemary
> ½ level teaspoon salt
> pepper
> 4 chicken breast joints, each about 5 oz/150 g in weight
> 1 level teaspoon gelatine
> 1 level teaspoon tomato ketchup
> ¼ pint/125 ml thick mild mayonnaise
> 1 piece cucumber skin
> 3 stuffed olives
> shredded lettuce
> 1 tomato

1. Place the lemon juice, rosemary, ½ pint/250 ml water, salt and a shake of pepper in a large saucepan.
2. Bring to the boil, add the chicken. Cover and simmer very gently for 15-20 minutes.
3. Remove the saucepan from the heat; leave the chicken to cool in the stock.
4. Remove the chicken from the saucepan, take off the skin and remove the bones. Place the chicken on a wire rack over a plate or tray.
5. Measure 2 tablespoons water into a small basin; add the gelatine and stir. Place the basin in a saucepan of water over a moderate heat. Stir until the gelatine has dissolved; stir in the ketchup. Remove from the pan.
6. Quickly stir the mayonnaise into the gelatine mixture; mix well.
7. Spoon the mayonnaise over each chicken piece to coat evenly; leave the chicken on a wire rack until the dressing has set.
8. To garnish the chicken, cut 4 thin strips of cucumber skin; place a strip on top of each piece of chicken to represent a stem. Cut 8 small diamond shapes to represent leaves and place 2 on each stem. Slice the olives; place a slice of olive at the top of each stem. Cut 4 slices in halves and place a half on each side of each stem.
9. Serve on shredded lettuce with tomato wedges.

Replace half of the mayonnaise with low-fat thick natural yoghurt. Mix some high-fibre vegetables into the shredded lettuce such as grated carrot, shredded spinach, cooked peas or sweetcorn.
CHO: 2 g Calories: 235

No change necessary but check that the mayonnaise contains no starch.

No change necessary if the mayonnaise is made with polyunsaturated oil.

Use home-made mayonnaise and a free-range chicken.

Mix in high-fibre vegetables as for diabetic.

Plaice Mayonnaise
Replace the chicken with rolled, skinned fillets of plaice and poach in lemony stock for 5 minutes. Replace the gelatine with agar-agar.

Roast Duck with Orange and Port Sauce

Serves 4: 300 calories per portion

    1 oven-ready duck
salt
    2 medium-sized oranges

Sauce:

    1 small orange
    1 small onion
    1 rasher lean streaky bacon
    ½ oz/15 g polyunsaturated margarine
    knob of lard
    1 level tablespoon plain flour
    8 fl oz/200 ml giblet stock
    2 fl oz/50 ml port
    1 rounded teaspoon redcurrant jelly
    salt and pepper

    watercress

1. Pre-heat a moderately hot oven (400°F/200°C/Gas 6).

2. Remove the giblets; rinse the inside of the duck with cold water and dry with kitchen paper. Place the giblets in a saucepan, cover with water, bring to the boil and simmer for 1 hour. Drain and reserve 8 fl oz/200 ml for sauce.

3. Weigh the duck and calculate the cooking time by allowing 15 minutes per lb/500 g.

4. Truss the duck with fine string, then place it on a rack in a roasting tin, prick the skin and sprinkle with salt, then cook in the centre of the oven for the calculated time.

5. Segment 2 medium-sized oranges; using a sharp or serrated knife cut the peel and pith from the fruit; cut out the segments and reserve.

6. To make the sauce, scrub a small orange, pare the rind with a potato peeler or sharp knife. Shred half of the pared rind and reserve; squeeze the juice from the orange and the reserved flesh. Peel and chop the onion. Remove the rind and bone from the bacon; chop the bacon.

7. Melt the margarine in a medium-sized saucepan, add the onion and bacon and fry for 3-4 minutes. Stir in the flour and gradually add

Special Diets

Remove all the fat. Replace the port with dry red wine and omit the redcurrant jelly.
CHO: 7.5 g Calories: 280

Replace the plain flour with maize flour or potato flour.

Remove all fat and skin from the duck. Use very lean bacon.

No change necessary.

In step 5, leave the skin and pith, if thin, on the orange, cut in thin slices, then halve the slices.

Baked Mackerel with Orange and Port Sauce
Serve the sauce with baked mackerel. Bake one mackerel per portion in a roasting tin for 15 minutes. Use the fish juices for the sauce.

the reserved stock, port, orange juice and pared rind. Bring to the boil, cover and simmer for 10 minutes. Place the orange shreds in a small saucepan, cover them with water, bring to the boil and cook for 5 minutes until tender; drain.

8. Strain the sauce; add the orange shreds and redcurrant jelly. Taste and season with salt and pepper.

9. Remove the duck from the oven and place on a warmed serving plate. Remove the trussing string. Place the orange segments and sprigs of watercress around the duck. Re-heat the sauce and place in a warmed sauceboat.

Golden Glazed Turkey

Serves 6: 380 calories per portion

> 3 oz/75 g dried apricots
> 1 turkey breast joint (about 1¼-1½ lb/550-650 g)
> 1 large orange
> 2 oz/50 g polyunsaturated margarine
> 6 oz/175 g fresh breadcrumbs
> ½ level teaspoon salt
> pepper
> 1 egg
> 2 level tablespoons clear honey
> 1 teaspoon vinegar
> parsley sprigs

1. Place the apricots in a small saucepan; cover with cold water. Bring to the boil and simmer for 10 minutes; then remove from the heat.
2. To make the stuffing, drain the apricots, place on a board and chop coarsely; place in a basin. Cut 3 slices from the centre of the orange; cut the slices into halves and reserve for garnish. Grate the rind and squeeze the juice from the remaining halves. Add the rind and 1 tablespoon juice to the basin; reserve the remaining juice for a glaze. Melt the margarine, add half to the apricot mixture in the basin with the breadcrumbs, salt, a shake of pepper and the egg; mix together and form into balls.
3. Pre-heat a moderately hot oven (400°F/200°C/Gas 6). Place the turkey in a small roasting tin, pour the remaining melted margarine over and cook in the centre of the oven for 30 minutes.
4. Meanwhile, make the glaze: measure the honey carefully, levelling off the spoon with the back of a knife and making sure there is none on the underside of the spoon. Mix in a basin with the vinegar and remaining orange juice.
5. Remove the turkey from the oven; pour the glaze over the meat and surround with the stuffing balls. Return the turkey to the oven and cook for a further 30-40 minutes until golden brown, basting with glaze occasionally.
6. To serve, place on a warmed serving plate and garnish with the parsley sprigs and the reserved orange slices. Serve with roast potatoes, peas and sweetcorn.

Use wholemeal breadcrumbs. Replace the margarine with 1 oz/25 g low-fat margarine. Reduce the honey to 1 teaspoon.
CHO: 38 g Calories: 330

Use crumbs made from gluten-free bread (see recipe, page 214). Use wine or cider vinegar.

Remove the fat from around the turkey joint and tie with string.

Use wholemeal breadcrumbs.

Replace the turkey with lentil loaf (see recipe, page 111). Serve hot, glazed and with stuffing balls (leave it to cool, then continue from step 4, cooking for 30 minutes).

Serves 4: 510 calories per portion

      2 oz/50 g polyunsaturated margarine
sunflower oil
      8 chicken drumsticks coated in crumbs
Corn fritters:
      5 oz/125 g plain flour
      ½ level teaspoon salt
      1 level teaspoon cream of tartar
      ½ level teaspoon bicarbonate of soda
      1 oz/25 g semolina
      1 egg
      3 tablespoons sunflower oil
      4 tablespoons semi-skimmed milk
      1 7-oz/148-g can sweetcorn with red and green peppers

      1 lb/450 g (4) medium-sized bananas
parsley

1. Heat 2 oz/50 g margarine and 1 tablespoon oil in a large frying pan. Add the chicken and cook for 20-25 minutes, turning once, until the chicken is golden brown and tender. Drain on kitchen paper and keep hot.
2. Meanwhile, to make the fritters, sift the flour, salt, cream of tartar and bicarbonate of soda into a bowl; add the semolina. Beat the egg in a basin and add the oil, milk and drained contents of the can of sweetcorn. Make a well in the centre of the flour, add the egg mixture and beat until well mixed.
3. Wash and dry the frying-pan; heat 1 oz/25 g margarine and 1 tablespoon oil in the pan. Place spoonsful of the mixture in the frying-pan, allowing room for the fritters to spread slightly. Cook for 2-3 minutes until the underside is golden brown. Turn over, press down with a palette knife and cook until golden brown. Place on a plate; keep warm.
4. Peel the bananas, cut in halves lengthwise and fry until golden brown.
9. Arrange the chicken pieces, fritters and bananas in a paper-lined basket or on a warmed serving dish. Garnish with a sprig of parsley and serve at once.

Buy uncoated drumsticks, remove the skin and coat in natural bran or rolled oats. Fry in oil and 1 oz/25 g margarine. Use wholemeal flour and wholemeal semolina for the fritters. Use skimmed milk. Cook in a very little oil in a non-stick pan.
CHO: 42 g Calories: 510

Buy uncoated drumsticks and coat with beaten egg and crumbs made from gluten-free bread (see recipe, page 214) or split-pea flour. Replace the flour, cream of tartar and bicarbonate of soda in the fritters with 4 oz/100 g Trufree or Jubilee no.7 self-raising flour. Replace the semolina with ground rice.

Buy uncoated drumsticks and remove the skin. Coat in egg and crumbs. Fry in polyunsaturated oil.

Buy uncoated drumsticks and coat with egg and breadcrumbs.

Use wholemeal flour and semolina in the fritters.

Courgettes Maryland
Omit the chicken. Coat thick slices of courgette in egg and sesame seeds. Fry in a little fat. Serve with corn fritters, bananas and chilli sauce.

Turkey Escallops Dutch-style

Special Diets

Serves 4: 340 calories per portion

>   4 turkey escallops
>   1 egg
>   2 oz/50 g fresh breadcrumbs
>   2 oz/50 g butter
>   8-oz/250-g packet frozen beans
>   1 small onion
>   1 red pepper
>   4 oz/100 g Gouda cheese
>   4 oz/100 g mushrooms
>   salt
>   pepper

1. Wet a sheet of greaseproof paper, place on a board, wet side up, arrange the turkey escallops over the paper and cover with another sheet of wetted greaseproof paper, wet side down. Beat well with the side of a rolling-pin to flatten and make thinner.
2. Beat the egg and pour into a shallow dish. Coat the turkey pieces in egg and breadcrumbs. Melt 2 oz/50 g butter in a large frying-pan and gently fry the coated turkey for about 8 minutes, turning once, until golden brown. Place the turkey down the centre of a warmed serving dish; keep warm.
3. Cook the beans as directed on the packet; arrange on the side of the dish. Dot with flakes of butter and keep warm.
4. Peel and finely chop the onion. Cut the pepper in half lengthwise, discarding the seeds, core and white pith; slice lengthwise and reserve 6 slices for garnish. Cut the cheese into 2-inch/5-cm matchsticks. Wash and quarter the mushrooms.
5. Melt a knob of butter in the frying-pan; add the onion and pepper; fry until soft but not browned. Add the mushrooms to the pan and fry gently until just tender; stir in the cheese and some salt and pepper.
6. Arrange the cheese mixture down the centre of the turkey pieces; garnish with the reserved pepper slices.

Use wholemeal crumbs. Replace 1 oz/25 g butter with 1 tablespoon polyunsaturated oil. Reduce the cheese to 2 oz/50 g.
CHO: 9 g Calories: 305

Use crumbs from gluten-free bread (see recipe, page 214).

Replace the butter with polyunsaturated margarine and oil. Replace the Gouda cheese with cottage cheese.

Use wholemeal crumbs or natural bran for coating the escallops.

Replace the turkey escallops with sliced tofu.

Turkey and Vegetable Pie

Serves 4: 605 calories per portion

1 turkey wing or leg joint
1 medium onion
½ level teaspoon salt
1 level teaspoon mixed dried herbs
pepper
½ pint/250 ml boiling water
milk
8 oz/200 g skinless pork sausages
knob of butter or turkey dripping
1 oz/25 g plain flour
8 oz/225 g frozen mixed vegetables
1 7½-oz/212-g packet frozen puff pastry, just thawed
egg or milk to glaze

1. Place the turkey in a medium-sized saucepan. Peel and quarter the onion and add to the pan with the salt, mixed herbs, a shake of pepper and the boiling water.
2. Bring to the boil, cover and simmer for 45 minutes. Remove from the heat. Strain the stock into a measuring jug; make up to ½ pint/250 ml with milk, if necessary. Reserve the onion from the stock.
3. Remove the skin and bones from the meat; cut the meat into large pieces and reserve. Pre-heat a hot oven (425°F/220°C/Gas 7).
4. Cut each sausage into 3 pieces. Melt the butter or dripping in a saucepan and fry the sausage pieces until lightly browned.
5. Add the flour to the pan; cook for a further 2 minutes.
6. Add the stock gradually, stirring. Bring to the boil, cook for 2 minutes. Add the turkey pieces, reserved onion and mixed vegetables to the pan; mix well. Pour into a 1½-pint/850-ml pie-dish.
7. Roll out the pastry until it is 1 inch/2.5 cm larger all round than the pie-dish. Cut a ½-inch/1-cm rim from around the edge of the pastry. Brush the edge of the pie-dish with water and press the pastry strip in position on the edge; brush with water. Support the remaining pastry on the rolling pin and lift on to the filling; press the edges together firmly and trim with a knife. Using the back of a knife, cut up the edge to form flakes. Flute the edge, make a hole in the centre and brush with egg or milk. Cut 'leaves' from the pastry trimmings and arrange on the pastry.
8. Bake in the centre of the oven for 25-30 minutes.

Replace the sausages with mushrooms. Use wholemeal puff pastry. CHO: 30 g Calories: 405

Use gluten-free pastry (see recipe, page 217). Replace the sausages with chopped bacon. Replace the plain flour with ground rice.

Replace the sausages with mushrooms and the butter with polyunsaturated margarine. Use home-made puff pastry (see recipe for steak and kidney pie, page 98).

Replace the sausages with chopped bacon.

Use wholemeal puff pastry; add a 7-oz/198-g can sweetcorn.

Replace the turkey meat with cooked or canned chick peas. Replace the sausages with 3 hard-boiled eggs. Use yeast extract or Vecon to make stock. Use vegetable margarine and vegetarian puff pastry (or home-made using vegetable fat).

Roast Goose with Sage and Apple Stuffing

Special Diets

Serves 8: 630 calories per portion

    1 oven-ready goose, about 7 lb/3.5 kg in weight

Stuffing:

- 2 medium onions
- 1 oz/25 g polyunsaturated margarine
- 1 level teaspoon dried sage
- 4 oz/100 g fresh breadcrumbs
- salt and pepper
- 1 small cooking apple
- 1 egg

- 2 medium eating apples
- 1 oz/25 g margarine
- 1 tablespoon oil
- cranberry sauce
- 1 rounded teaspoon plain flour

1. Pre-heat a moderate oven (375°F/190°C/Gas 5).

2. Remove the giblets and fat from inside the carcass; rinse the inside of the goose with cold water and dry with kitchen paper. Place the giblets in a saucepan, cover with water, bring to the boil and simmer for 1 hour; strain.

3. To make the stuffing, peel and finely chop the onions, melt the margarine in a saucepan, add the onion and cook for 5 minutes. Remove from the heat and stir in the sage, breadcrumbs, salt and a shake of pepper.

4. Peel, core and finely chop the cooking apple. Lightly beat the egg, add to the stuffing with the apple and mix well.

5. Stuff the neck end of the goose and place any remaining stuffing in the body cavity.

6. Draw the skin backwards over the neck and sew the skin flap underneath with a trussing needle and fine string. Tuck the tail under the skin at the other end of the goose and secure by sewing up with the string. Weigh the goose and calculate the cooking time by allowing 15 minutes per lb/500 g.

7. Place the goose on a wire rack in a roasting tin. Prick the skin and rub in the salt. Place in the centre of the oven; cook for the calculated

Reduce fat by boiling the onions instead of frying them and poaching the apple slices in a little water. Drain all the fat from the roasting tin. Use wholemeal breadcrumbs. Make the cranberry sauce from fresh fruit, and sweeten after cooking with liquid sweetener.
CHO: 15 g Calories: 570

Use crumbs from gluten-free bread. Replace the flour with potato flour.

Use polyunsaturated margarine for the stuffing. Poach the apples. Drain all the fat from the roasting tin and skim with kitchen paper, leaving just the juices for the gravy.

No change necessary.

Leave the skin on the cooking apple. Use wholemeal breadcrumbs.

time. Pour off the fat from the tin during cooking.

8. Cut each eating apple into 4 slices and remove the cores.

9. Heat the margarine and oil in a frying-pan, add the apple slices and fry, turning once until golden brown. Drain on kitchen paper.

10. To serve the goose, lift it on to a warmed serving dish; remove the trussing string. Place slices of apple around the goose and fill the centres with cranberry sauce; keep hot.

11. Pour off most of the fat from the roasting tin; stir the flour into the remaining fat and add ½ pint/250 ml giblet stock; bring to the boil, stirring occasionally; simmer for 3 minutes. Taste and season with salt and pepper. Place in a warmed gravy boat. Serve with the roast goose, roast potatoes and brussels sprouts.

Stuffed Vegetable Platter

Serve the stuffing with a platter of vegetables: tomatoes, courgettes, halved peppers, cabbage leaves and large, flat mushrooms. Blanch each vegetable, if necessary, until just tender, in boiling water. Arrange in a roasting tin, fill with stuffing, sprinkle with sesame seeds and bake under a piece of oiled greaseproof paper for ½ hour. Serve with jacket potatoes topped with soured cream.

Turkey and Paprika Braise

Serves 4: 270 calories per portion

1 turkey leg joint (thigh and drumstick),
   about 1½ lb/675 g in weight
1 rounded tablespoon plain flour
1 tablespoon paprika
salt and pepper
2 oz/50 g butter or turkey dripping
2 medium-sized onions
2 sticks celery
½ level teaspoon mixed dried herbs
15-oz/425-g can tomatoes

1. Pre-heat a cool oven (325°F/170°C/Gas 3). Cut the turkey leg through the joint into two. Mix the flour, paprika, 1 level teaspoon salt and a shake of pepper on a plate; coat the joints in seasoned flour.
2. Melt the butter or dripping in a large frying-pan; fry the turkey slowly, turning occasionally, for about 10 minutes. Place the joints in a 4-pint/2-litre casserole.
3. Peel the onions and slice finely. Wash and slice the celery. Fry the onion and celery in the remaining butter in a frying-pan for 5 minutes; stir in any remaining seasoned flour, the mixed herbs and tomatoes. Bring to the boil, stirring; pour over the turkey joints. Cover the casserole and cook in the centre of the oven for 1¾-2 hours until the meat is tender. Taste, and add more seasonings if needed. Cut the meat off the bone to serve.

Use wholemeal flour, omit the butter and use 1 oz/25 g polyunsaturated margarine.
CHO: 10 g Calories 215

Replace the plain flour with ground rice.

Remove the skin from the turkey; replace the butter with polyunsaturated margarine.

No change necessary.

Add a small can of butter beans towards the end of the cooking time.

Replace the turkey with 1 large bulb fennel, cooked in boiling salted water for 10 minutes and quartered. Use vegetable margarine. Cook with the sauce for ½ hour.

Beany Pork Cobbler

Serves 4: 507 calories per portion

> 1 lb/500 g lean boneless pie pork
> 1 oz/25 g plain flour
> 1 medium onion
> 1 tablespoon sunflower oil
> 1 15-oz/425-g can baked beans with tomato sauce
> 1 level tablespoon tomato ketchup
> salt and pepper

Topping:

> 4 oz/100 g self-raising flour
> 2 oz/50 g polyunsaturated margarine
> ½ level teaspoon salt
> pinch of dried sage
> semi-skimmed milk

1. Pre-heat a moderate oven (350°F/180°C/Gas 4).
2. Cut the pie pork into ½-inch/2.5-cm cubes; coat in plain flour. Peel and chop the onion.
3. Heat the oil in a frying-pan and fry the pork and onion until lightly browned. Stir in the remaining flour.
4. Drain the tomato sauce from the baked beans and make up to ½ pint/225 ml with water. Add to the pan with the tomato ketchup and bring to the boil, stirring. Add a little salt and pepper and pour into a 2-pint/1-litre casserole; cover and cook in the centre of the oven for 1 hour. Stir in the baked beans.
5. To prepare the topping, place the self-raising flour in a bowl, add the margarine, cut into small pieces, and rub in with the fingers until the mixture resembles fine breadcrumbs. Add the salt and sage. Stir in about 4 tablespoons milk to make a soft dough.
6. Turn out on to a floured board and knead lightly. Roll out to ¾ inch/2 cm thick and cut into 2-inch/5-cm rounds. Arrange on top of the casserole; brush with milk.
7. Return to the oven and cook, uncovered, for a further 20 minutes until the topping is golden brown. Serve hot.

Trim off all the visible fat; use wheat-meal 81% extraction self-raising flour in the cobbler.
CHO: 39 g Calories: 502

Replace the plain flour with potato flour. Use gluten-free beans (e.g. Heinz). Use recipe for gluten-free plain scones (see recipe, page 215), and roll out with special flour.

Cut all the fat off the meat and use polyunsaturated margarine. Use skimmed milk.

No change necessary.

Use fine wholemeal self-raising flour.

Vegetable Cobbler
Replace the pork with extra vegetables such as cubed aubergine, sliced courgettes and sliced celeriac. Cook in the oven for ½ hour. Make the topping with wholemeal flour and vegetable margarine. Add 2 oz/50 g grated cheese to the mixture and sprinkle with cheese.

Roast Pork with Fruit Stuffing

Serves 5: 423 calories per portion

       2 lb/1 kg belly pork

Stuffing:
- 1 medium orange
- 1 medium cooking apple
- 3 oz/75 g fresh breadcrumbs
- 1 level tablespoon chopped parsley
- 1 level teaspoon salt
- 1 egg

       gravy powder
       salt and pepper

1. Ask the butcher to bone the meat and score the skin. Place the bones in a saucepan, cover with water and simmer for 1 hour. Strain and use the stock for the gravy.

2. Pre-heat a moderate oven (375°F/190°C/Gas 5).

3. Scrub the orange, then grate the rind and squeeze the juice. Peel, core and dice the apple.

4. Place the breadcrumbs, parsley, orange rind, diced apple and salt in a basin. Beat and add the egg, with sufficient orange juice to bind the stuffing. Place along the centre of the meat. Roll up and tie with string.

5. Place the pork on a small rack in a roasting tin and cook in the centre of the oven for 1¼-1½ hours. Place the meat on a serving dish, remove the string and keep hot. Pour off the fat from the tin. Stir in the gravy powder, then add ½ pint/250 ml stock. Bring to the boil, stirring, and simmer for 3 minutes; taste and season with salt and pepper, then pour into a warm gravy boat.

Special Diets

Choose a lean piece of thick end belly and cut off all the visible fat and the skin. Use wholemeal or malted wholemeal breadcrumbs. Leave the skin on the apple.
CHO: 12.5 g Calories: 320

Use breadcrumbs from gluten-free bread or replace with 3 oz/75 g cooked rice. Use potato flour to thicken the gravy instead of gravy powder.

Choose a lean piece of thick end belly and cut off all the fat and skin.

Replace the gravy powder with flour.

Use wholemeal breadcrumbs and leave the skin on the apple. Grate the orange rind, then cut off the pith and use all of the orange, chopped.

Not suitable.

Home-made Sausages

Makes 10: 105 calories each

1 lb/450 g lean belly pork
3 slices bread from a large white loaf
1 level teaspoon salt
¼-½ level teaspoon pepper
½-¾ level teaspoon mixed dried herbs
1½ oz/40 g breadcrumbs, browned under the grill

1. Remove the bones and skin from the pork; cut the meat into thin strips.
2. Finely mince the meat and bread. Place in a bowl; add the salt, pepper and herbs; mix.
3. Turn the mixture out on to a floured board; divide into 10 pieces; roll each between the hands to form a sausage shape, about 3½ inches/9 cm long. Alternatively, roll into balls, then flatten to form sausageburgers. Place the browned breadcrumbs on a large plate and roll the sausages in them to coat.
4. Melt a little fat in a frying-pan, add the sausages and cook over a low heat for 15-20 minutes, turning until evenly browned. Alternatively, grill under a moderate heat.
To freeze, place the sausages on a baking tray, chill, then open-freeze for about 1 hour. Pack into freezer bags or boxes, label and store in the freezer for up to 2 months.

Special Diets

Use wholemeal breadcrumbs and cut all visible fat from the meat.
CHO: 5.5 Calories: 95

Use crumbs made from gluten-free bread, both fresh and browned.

Cut all visible fat from the pork. Cook by grilling. Serve with tomatoes or a moist vegetable because lack of fat will make the sausages dry. A knob of polyunsaturated margarine may be added to the meat, if preferred.

No change necessary.

Use wholemeal breadcrumbs and roll in natural wheat bran, crushed All-bran or rolled oats.

Replace the pork with 8 oz/225 g each cooked brown lentils and chopped nuts. Bind with an egg.

Roast Pork with Sage and Onion Stuffing and Apple Sauce

Special Diets

Roasting times:
Moderate oven (350°F/180°C/Gas 4).
All joints 35 minutes per lb/450 g plus 35 minutes.
For a crisp crackling, rub a little oil into the scored skin and press salt all over. Place the joint on a rack in a roasting tin.

Sage and Onion Stuffing

Serves 6: 104 calories per portion

   4 oz/100 g onions, chopped
   1 oz/25 g polyunsaturated margarine
   1 teaspoon dried sage
   4 oz/100 g fresh breadcrumbs
   salt and pepper
   1 egg, beaten

1. Cook the onions in the margarine in a covered pan for 5 minutes, shaking the pan occasionally. Remove from the heat.
2. Add the sage, breadcrumbs and some salt and pepper. Mix in the egg and use to stuff the joint; alternatively, form the mixture into small balls and cook around the meat for the last ½ hour.

Omit the margarine and cook the onion in 1 teaspoon oil in a non-stick saucepan. Use wholemeal breadcrumbs.
CHO: 8 g Calories: 72

Use bread made from gluten-free flour and crumble with the fingers.

Use polyunsaturated margarine

No change necessary.

Use wholemeal breadcrumbs and add 1 teaspoon oat or wheat bran softened in 3 teaspoons water.

Not suitable. Serve stuffing sprinkled over a vegetable hotpot.

Apple Sauce

    8 oz/250 g cooking apples
    1 oz/25 g sugar

Cook the prepared apples in 2 tablespoons water with the sugar in a covered pan until tender. Pour into a sauceboat and serve with roast pork.

Replace the sugar with a shake of low-calorie sweetener after cooling.

No change necessary.

No change necessary.

No change necessary.

No change necessary.

No change necessary.

Toad-in-the-hole

Special Diets

Serves 4: 630 calories per portion

    1 oz/25 g lard or dripping
    1 lb/450 g pork sausages
    4 oz/100 g plain flour
    1 teaspoon salt
    1 large egg, size 2
    ½ pint/250 ml semi-skimmed milk and water mixed

1. Pre-heat a hot oven (425°F/220°C/Gas 7). Place the lard and sausages in an 11 × 7-inch/28 × 18-cm roasting tin; place on the top shelf in the oven.

2. Place the flour and salt in a bowl. Make a well in the centre of the flour and add the egg. Stir in half the diluted milk gradually. Mix well, using a wooden spoon, and beat until smooth. Stir in the remaining diluted milk; pour over the sausages.

3. Bake for 35-40 minutes until well risen, crisp and golden brown. Serve hot with vegetables.

Use a non-stick tin, lightly greased; omit the lard and use low-fat sausages. Replace 2 oz/50 g plain flour with wholemeal flour.
CHO: 41 g Calories: 365

Use Trufree or Jubilee no.7 self-raising flour and 1 tablespoon oil to batter. Cook in a hot oven (475°F/245°C/Gas 9) for 5 minutes, then reduce to 425°F/220°C/Gas 7 for 30 minutes. Replace the sausages with balls of seasoned minced pork.

Use polyunsaturated oil instead of lard. Make the sausages with 12 oz/350 g lean minced pork mixed with 2 oz/50 g wholemeal breadcrumbs, ½ teaspoon salt, pepper and 1 teaspoon mixed dried herbs, and bind with an egg.

Make sausages as above.

Replace 2 oz/50 g flour with wholemeal flour.

Use vegetable fat instead of lard. Replace the sausages with sliced onion, 4 whole tomatoes and 2 teaspoons mixed dried herbs. Serve sprinkled with parmesan cheese.

Sweet and Sour Pork

Special Diets

Serves 4: 600 calories per portion

2 lb/1 kg lean loin of pork
8-oz/227-g can pineapple pieces in syrup

Sauce:

1 small onion
2 tablespoons mango chutney
1 tablespoon sunflower oil
2 teaspoons tomato purée
2 teaspoons clear honey
2 teaspoons soy sauce
1 tablespoon vinegar
1 teaspoon cornflour
¼ pint/125 ml water
1 green pepper

1. Ask your butcher to chine the meat and remove the skin. Cut off all the visible fat.
2. Pre-heat a moderately hot oven (400°F/200°C/Gas 6).
3. Place the pork in a roasting tin, drain the pineapple and pour the syrup over the pork. Roast for 1¼ hours, basting occasionally.
4. Meanwhile, to prepare the sauce, finely chop the onion and chutney and place in a small saucepan with the oil. Cook for 3-4 minutes, then add the tomato purée, sugar, soy sauce and vinegar.
5. Blend the cornflour with a little of the water and add with the remaining water to the pan. Bring to the boil, stirring; simmer for 15 minutes.
6. Remove the seeds from the green pepper and cut into thin strips. Place in a saucepan, cover with cold water and bring slowly to the boil. Drain off the water and add with the pineapple pieces to the sauce; re-heat.
7. Place the pork on a warm serving dish, spoon a little sauce around and pour the remainder into a sauce-boat.

Use pineapple pieces in their own juice; replace the honey with low-calorie liquid sweetener.
CHO: 7 g Calories: 575

Replace the cornflour with potato flour and soy sauce with Worcestershire sauce. If the mango chutney includes starch, replace with marmalade and increase the vinegar (use wine or cider vinegar) to 2 tablespoons.

Cut all the fat off the meat.

Replace the soy sauce with Worcestershire sauce.

Add a small can of sweetcorn to the sauce.

Sweet and Sour Eggs
Replace the pork with 2 hard-boiled eggs on 2 oz/50 g wholewheat spaghetti per portion.

Serves 8: 45 calories per portion

Roasting times:
Slow roast for small joints and aitchbone, top rump, topside, back rib and top rib.
Moderate oven (350°F/180°C/Gas 4).
Minutes per lb/450 g
Rare: 25 minutes + 25 minutes
Medium: 30 minutes + 30 minutes
Well done: 35 minutes + 35 minutes
Fast roast for sirloin, wing rib, rump, fillet.
Hot oven (425°F/220°C/Gas 7).
Minutes per lb/450 g
Rare: 15 minutes + 15 minutes
Medium: 20 minutes + 20 minutes
Well done: 25 minutes + 25 minutes
Wipe the meat, cut off all visible fat and place on a rack in a roasting tin.

Horseradish Sauce

Serves 8: 45 calories per portion

> 1 horseradishroot (about 8 oz/250 g)
> 6 tablespoons single cream
> salt and pepper

1. Horseradish is strong and can make you weep. Peel it under water, then cut in pieces and chop in a food processor or with water in a liquidizer.
2. Drain well, blot on kitchen paper, then mix with top of the milk or cream and add some salt and pepper.

Replace the cream with thick low-fat yoghurt.
CHO: 5 g Calories: 23

No change necessary.

As for diabetic.

No change necessary.

No change necessary.

No change necessary.

Yorkshire Pudding

Serves 6: 120 calories per portion

>   lard
>   4 oz/100 g plain flour
>   ½ level teaspoon salt
>   1 egg
>   ½ pint/250 ml semi-skimmed milk

1. Pre-heat a hot oven (450°F/230°C/Gas 8). Place a little lard in 12 individual Yorkshire pudding tins (or deep bun tins) or a 7-inch/18-cm square tin and leave in the oven until melted and hot.
2. Place the flour and salt in a bowl. Make a well in the centre and add the egg. Stir in half the milk gradually. Mix well, using a wooden spoon, and beat until smooth. Add the remainder of the milk; pour into a jug. Alternatively, mix all the ingredients in a food processor or liquidizer.
3. Pour the batter into the tins (or tin) and bake on the top shelf of the oven for 10-15 minutes if using individual pudding tins, 30-40 minutes if using a large tin, until risen and golden brown. Serve with roast beef.

Use non-stick tins, lightly greased. Use a large egg and replace 2 oz/50 g plain flour with wholemeal. Use skimmed milk.
CHO: 16 g Calories: 85

Use Trufree or Jubilee no.7 self-raising flour and add 1 tablespoon oil to the batter. Cook in a hot oven (475°F/245°C/Gas 9) for 5 minutes then reduce to 425°F/220°C/Gas 7 for 30 minutes.

Use polyunsaturated oil instead of lard.

No change necessary.

Use a large egg and wholemeal flour as for diabetic.

Use vegetable fat instead of lard.

Mustard
For gluten-free diets, use coarse-grain mustard and check the ingredients list to make sure no flour is present.

Lasagne

Serves 8: 315 calories per portion

1 large onion, chopped
1 tablespoon oil
1 lb/450 g lean mince
14-oz/400-g can tomatoes
1 beef stock cube
1 clove garlic, crushed
1 teaspoon mixed dried herbs
8 oz/225 g carrots, chopped
salt and pepper
2 tablespoons cornflour

Sauce:

8 peppercorns
1 bay leaf
½ teaspoon (or a sprig) thyme
1 onion, sliced
1 pint/500 ml skimmed milk
1 oz/25 g plain flour
1 oz/25 g soft margarine
8 oz/225 g egg lasagne
2 oz/50 g parmesan cheese

1. Pre-heat a moderate oven (375°F/190°F/Gas 5). Fry the onions quickly in oil until browned, add the meat and fry until browned; drain off any fat. Add the tomatoes and juice, then re-fill the can with water and add with the stock cube, garlic, herbs, carrots and some salt and pepper. Cover and cook over a low heat for ½ hour.
2. Blend the cornflour with a little water and add to the pan.
3. Place the peppercorns, bay leaf, thyme and onion in a saucepan with the milk and simmer for 10 minutes. Blend the margarine and flour together. Strain the milk, then return to the pan and whisk in the margarine and flour. Stir until thickened.
4. Cook the lasagne as directed, if necessary. Spread a layer of the meat mixture in a large, shallow ovenproof dish and cover with lasagne, cutting to fit. Repeat with a layer of sauce, then lasagne, then two more layers of meat and lasagne. Finish with a layer of sauce, top with cheese and bake for 40-50 minutes until golden.
Note Freeze after stage 4, if desired. Cook for 1½ hours from frozen.

Special Diets

Use wholemeal lasagne and flour, and lean mince.
CHO: 30 g Calories: 315

Use gluten-free pasta (see recipe, page 216). Thicken the mince and sauce with ground rice. Check that the stock cube does not contain starch.

Use very lean mince and low-fat cheese or cottage cheese. Omit the margarine from sauce.

Replace the beef stock cube with yeast extract.

Use wholemeal lasagne and wholemeal flour; thicken the mince with 1 tablespoon natural bran.

Replace the mince with 1 lb/500 g smoked haddock mixed with 1 pint/500 ml white sauce, or replace the mince with 1 lb/500 g red and green peppers and 1 lb/500 g tomatoes, cooked together.

Serves 4: 660 calories per portion

Filling:
- 1 lb/450 g stewing steak
- 4 oz/100 g ox kidney
- 1 round tablespoon plain flour
- salt and pepper
- ¼ pint/125 ml stock or water

Suet pastry:
- 8 oz/200 g self-raising flour
- 1 level teaspoon salt
- 4 oz/100 g shredded suet
- 7-8 tablespoons cold water

1. Prepare a steamer. Grease a 1½-pint/750-ml pudding basin and a double thickness of greaseproof paper, to cover.
2. Cut the steak into 1-inch/2.5-cm cubes and the kidney into small pieces. Mix the flour, salt and pepper together on a plate. Coat the meat in seasoned flour.
3. Place the self-raising flour and salt in a bowl, stir in the suet and mix with water to form a soft but not sticky dough.
4. Cut off a third of the pastry and roll to the size of the top of the basin for a lid. Roll out the remainder; line the basin.
5. Fill the basin with the meat and add sufficient stock or water to come half-way up the meat. Dampen the edges of the pastry lid; cover the meat. Seal the edges well.
6. Cover the pudding and tie down securely with string, making a loop over the top of the basin to form a handle.
7. Cook for 3-3½ hours. Re-fill the saucepan with boiling water when necessary.
8. Remove the cover and turn out the pudding on to a warmed serving plate.

Use wholemeal flours. Reduce the suet to 3 oz/75 g.
CHO: 44 g Calories: 580

In the filling, replace the flour with potato flour or maize flour. Use butcher's suet or margarine. Pre-cook until the meat is tender (about 1 hour). Replace the pastry with 3 oz/75 g soft margarine, 6 oz/150 g ground rice and 4½ oz/125 g un-peeled finely grated cooking apple, mix, press together, reserve one-third for the lid and press the remainder over the greased base and sides of the basin. Add the filling, press out the lid piece and lift with a spatula. Steam for ¾ hour.

Replace the suet with polyunsaturated margarine.

No change necessary.

Use wholemeal flours.

Vegetable Pudding
Use vegetable suet for the pastry. Line the pastry with blanched spinach leaves; replace the meat with layers of courgettes, sliced peppers, sliced onion, parsnip, celery and tomato. Season with soy sauce. Cook for 1½ hours.

Steak, Kidney and Mushroom Pie

Special Diets

Serves 6: 764 calories per portion

Filling:

> 1½ lb/675 g blade or chuck steak
> 8 oz/225 g ox kidney
> 8 oz/225 g carrots
> ½ level teaspoon salt
> ¼ level teaspoon pepper
> 1 level tablespoon cornflour
> 4 oz/50 g button mushrooms

Flaky pastry:

> 9 oz/250 g lard and margarine mixed
> 12 oz/350 g plain flour
> ½ level teaspoon salt
> 3 teaspoons lemon juice
> 8-10 tablespoons cold water
> beaten egg to glaze

1. Remove the fat from the meat; cut the meat into 1-inch/2-cm cubes. Wash the kidney, remove the skin and core and cut into small pieces. Peel the carrots and cut into sticks. Place in a saucepan with ½ pint/275 ml water, salt and pepper. Bring to the boil, cover and simmer for 1-1½ hours until the meat is tender. Alternatively, cook at high pressure for 30-35 minutes. Taste and season with more salt and pepper if necessary. Blend the cornflour with a little water; stir into the saucepan to thicken the gravy. Wipe the mushrooms and add to the steak and kidney.

2. To make the pastry, blend the fats on a plate and divide into quarters; then sift the flour and salt into a bowl and add one-quarter of the fat. Cut the fat into small pieces and rub in with the fingertips until the mixture resembles fine breadcrumbs. Mix the lemon juice with cold water and add to the bowl; mix with a fork to form a soft dough.

3. Turn out on to a floured board and knead lightly until smooth. Place the pastry on a plate, cover with polythene and place in the refrigerator with the remaining fats for 15-20 minutes.

4. Roll out the pastry to an oblong about 18 × 9 inches/46 × 23 cm;

Replace the cornflour with wholemeal flour.

For the pastry, use half the quantity; replace half of the plain flour with wholemeal flour and use as a top crust only.

CHO: 25 g Calories: 535

In the filling, replace the cornflour with maize flour. For the pastry, make shortcrust pastry with Trufree or Jubilee no.6 plain flour (see recipe, page 217).

For the pastry, use polyunsaturated margarine instead of the lard and margarine mixture.

No change necessary.

In the filling, use wholemeal flour.

For the pastry, replace half of the plain flour with wholemeal flour.

In the filling, replace the meat and kidney with a savoury vegetable mixture, of 1 sliced onion, 2 sticks celery, 2 carrots and 1 blanched red pepper fried together. Add a large can of baked beans and 8 oz/225 g cubed mature Cheddar cheese.

brush off the surplus flour. Take a portion of fat, cut into small pieces and cover the top two-thirds of the dough to within ½ inch/1.25 cm of the edges. Fold the bottom third up to cover the fat and fold the top third over the folded dough; press to seal the edges with a rolling-pin.

5. Turn the dough so the right-hand edge faces you and flatten the dough slightly by pressing down with the rolling-pin in several places. Repeat the rolling and folding using another portion of fat. Cover and place in the refrigerator for 20 minutes. Repeat the rolling and folding using the remaining fat, then repeat the rolling and folding without any fat. Cover the pastry and chill for at least 20 minutes before using.

6. Pre-heat a hot oven (425°F/220°C/Gas 7). Cut the pastry in half, roll out one-half on a lightly floured board and line a 9-inch/22.5-cm ovenproof pie-plate; trim off the surplus pastry with a knife. Brush the edge with water. Place the cooled meat over the pastry (reserve the gravy to serve separately).

7. Roll out the remaining pastry and cover the pie. Press the edges together and trim off the surplus pastry. Cut up the edges of pastry to form flakes and flute the edge with the fingers. Make a hole in the centre of the pie to allow steam to escape.

8. Using trimmings, cut out 6 pastry leaves and mark 'veins' with a knife; arrange on the centre of the pie covering. Make a centre tassel and place over the hole in the pie. Brush the pastry with beaten egg and place the pie on a baking sheet.

9. Bake on the second shelf from the top of the oven for 35-40 minutes until the pastry is well risen and golden brown. Serve hot with gravy, sprouts and root vegetables.

Beef and Bacon Olives

Special Diets

Serves 4: 385 calories per portion

 4 thin slices topside of beef (about 1 lb/450 g in weight)
 4 rashers streaky bacon
 1 small onion
 2 oz/50 g polyunsaturated margarine
 2 oz/50 g fresh breadcrumbs
 1 level teaspoon dried marjoram or mixed dried herbs
 1 oz/25 g plain flour
 1 beef stock cube
 ¾ pint/425 ml boiling water
 2 level teaspoons tomato purée

1. Place each slice of meat between 2 small pieces of greaseproof paper; beat with a rolling-pin until thin. Remove the rind and bone from the bacon; cut into small pieces. Peel and finely chop the onion.
2. Melt 1 oz/25 g margarine in a small saucepan and fry the bacon and onion for 3 minutes. Remove from the heat and stir in the breadcrumbs and marjoram or mixed dried herbs.
3. Divide the stuffing into 4. Place a portion of stuffing on each slice of the meat and roll up tightly; tie securely with cotton.
4. Melt the remaining 1 oz/25 g margarine in a 2-pint/1-litre flameproof casserole. Brown the meat quickly all over in a casserole, then remove. Add the flour to the casserole; cook for 2 minutes. Dissolve the stock cube in boiling water and add, together with the tomato purée; bring to the boil, stirring. Return the meat to the casserole; cover and simmer for 1 hour, or until the meat is tender; remove the cotton. Serve with creamed potato.

Use wholemeal breadcrumbs and cut the fat off the bacon. Reduce the margarine to half.
CHO: 12 g Calories: 330

Replace the breadcrumbs with cooked brown rice and the cornflour with potato flour or mashed potato. Check that the stock cube does not contain starch or MSG.

Cut off all the fat from the meat and bacon.

Replace the stock made from a cube with home-made bone stock or water.

Use wholemeal breadcrumbs and serve with brown rice.

Replace the meat with plaice fillets or large cabbage leaves that have been cooked in boiling water for 1 minute. Omit the margarine and browning in step 4. Cook for ½ hour.

Beef and Bean Hotpot with Parsley Dumplings

Serves 4: 590 calories per portion

1 lb/500 g stewing steak
1 oz/25 g plain flour
4 oz/100 g carrots
4 oz/100 g turnips
2 small onions
2 tablespoons oil
¾ pint/375 ml water
1 beef extract cube
salt
pepper
bay leaf
15-oz/425-g can beans in tomato sauce

Parsley dumplings:
4 oz/100 g self-raising flour
2 oz/50 g shredded suet
½ teaspoon salt
1 tablespoon chopped parsley

1. Pre-heat a cool oven (325°F/160°C/Gas 3).
2. Trim all visible fat from the meat, cut into 1-inch/2.5-cm cubes and coat in flour. Peel and slice the carrots, peel the turnips and cut into small cubes. Peel and quarter the onions.
3. Heat the oil in a frying-pan and fry the meat and vegetables for 4 minutes. Stir in the remaining flour. Add the water and the crumbled beef extract cube and bring to the boil, stirring. Add the seasonings, bay leaf and beans.
4. Pour into a 3-pint/1.4-litre casserole, cover and cook in the oven for 1½ hours. Remove the bay leaf.
4. Sift the self-raising flour into a basin and stir in the suet, salt and parsley. Mix to a soft, but not sticky, dough with water. Form into 8 small balls.
6. Place on top of the stew, cover and cook for a further 15-20 minutes until well risen. Serve at once.

Use wholemeal flour. Replace the suet with 1 oz/25 g polyunsaturated margarine.
CHO: 47 g Calories: 520

In the hotpot, replace the flour with rice flour. For the dumplings, grate 8 oz/250 g scrubbed potatoes, mix in 1 tablespoon rice flour, 1 tablespoon chopped fresh parsley, salt, pepper and 1 egg. Fry tablespoonsful in a greased non-stick pan and add to the hotpot just before serving. Check the ingredients list of the beef extract.

Remove all the fat from the meat and use polyunsaturated oil. Replace the suet with polyunsaturated margarine and rub in.

Use bone stock or yeast or vegetable extract (check ingredients list).

Use wholemeal flour.

Omit the beef and beef extract cube; add 2 oz/50 g barley, 1 rounded tablespoon yeast extract, 1 clove garlic crushed, 1 teaspoon dried oregano. Cook for ½ hour, then add the contents of a large can of sweetcorn with red and green peppers, before the dumplings. Sprinkle with flaked almonds before serving.

Crispy-topped Lamb

Serves 4: 450 calories per portion

1½ lb/675 g potatoes
1 oz/25 g cooking fat
2 lb/900 g lean half shoulder of lamb
2 oz/50 g fresh breadcrumbs
grated rind of 1 small lemon
1 level tablespoon chopped parsley
garlic salt (optional)
pepper

1. Pre-heat a moderate oven (350°F/190°C/Gas 4).
2. Peel the potatoes and cut into even-sized pieces. Place in boiling, salted water and cook for 5 minutes; drain. Melt the fat in a roasting tin; add the potatoes, then coat in fat.
3. Wipe the meat and trim off all the visible fat. Place in the centre of the roasting tin. Cook in the centre of the oven for 1 hour (allowing 30 minutes per lb/500 g).
4. Mix together the breadcrumbs, lemon rind, parsley, garlic salt, if using, pepper and 2 level tablespoons dripping from the roasting tin. Press the mixture over the lamb.
5. Set the oven to hot (425°F/220°C/Gas 7) and cook the lamb for a further 15-20 minutes, until golden brown and crisp. Place the meat on a warmed serving dish with the potatoes. Serve with mint sauce, a green vegetable and gravy made from the drippings in the tin.

Special Diets

Leave the skins on the potatoes. Use wholemeal breadcrumbs.
CHO: 40 g Calories: 465

Omit the breadcrumbs.

Cut all the fat off the meat; replace the cooking fat with polyunsaturated oil.

Scrub the lemon thoroughly using a small brush and dry before grating.

As for diabetic.

Leave the skins on the potatoes and roast for 1 hour. Add 6 oz/150 g drained, sliced tofu and cook on each side until browned. Add 4 oz/100 g grated cheese to the breadcrumb mixture and sprinkle over the tofu. Bake until crisp.

Lamb Hotpot

Serves 4: 390 calories per portion

8 lean neck of lamb chops
1 large onion, sliced
2 sticks celery, sliced
1 cooking apple, sliced
1½ lb/675 g potatoes, sliced
salt and pepper
½ pint/275 ml meat stock
freshly chopped parsley

1. Pre-heat a moderate oven (375°F/180°C/Gas 5). Trim the excess fat from the meat.
2. Make two layers of chops, onion, celery, apple and potato in a 3-pint/1.5-litre ovenproof dish, finishing with a layer of potatoes and seasoning each layer with salt and pepper.
3. Pour the stock down the side of the dish, then brush the potato with oil and cover with a lid or a piece of foil.
4. Cook in the centre of the oven for 1 hour. Remove the lid and cook, uncovered, for a further 15 minutes. Sprinkle with parsley and serve with a green vegetable.

Special Diets

No change necessary.
CHO: 43 g Calories: 390

No change necessary.

Remove all the fat from the lamb.

Use home-made stock from boiling meat or bones or dissolve yeast extract in ½ pint/275 ml boiling water.

Scrub the potatoes but do not peel before slicing.

Vegetable Hotpot
Replace the lamb with 4 oz/100 g chopped salted peanuts and a 15-oz/439-g can baked beans in tomato sauce.

Lamb and Lentil Stew

Special Diets

Serves 4: 440 calories per portion

8 oz/225 g brown lentils
2 medium-sized onions
1 lb/450 g carrots
2 sticks celery
2 lb/1 kg middle neck of lamb, cut into chops
2 level tablespoons chopped parsley
salt and pepper
1½ pints/800 ml water

1. Wash the lentils and place in a basin. Cover with water and soak overnight.
2. Peel and chop the onions; peel and slice the carrots. Wash and slice the celery.
3. Drain the lentils and place in a large 5-6-pint/2.4-3-litre saucepan with the meat, onions, celery, carrots, parsley and some salt and pepper.
4. Add the water, bring to the boil, cover tightly and simmer for 1½-2 hours, stirring occasionally.

Cut all the fat off the meat.
CHO: 46 g Calories: 440

No change necessary.

Cut all the fat off the meat (it may be easier to use boned neck of lamb fillet with all the fat removed). Sprinkle thickly with fresh chopped parsley.

No change necessary.

Stir in a medium can of baked beans in tomato sauce for the last 10 minutes.

Omit the meat and cook the other ingredients as directed for 1 hour adding 1 teaspoon mixed dried herbs. Add 1 tablespoon tomato purée, 8 oz/225 g prepared leeks and 3 oz/75 g wholemeal pasta shells (cooked). Cook for 15 minutes and season to taste. Serve sprinkled with freshly chopped parsley.

Serves 4: 300 calories per portion

      1½ lb/750 g middle neck of mutton
      1½ lb/750 g small potatoes
      2 large onions
      salt and pepper
      1 beef stock cube
      ¾ pint/725 ml boiling water

1. Wipe the meat and cut into even-sized pieces. Peel and quarter the potatoes; peel and slice the onions.
2. Arrange the meat and vegetables in alternate layers in a saucepan, seasoning each layer with salt and pepper.
3. Dissolve the stock cube in boiling water; add to the saucepan and bring to the boil. Skim, cover with a tight-fitting lid and simmer for about 1½ hours, until the meat is tender.
4. Stir occasionally and add extra stock, if necessary. Serve with carrots and a green vegetable.

Leave the skins on the potatoes. Remove all the fat from the meat.
CHO: 36 g Calories: 300

No change necessary, but check the ingredients list of the stock cube. Replace with bone stock if necessary.

Cut all the fat off the meat very thoroughly.

Replace the beef stock cube and water with bone stock.

Leave the skins on the potatoes. Add some barley.

Vegetable Irish Stew
Replace the meat with a mixture of 4 oz/100 g each of grated cheese, sliced celery and muesli, mixed. Replace the beef stock cube with 2 tablespoons vegetable extract and mix with a can of tomatoes.

Roasting times:
Moderate oven (350°F/180°C/Gas 4).
Small joints: 30 minutes per lb/500 g
Large joints: 25 minutes per lb/500 g
Stuffed joints: 40 minutes per lb/500 g
Wipe the surface of the meat with a piece of moistened kitchen paper. Weigh the meat and calculate the cooking time. Place in a roasting tin, fat side uppermost. Accompaniments to serve with roast lamb: mint sauce, redcurrant jelly (not suitable for diabetics, and those avoiding non-essential additives should check the label), onion sauce, gravy and roast potatoes.

Mint Sauce

> 1 teacup loosely-packed mint leaves
> 1 teaspoon caster sugar
> 2 tablespoons boiling water
> 4 tablespoons malt vinegar

1. Wash and finely chop the mint leaves. Place in a small basin and add the caster sugar and boiling water; stir until the sugar has dissolved.
2. Add the vinegar; pour into a sauceboat.

Omit the sugar and add low-calorie sweetener to taste.
CHO: – Calories: –

Use cider or wine vinegar instead of malt vinegar in the sauce.

No change necessary.

No change necessary.

No change necessary.

Serve a lentil loaf instead, without the mint sauce.

106

Onion Sauce

1 large onion
¼ pint/125 ml semi-skimmed milk
3 level tablespoons plain flour
1 oz/25 g butter
salt and pepper
2 tablespoons top of the milk or single cream

1. Peel and slice the onion. Place in a saucepan with ¼ pint/125 ml water, bring to the boil, cover and simmer for 10 minutes.
2. Add the milk, then whisk in the flour and butter, bring to the boil and cook for 2 minutes. Add salt and pepper to taste and top of the milk or cream.

Omit the top of the milk or cream and reduce the butter by half.

Replace the plain flour with 1 oz/25 g Trufree or Jubilee no.6 plain flour.

Omit the butter and top of the milk or single cream. Use skimmed milk plus 1 extra tablespoon low-fat dried milk.

No change necessary.

Mix in 2 heaped tablespoons canned sweetcorn.

Use polyunsaturated margarine.

Braised Stuffed Hearts

Special Diets

Serves 4: 440 calories per portion

　　　　4 lambs' hearts
Stuffing:
　　　　2 oz/50 g wholemeal breadcrumbs
　　　　½ level teaspoon grated lemon rind
　　　　2 level tablespoons chopped parsley
　　　　½ level teaspoon dried thyme
　　　　2 tablespoons semi-skimmed milk
　　　　salt and pepper

　　　　3 carrots
　　　　2 sticks celery
　　　　2 turnips
　　　　1 tablespoon sunflower oil
　　　　¾ pint/400 ml boiling stock or water
　　　　1 level tablespoon cornflour

1. Pre-heat a moderate oven (350°F/180°C/Gas 4).
2. Wash the hearts and cut out the tubes from the tops.
3. Mix the breadcrumbs, lemon rind, parsley, thyme, milk and some salt and pepper together in a bowl. Stuff the cavities in the hearts with the mixture.
4. Peel the carrots and cut into rings. Peel and slice the onions. Wash and slice the celery. Peel and dice the turnips. Place the vegetables in a 3-pint/1.4-litre casserole.
5. Melt the oil in a frying-pan and fry the hearts lightly on all sides. Arrange on top of the vegetables. Pour the stock or water into the casserole; cover and cook until the hearts are tender (about 1¾ hours).
6. To serve, arrange the hearts on a warm dish with the vegetables round the edge; keep hot. Blend the cornflour to a smooth paste with a little cold water. Stir into the gravy in the casserole and return to the oven for 2-3 minutes. Pour over the hearts.

Use wholemeal breadcrumbs.
CHO: 16 g Calories: 423

Use special gluten-free breadcrumbs or replace with 2 oz/50 g cooked brown rice. Thicken the gravy with potato flour (add straight to the casserole: no need to blend).

Use polyunsaturated oil and skimmed milk.

Use bone stock or yeast extract and water.

Use wholemeal breadcrumbs and add 1 heaped tablespoon natural bran or muesli to the stuffing.

Braised Stuffed Peppers
Replace the hearts with 4 small red or green peppers. Cut off the tops, scoop out the seeds, then blanch in boiling water for 2 minutes. Add 3 oz/75 g grated Cheddar cheese to the stuffing and fill the peppers. Place on top of the vegetables in the casserole and cook until the vegetables are tender (about ¾ hour).

Liver and Bacon Hotpot

Serves 4: 512 calories per portion

> 1 lb/450 g ox liver
> 1 rounded tablespoon plain flour
> salt and pepper
> 4 rashers lean streaky bacon
> 1 large onion
> 1 oz/25 g lard
> ½ pint/250 ml water
> 2 lb/1 kg potatoes

1. Pre-heat a moderate oven (350°F/180°C/Gas 4). Cut the liver into thin strips, about 1 inch/2.5 cm long. Sprinkle the flour on a plate; mix in some salt and pepper; coat the liver in the seasoned flour.
2. Remove the rind and bone from the bacon; cut into strips. Peel and slice the onion.
3. Heat the lard in a large frying-pan and fry the liver, onion and half the bacon slowly (about 5 minutes). Stir in any remaining flour and gradually add the water, stirring continuously. Bring to the boil, stirring, then pour into a deep 3-pint/1.4-litre ovenproof dish.
4. Peel and thinly slice the potatoes; spread over the liver, seasoning each layer with a little salt and pepper. Spread the remaining bacon pieces over the top. Cover with buttered paper, place on a baking sheet and cook in the centre of the oven for 1½ hours.

Cut off all visible fat from the bacon. Leave the skin on the potatoes. Replace the lard with polyunsaturated margarine.
CHO: 54 g Calories: 511

Use potato flour instead of plain flour.

Replace the lard with polyunsaturated oil and cut off all visible fat.

No change necessary.

Use wholemeal flour and leave the skins on the potatoes.

Chilli-bean Hotpot
Replace the liver and bacon with the following mixture. Fry 1 sliced onion in 2 tablespoons oil, add a 15-oz/425-g can tomatoes, a 15-oz/425-g can kidney beans in chilli sauce, 2 cloves garlic, crushed, ½ pint/250 ml yeast extract stock and 4 oz/100 g tvp mince. Bring to the boil, pour into the casserole and top with potatoes. Cook for ¾-1 hour until the potatoes are tender.

French-style Liver and Bacon

Serves 4: 460 calories per portion

4 rashers lean streaky bacon
1 rounded tablespoon plain flour
salt and pepper
1¼-1½ lb/550-675 g lamb's liver, cut into 8 slices
6 level tablespoons sage and onion stuffing
boiling water
1 oz/25 g margarine
1½ lb/675 g potatoes, boiled and mashed
1 1-lb 3 oz/525-g can whole small carrots
watercress

1. Pre-heat a moderate oven (375°F/190°C/Gas 5).
2. Remove the rind and bone from the bacon; cut each rasher across in half. Mix the flour and some salt and pepper on a plate and coat each liver slice in seasoned flour. Make the stuffing as directed on the packet, using boiling water.
3. Melt the margarine in a frying-pan and quickly fry the liver until browned. Place in a shallow 2-pint/1-litre casserole. Stir the remaining flour, then ½ pint/275 ml water, into the frying-pan. Bring to the boil, stirring, and pour around the liver.
4. Spread the stuffing evenly on the liver and arrange the halved bacon rashers on top. Cover with a lid or greased kitchen foil. Bake in the centre of the oven for 30 minutes. Remove the lid and cook for a further 20-30 minutes until tender, depending on the thickness of the liver.
5. To serve, place the mashed potato down the centre of a warmed serving dish. Arrange 4 slices of liver and bacon on either side of the potato. Heat the carrots, drain, and arrange round the edge of the dish. Place a small bunch of watercress at each end of the dish. Pour the gravy into a warmed gravy boat and stir in a little gravy browning, if desired. Serve with the remaining carrots and sweetcorn.
Note For a larger quantity of gravy, stir in the carrot liquor before serving.

Special Diets

Replace the plain flour with natural bran; use very lean bacon. Replace the packet stuffing with 6 rounded tablespoons wholemeal breadcrumbs mixed with ½ teaspoon dried sage and 1 small chopped onion.
CHO: 53 g Calories: 455

Replace the plain flour with maize flour and stuffing with 4 oz/100 g cooked brown rice mixed with chopped onion, ½ teaspoon sage and half a beaten egg.

Use back bacon and cut off all the fat; use polyunsaturated margarine.

Replace packet stuffing as for diabetic.

As for diabetic.

Replace the liver and bacon with fish fillets or cutlets, or with sliced tofu, and adjust the cooking time.

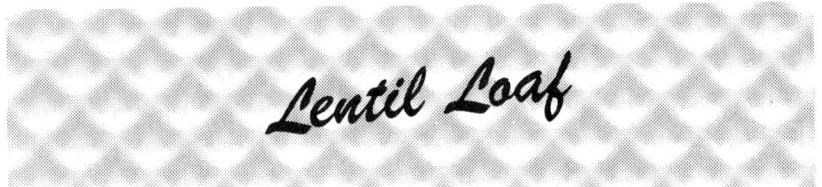

Lentil Loaf

Serves 6: 235 calories per portion

8 oz/225 g lentils
1 clove garlic, crushed
1 sachet bouquet garni herbs
1 large onion
2 sticks celery, sliced
1 8-oz/225-g can peeled tomatoes
4 oz/100 g red Leicester cheese
2 eggs
1 rounded teaspoon vegetable or yeast extract
1 level teaspoon salt
freshly ground black pepper
1 tablespoon sesame seeds (optional)

1. Soak the lentils overnight, then drain, rinse and place in a saucepan with the garlic and herbs. Cover with water and simmer for ½ hour, drain and remove the herb sachet.
2. Chop the onion and add with the celery, tomatoes and cheese. Beat the eggs with the vegetable or yeast extract, salt and a generous grind of pepper. Grease a 1-lb/500-g loaf-tin and sprinkle with sesame seeds. Pour the mixture into the loaf-tin, cover with foil and bake in a moderate oven (350°F/180°C/Gas 4) for 1 hour.
3. Turn on to a warm serving dish if serving hot, or leave in the tin for 10 minutes then turn out and cool. If possible chill overnight to allow the flavours to blend, then serve sliced.

No change necessary. Best served cold with salad.
CHO: 23 g Calories: 235

No change necessary.

Replace the cheese with chopped lean ham or smoked bacon.

No change necessary.

No change necessary.

No change necessary.

Snacks and Suppers

It is tempting to fill up on coffee and buns for casual meals, but these recipes show that wholesome, tasty food need not take long to prepare. Some dishes can be frozen and then cooked traditionally or in a microwave oven.

Golden Brunch

Special Diets

Serves 4: 230 calories per portion

i3l2 tomatoes
1 lb/450 g smoked haddock fillet
4 eggs
4 tablespoons semi-skimmed milk
salt and pepper
1 oz/25 g butter

1. Place the tomatoes in a bowl and cover with boiling water. Leave for 1 minute; drain, then peel and chop.
2. Wash and trim the fish. Place in a frying-pan and cover with water. Bring to the boil and cook gently for about 5 minutes until the fish is tender; drain and arrange on a warmed serving dish; keep warm.
3. Beat the eggs and milk together, with some salt and pepper. Melt the butter in a saucepan, add the egg mixture and scramble lightly; stir in the tomatoes. Top each fish cutlet with the egg mixture and serve immediately.

Leave the skins on the tomatoes; use low-fat spread instead of butter. Serve with wholemeal bread.
CHO: 1 g Calories: 205

No change necessary.

Use skimmed milk and polyunsaturated margarine.

Replace the smoked haddock with fresh haddock or boned herring.

Leave the skins on the tomatoes. Serve with wholemeal bread.

Replace the butter with vegetable margarine.

Aberdeen Fish Cakes

Serves 4: 420 calories per portion

    1 lb/450 g potatoes
    12 oz/300 g smoked cod
    1 oz/25 g butter
    5 eggs
    salt and pepper
    fresh or browned breadcrumbs
    groundnut oil for frying

1. Cook the potatoes in boiling, salted water until tender; drain, dry over a low heat, then mash.

2. Wash and trim the fish. Place with ½ pint/250 ml water in a large saucepan, bring to the boil and cook for 5 minutes. Remove, place skin side uppermost on a plate and remove the skin and bones. Add to the potatoes with the butter.

3. Hard-boil 4 of the eggs for 10 minutes, crack and leave to cool. Remove the shells, chop and add to the potato mixture. Taste and add salt, if necessary, and about ½ teaspoon pepper.

4. Turn out on to a floured board and form into eight flat cakes.

5. Beat the remaining egg; place on a deep plate. Place the breadcrumbs on a large sheet of greaseproof paper.

6. Coat the fish cakes in egg, then toss in the breadcrumbs; press the breadcrumbs on with a knife. Freeze or chill at this stage, if desired.

7. Heat sufficient oil, to a depth of ½ inch/1.25 cm, in a large frying-pan. Fry the cakes for about 8 minutes over a gentle heat, turning once. Drain on kitchen paper and serve hot.

As for higher-fibre and saturated fat-free.
CHO: 30 g Calories: 418

Omit the flour for shaping and the breadcrumbs. Use chopped nuts or sesame seeds for the coating.

Use polyunsaturated margarine and sunflower oil (but keep the frying temperature low).

Replace the smoked cod with cod fillet or frozen portions. Add 2 rounded tablespoons chopped fresh parsley for extra flavour.

Add 1 oz/25 g natural bran to the mixture and use natural bran or wholemeal breadcrumbs for the coating.

Use polyunsaturated margarine instead of butter.

Kipper Pizza

Serves 12: 195 calories per portion

Scone base:

    8 oz/225 g self-raising flour
    ½ level teaspoon salt
    2 oz/50 g polyunsaturated margarine
    ¼ pint/150 ml semi-skimmed milk

Cheese sauce:

    6 oz/175 g Cheddar cheese, grated
    1 oz/25 g polyunsaturated margarine
    1 oz/25 g plain flour
    ½ pint/275 ml semi-skimmed milk
    salt and pepper

Topping:

    8-oz/225-g packet kipper fillets
    3 firm tomatoes
    endive or watercress to garnish

1. Pre-heat a moderately hot oven (400°F/200°C/Gas 6). Lightly grease a baking sheet.

2. Place the flour and salt in a bowl. Add 2 oz/50 g margarine, cut into small pieces, and rub in with the fingertips until the mixture resembles fine breadcrumbs. Add ¼ pint/150 ml milk and stir with a fork until just mixed. Turn out on to a floured board and knead lightly.

3. Roll out to an oblong 13 × 9 inches/32 × 23 cm. Brush a 1½-inch/4-cm-wide border around the edge of the dough with water and fold about ½ inch/1.25 cm of the edge over; fold over again to form a raised edge. Pinch the edge firmly between finger and thumb. Carefully lift the dough on to a baking sheet.

4. Place the margarine in a small saucepan with flour and ½ pint/275 ml milk and bring to the boil, stirring or whisking continuously; cook for 2 minutes. Remove from the heat; add half the grated cheese to the sauce and stir until melted. Taste and season with salt and pepper.

5. Cool the sauce slightly, then spread evenly over the dough.

6. Peel away the skin from the kipper fillets. Cut each kipper fillet in

Use fine wholemeal self-raising flour and skimmed milk. Use 3 oz/75 g strong Cheddar cheese.
CHO: 16 g Calories: 162

Use double quantity gluten-free scone base for pizza (see recipe, page 215). Thicken sauce with cornflour instead of wheat flour.

Use polyunsaturated margarine. Replace the Cheddar cheese with 3 oz/75 g cottage cheese and add the rind and juice of half a lemon and ½ teaspoon dried basil to the sauce.

Use undyed kippers or replace with herrings.

Use fine wholemeal self-raising flour.

Use rennet-free cheese and vegetable margarine.

half lengthwise. Arrange in a lattice pattern on the cheese sauce. Cut the tomatoes into quarters. Place a tomato quarter in the centre of each square made by the kipper fillets. Sprinkle with the remaining grated cheese.

7. Bake in the centre of the oven for 25-30 minutes until risen and golden brown. Remove from the oven and leave to cool for 2 minutes. Using a sharp knife, cut into 12 squares. Pile the squares on a tray or on a board. Garnish with sprigs of endive or watercress. Serve with a green salad.

Soused Herrings or Mackerel

Serves 4: 260 calories per portion

> 4 herrings or mackerel
> salt and pepper
> 1 small onion
> 1 level dessertspoon mixed pickling spice
> ½ pint/275 ml malt vinegar and water, mixed
> 4 small bay leaves

1. Pre-heat a moderate oven (350°F/180°C/Gas 5). Cut the heads off the herrings, using a sharp knife.

2. Scrape the skin with a round-ended knife from tail to head to remove scales. Wash the fish under running water.

3. Cut along the underside of each fish from head to tail. Remove the roe and put to one side. Gently scrape away the gut and discard.

4. Open the fish and place, skin side uppermost, on a board. Press firmly all the way along the centre back of the fish to loosen the backbone.

5. Turn the fish over and ease away the backbone from the flesh, starting at the head end. Cut off the tail. Sprinkle the flesh with a little salt and pepper; roll up from the tail end. Peel and slice the onion. Place half the onion and half the pickling spice in an ovenproof dish. Arrange the fish close together on top. Pour over the vinegar and water. Sprinkle with the remaining pickling spice. Add the bay leaves and remaining onion. Cover with a piece of foil or a lid and bake in the centre of the oven for 1 hour. Leave to cool in the dish.

No change necessary.
CHO: 1 g Calories: 260

Use wine vinegar.

No change necessary.

No change necessary.

Serve with high-fibre accompaniments – wholemeal rolls, salads containing peas, sweetcorn, beans.

No change necessary.

Cod Quiche

Serves 4: 400 calories per portion

4 oz/100 g cream crackers
2 oz/50 g polyunsaturated margarine
6 oz/175 g Cheddar cheese
10 oz/275 g cod fillet
1 egg
5½ fl oz/150 g natural low-fat yoghurt
salt and pepper
sprig of parsley to garnish

1. Pre-heat a moderate oven (375°F/190°C/Gas 5). Grease an 8½-inch/21-cm ovenproof pie-plate.
2. Place the biscuits in a paper bag and crush with the hands. Melt the margarine in a small saucepan. Remove from the heat and stir in the crushed biscuits. Press on to the base and sides of the pie-plate.
3. Cut the cheese into ½-inch/1.25-cm cubes. Wash the cod and remove the skin; cut into 1-inch/2.5-cm cubes. Mix the cheese and cod together and spread into the pie-plate.
4. Beat together the egg, yoghurt and some salt and pepper; pour over the fish mixture.
5. Place on a baking sheet and bake in the centre of the oven for 30-35 minutes, until set and golden. Garnish with a sprig of parsley. Serve hot with a green salad.

Special Diets

Use wholewheat crackers, and low-fat spread instead of margarine. Use 3 oz/75 g low-fat Cheddar cheese.
CHO: 7.5 g Calories: 235

Replace the cream crackers with 1 lb/500 g potatoes, peeled and finely sliced. Generously brush the dish with melted margarine and cover with layers of potato, brushing between the layers with melted margarine and sprinkling with salt and pepper. Cook the potato case for 10 minutes before adding the fish.

Replace the Cheddar cheese with cottage cheese with chives.

No change necessary.

Use wholemeal crackers and add 4 oz/100 g frozen peas.

Use vegetable margarine and rennet-free cheese.

Haddock and Cheese Charlotte

Serves 4: 340 calories per portion

1 small onion
2 sticks celery
4 oz/100 g Cheddar cheese
1¼ lb/550 g haddock fillet
2 level tablespoons plain flour
salt and pepper
2 oz/50 g fresh white breadcrumbs
1 oz/25 g polyunsaturated margarine
14-oz/400-g can peeled tomatoes

1. Pre-heat a moderate oven (375°F/190°C/Gas 5).
2. Peel and finely chop the onion; wash and slice the celery; grate the cheese. Wash the haddock and remove the skin; cut into pieces. Mix the flour and some salt and pepper on a plate. Coat the haddock in the seasoned flour. Mix the breadcrumbs, grated cheese and some salt and pepper together.
3. Melt the margarine in a frying-pan. Add the onion and celery and cook for 3 minutes, until the onion is tender. Add the haddock to the pan and turn carefully until browned. Turn into a 2-pint/1-litre casserole. Add the tomatoes to the pan and bring to the boil, stirring. Pour over the fish mixture. Cover with the breadcrumb and cheese mixture.
4. Bake in the centre of the oven for 40-45 minutes, until golden brown. Serve hot with potatoes and peas.

Special Diets

Use wholemeal flour and breadcrumbs. Use only 1 oz/25 g cheese.
CHO: 12.5 g Calories: 250

Replace the flour with potato flour or rice flour; replace the breadcrumbs with 6 oz/175 g grated potato or breadcrumbs from gluten-free bread.

Omit the cheese. Replace with 1 oz/25 g polyunsaturated margarine mixed with 1 tablespoon yeast extract, then the breadcrumbs.

No change necessary.

Use wholemeal flour and breadcrumbs. Serve with jacket potatoes.

Use vegetarian cheese.

Hamburger Loaf

Serves 6: 380 calories per portion

> 1 lb/500 g lean chuck steak or braising steak
> 4 oz/100 g lean bacon or bacon pieces
> 3 slices of bread from a large loaf
> ¼ level teaspoon mixed dried herbs
> 1 level tablespoon chopped parsley
> salt and pepper
> cucumber and radishes

1. Pre-heat a moderate oven (350°F/180°C/Gas 4).
2. Remove any excess fat or gristle from the steak and remove the rind and bone from the bacon; finely mince or chop in a food processor with the bread.
3. Mix thoroughly with the herbs, parsley and some salt and pepper.
4. Press the mixture into a 1-lb/500-g loaf-tin and level the top; cover with a piece of foil and cook for 1¼ hours.
5. Leave to cool in the tin. Chill for at least 2 hours, then turn out, garnish with cucumber and radishes and serve sliced with salad. Cover the loaf and store for up to 5 days in the refrigerator.

Use lean meat and bacon and cut off all the fat. Use wholemeal bread. Add 1 oz/25 g natural bran.
CHO: 7 g Calories: 200

Use special gluten-free breadcrumbs or replace with 4 oz/100 g cooked brown rice.

Use lean meat and cut off all the fat.

No change necessary.

Use wholemeal bread. Replace 1 slice with 1 oz/25 g natural bran.

Savoury Nut Loaf
Replace the meat and bacon with 4 oz/100 g each of ground salted peanuts, walnuts, wholemeal breadcrumbs and a finely chopped onion. Add the herbs and 1 heaped teaspoon yeast extract or Vecon with 3 beaten eggs and 6 fl oz/150 ml natural yoghurt. Season well and spread in the loaf-tin. Line the tin with blanched spinach or cabbage leaves (for an attractive appearance). Leave for ½ hour before baking at 325°F/160°C/Gas 3 for 1 hour. Place the loaf-tin in a roasting tin containing 1 inch/2.5 cm water.

Macaroni Supper Dish

Serves 4: 460 calories per portion

> 1 small green pepper
> 8 oz/225 g lean cooked ham or bacon
> 4 tomatoes
> 8 oz/225 g quick-cooking macaroni
> 10-oz/275-g can condensed mushroom soup
> salt and pepper
> 2 oz/50 g Cheddar cheese, grated

1. Cut the pepper in half, remove the seeds and white pith; cut into dice. Place in a basin, cover with boiling water and leave for 1 minute; drain.
2. Cut the ham or bacon into small dice. Wash and slice the tomatoes.
3. Cook the macaroni in boiling, salted water for 7 minutes; drain and rinse with hot water. Pre-heat a hot grill.
4. Make up the soup as directed on the can; bring slowly to the boil, stirring. Remove from the heat and add the macaroni, ham, green pepper and some salt and pepper, then turn into a shallow, 2-pint/1-litre ovenproof dish. Sprinkle with cheese and arrange a row of tomato slices, slightly overlapping, at each side of the dish.
5. Grill until golden brown and bubbling. Serve immediately.
Note If desired, this dish can be made in advance and re-heated in a moderate oven.

Use wholemeal macaroni and low-fat Cheddar cheese.
CHO: 56 g Calories: 420

Make gluten-free pasta (see recipe, page 216). Replace the mushroom soup with a can of mushrooms. Thicken the liquor in the can with potato flour.

Use lean ham and remove all the fat. Replace the mushroom soup with a can of mushrooms; thicken the liquor with 1 tablespoon cornflour. Omit the cheese and top with 10 black olives.

Replace the mushroom soup with 4 oz/100 g sliced mushrooms and ½ pint/250 ml milk thickened with 1 oz/25 g cornflour. Add salt and pepper.

Use wholemeal macaroni. Stir in 1 oz/25 g wheat or oat bran.

Omit the cooked ham or bacon. Replace with 2 oz/50 g peanuts. Use vegetarian cheese.

Baconburgers

Serves 8: 135 calories each

12 oz/350 g collar or forehock bacon
1 medium-sized onion
3 oz/75 g fresh white breadcrumbs
1 level teaspoon made mustard
pepper
1 egg
oil

1. Remove the rind and bone from the bacon. Peel and quarter the onion. Finely mince or chop the bacon and onion in a food processor; place in a large bowl. Add the breadcrumbs, mustard, a shake of pepper and egg; mix well together.
2. Turn the mixture out on to a floured board; shape into 8 even-sized cakes.
3. Heat a little oil in a frying-pan and fry the baconburgers over a gentle heat for 7-8 minutes, turning once.
4. Serve in warm buttered rolls with slices of tomato and gherkin.

Special Diets

Remove all the fat from the bacon. Use wholemeal breadcrumbs and add 1 tablespoon wheat bran.
CHO: 6 g Calories: 140

Use crumbs from special gluten-free bread (see recipe, page 214). Use Dijon mustard and check that it contains no wheat-based thickener. Serve with salad or in gluten-free rolls.

Cut all the fat off the bacon and use polyunsaturated oil for frying.

No change necessary.

Use wholemeal breadcrumbs and add 1 tablespoon wheat bran or muesli.

Chick-pea Burgers
Replace the bacon with 2 cans (15.2 oz/432 g) chick peas, drained and mashed with the rind and juice of ½ lemon. Replace the breadcrumbs with 1 oz/25 g chopped walnuts. Add 1 tablespoon chopped fresh mint and some salt and freshly ground black pepper. These store for up to 3 days in the refrigerator or 3 months in the freezer.

Serves 4: 285 calories per portion

> 4 oz/100 g streaky bacon or bacon pieces
> knob of margarine
> 1 lb/500 g potatoes, cooked and diced
> salt and pepper
> 2 eggs, beaten
> 10-oz/283-g packet frozen stir-fry vegetables

1. Remove the rind and bone from the bacon and cut in strips. Fry in the margarine until crisp. Remove from the pan and fry the vegetables as directed.
2. Add the potatoes and stir-fry to heat, then return the bacon to the pan, add some salt and pepper and the eggs. Cook slowly until set. Cut into four to serve.

[d]

Leave the skin on the potatoes; use lean bacon. Cook in a greased non-stick pan.
CHO: 25 g Calories: 210

[icon]

No change necessary.

[icon]

Use polyunsaturated margarine or oil.

[icon]

No change necessary.

[icon]

Leave the skins on the potato.

[icon]

Stir-fry Vegetable and Egg Cake
Replace the bacon with shredded brussels sprouts, cabbage and leek. Add a shake of soy sauce, 2 pieces chopped crystallized ginger, a shake of five-spice powder ('Chinese seasoning'), then the stir-fry vegetables and potatoes.

Cornish Pasties

Serves 4: 545 calories per portion

Filling:

    1 medium-sized potato
    1 medium-sized onion
    8-oz/200-g piece blade of beef or lean rump steak
    1 level teaspoon salt
    pepper

Shortcrust pastry:

    8 oz/200 g plain flour
    ½ level teaspoon salt
    2 oz/50 g polyunsaturated margarine
    2 oz/50 g lard
    cold water to mix

    beaten egg or milk to glaze

1. Pre-heat a hot oven (425°F/220°C/Gas 7).
2. Peel the potato and cut into small dice. Peel and chop the onion. Cut the meat into small cubes. Place in a basin with the onion, potato, salt and a shake of pepper.
3. Place the flour and salt in a bowl. Add the fats, cut into small pieces, and rub in with the fingertips until the mixture resembles fine breadcrumbs. Add about 2 tablespoons water and mix with a fork to form a firm dough. Turn out on to a floured board and knead lightly.
4. Divide the pastry into 4; lightly knead each quarter into a round. Roll out each round to the size of a tea-plate, about 6½ inches/16 cm across; trim the round by cutting round the edge of a tea-plate.
5. Divide the filling between the 4 rounds; brush the edges with water and draw up the pastry on each pasty, in a line over the centre of the filling. Seal firmly. Thicken the edges by cutting with the back of a knife; flute the edges with the fingers.
6. Place the pasties on a baking sheet, fluted edges uppermost. Brush each with a little beaten egg or milk. Bake in the centre of the oven for 40-45 minutes until golden brown. Serve hot or cold.

For the filling, leave the skin on the potatoes. Replace the lard with polyunsaturated margarine.

In the pastry, use wheatmeal 80% flour or replace 4 oz/100 g with wholemeal flour.

CHO: 47 g Calories: 512

No change necessary in the filling. Use gluten-free shortcrust pastry (see recipe, page 217).

Trim all the fat from the meat; use polyunsaturated fat for the pastry.

No change necessary.

As for diabetic.

For the filling, replace the meat with an equal weight of mixed vegetables: sliced pepper, celery, carrot and a tiny can of baked beans. Use vegetable margarine and white fat for the pastry.

Serves 4: 335 calories per portion

> 4 oz/100 g long spaghetti
> salt and pepper
> 2 eggs
> 4 oz/100 g red Leicester cheese
> 7-oz/198-g can chopped pork and ham
> 2 tablespoons sunflower oil
> 4 black olives
> 1 tomato
> watercress

1. Bring a large saucepan of salted water to the boil; gently lower the ends of the spaghetti into the pan, pressing them in further as the ends soften and curl round the pan. Boil, uncovered, for 15 minutes or until soft; test by pressing between the fingers. Drain in a sieve or colander and rinse with hot water.

2. Beat the eggs together in a large basin; grate the cheese, reserving 1 oz/25 g for garnish. Add the remaining cheese to the eggs with ¼ level teaspoon salt and a shake of pepper. Cut the meat into small dice, add to the egg mixture with the spaghetti and stir.

3. Heat the oil in a large frying-pan. Add the spaghetti mixture to the pan, press flat with the back of a metal spoon until the base of the pan is completely covered. Cook over a moderate heat for 6-8 minutes.

4. Place a plate on top of the pizza; invert the frying-pan; slip the pizza back into pan, cooked side uppermost. Cook for a further 6 minutes; remove from the heat.

5. Pre-heat a moderate grill. Turn the pizza out on to an ovenproof plate. Cut the olives in halves, remove the stones and reserve. Cut the tomato into 4 slices and place on top of the pizza. Sprinkle the surface with the reserved cheese and place under the grill for 2 minutes until the cheese starts to brown. Garnish with the halved olives and a sprig of watercress. Serve hot.

Use wholemeal spaghetti and low-fat hard cheese.
CHO: 24 g Calories: 285

Use gluten-free pasta (see recipe, page 216). Replace the canned chopped pork and ham with 8 oz/225 g cubed lean cooked ham.

Replace the Leicester cheese with skimmed-milk soft cheese and 1 teaspoon mixed dried herbs. Use polyunsaturated oil and replace the can of chopped pork and ham with 8 oz/225 g cubed lean cooked ham.

Replace the can of chopped pork and ham with 8 oz/225 g cubed lean cooked ham.

Use wholemeal spaghetti.

Use vegetarian cheese and replace the chopped pork and ham with a small can of pilchards in tomato sauce.

Country Pork Pâté

Serves 12: 225 calories per portion

 1½ lb/725 g piece thin end belly pork
 8 oz/225 g lean bacon pieces
 1 lb/500 g potatoes
 2 medium-sized onions
 8 oz/225 g pigs' liver
 8 oz/225 g reduced-fat pork sausagemeat
 1 level teaspoon salt
 ½ level teaspoon pepper
 ½ level teaspoon mixed dried herbs
 2 level teaspoons gelatine
 12 bay leaves
 3 lemon slices, quartered
 4 stuffed olives, sliced

1. Pre-heat a cool oven (325°F/160°C/Gas 3).
2. Bone the pork, place the bones in a saucepan with ½ pint/250 ml water. Remove the skin from the pork in one piece and reserve.
3. Remove the rind and bone from the bacon; peel the potatoes and onions. Cut all the ingredients into small pieces.
4. Using a medium blade, mince the pork, bacon, potatoes, liver and sausagemeat into a bowl. Add the salt, pepper and herbs and mix well. Alternatively, coarsely chop and mix in a food processor. Place in a 3-pint/1.5-litre casserole or ovenproof dish; level the top; place the pork skin, fat side downwards, over the pâté. Cover the dish and cook, in a roasting tin half-full of cold water, for 1½ hours.
5. Remove the pork skin, replace the lid or foil and cook for a further 20-30 minutes, until the pâté begins to leave the side of the dish.
6. Remove the pâté dish from the tin, uncover and place a small saucer or plate on the surface and place a 2-lb/1-kg weight on top. When cold, leave in the refrigerator overnight.
7. Bring the bones and water to the boil, cover and cook gently for 1 hour. Place the gelatine and 2 tablespoons water in a basin, pour ¼ pint/125 ml stock on to the gelatine and stir until dissolved. Add some salt and pepper to taste and leave until cold.
8. Pour half of the gelatine stock over the pâté and leave until almost set. Arrange the bay leaves, lemon slices and olive slices on top of the pâté, spoon the remaining gelatine stock over and leave to set.

Use lean pork and bacon.
CHO: 12 g Calories: 215

Replace the sausagemeat with cubed veal or turkey.

Use a leaner cut of pork, thick end of belly or shoulder, and remove all the fat. Remove the fat from the bacon. Replace the sausagemeat with cubed veal or turkey. Omit covering the pâté with pork fat in step 4.

Replace the sausagemeat with cubed veal or turkey.

Replace the sausagemeat with 3 oz/ 75 g lentils boiled to a purée.

Not suitable.

Spaghetti with Ham and Eggs

Serves 4: 580 calories per portion

Tomato sauce:

    1 medium-sized onion
    1 clove of garlic
    1 level teaspoon salt
    ½ oz/15 g polyunsaturated margarine
    1 level tablespoon plain flour
    1 chicken stock cube
    14-oz/198-g can tomatoes
    1 level teaspoon granulated sugar
    pepper

    6 oz/150 g lean cooked ham
    12 oz/325 g spaghetti
    1 oz/25 g butter
    2 eggs, beaten
    2 level tablespoon chopped parsley
    1 level tablespoon grated parmesan cheese
    salt
    black pepper

1. Peel and chop the onion; crush the garlic.
2. Melt the margarine in a saucepan; add the onion and garlic and fry for 3-4 minutes, until the onion is soft but not browned. Stir in the flour and cook for 1 minute. Add the stock cube, the canned tomatoes, sugar, a shake of pepper and ¼ pint/150 ml water. Bring to the boil, stirring. Cover and simmer for 15 minutes.
3. Meanwhile, cut the ham into even-sized pieces. Bring a large saucepan of salted water to the boil, gently lower the ends of the spaghetti into the pan, pressing them in further as the ends soften and curl round in the pan. Boil, uncovered, for 15 minutes, or until just soft when pressed between the fingers. Drain in a sieve or colander and rinse with hot water.
4. Melt the butter in a saucepan; add the ham and cook for 1 minute. Add the eggs, spaghetti, parsley, parmesan cheese, 1 level teaspoon salt and a shake of pepper to the pan. Stir over a medium heat until the eggs are cooked. Pile on to a warmed serving plate. Re-heat the tomato sauce and season with more salt and pepper, if necessary. Place in a warmed bowl and serve with the spaghetti.

Special Diets

Use wholemeal flour and spaghetti and omit the sugar from the sauce. Replace the butter with polyunsaturated margarine.
CHO: 78 g Calories: 565

Use spaghetti made with gluten-free flour (see recipe, page 216). Replace the flour with potato flour.

Use polyunsaturated margarine instead of butter. Use very lean ham and omit the parmesan cheese.

Use home-boiled ham and freshly grated parmesan cheese.

Use wholemeal flour and spaghetti.

Replace the ham with 4 oz/110 g tofu and 4 oz/100 g chopped walnuts.

Spicy Stuffed Eggs

Serves 4: 255 calories per portion

> 3 tablespoons mayonnaise
> 2 level teaspoons curry powder
> 8 hard-boiled eggs
> 4 stuffed olives, sliced
> lettuce
> watercress

1. Mix the mayonnaise and curry powder in a basin. Cut the eggs in half lengthwise, sieve the yolks into the basin and beat until smooth.
2. Place the mixture in a piping bag fitted with a large star tube and pipe the mixture into the cavities of the egg whites. Or fill with a teaspoon and swirl the tops with a fork.
3. Place a slice of olive on each and arrange four halves per portion on shredded lettuce and watercress.

Special Diets

Use low-calorie mayonnaise.
CHO: 0.5 g Calories: 225

Check that the curry powder and mayonnaise do not contain starch, or use home-made mayonnaise made from egg, oil and wine vinegar.

Make sure the mayonnaise is made from polyunsaturated oil.

Check that the curry powder does not contain artificial colouring. Use home-made mayonnaise.

Serve a mixture of cold cooked peas and sweetcorn in the salad. Serve with a jacket potato.

No change necessary.

Spicy Egg Fluff

Serves 4: 325 calories per portion

1 (2-3 serving) packet instant mashed potato
2 lb/1 kg fresh spinach
½ oz/15 g polyunsaturated margarine
¼ level teaspoon grated nutmeg
salt and pepper
4 eggs
4 oz/100 g Cheddar or Cheshire cheese, grated
¼ level teaspoon cayenne pepper

1. Pre-heat a moderately hot oven (400°F/200°C/Gas 6).
2. Make up the instant mashed potato, following the directions on the packet. Spread the potato over 4 greased ovenproof plates.
3. Wash the spinach thoroughly, removing all the coarse stalks. Place in a saucepan with just enough water to cover the base of the saucepan; cover and cook over a moderate heat for 10-12 minutes, or until tender.
4. Drain the spinach thoroughly in a sieve and press to remove excess water. Heat the margarine in a saucepan, add the nutmeg and some salt and pepper; return the spinach to the saucepan. Stir over a low heat until piping hot. Divide the spinach into 4 and pile on top of the potato in dishes; keep warm.
5. Separate the eggs and keep the yolks in the egg-shells. Add a pinch of salt to the egg whites and whisk until stiff. Using a metal spoon, fold in the grated cheese and cayenne pepper.
6. Divide the mixture into 4 and pile on top of the spinach; form into 'nests' with the back of a spoon. Carefully drop the egg yolks into the nests and top each with a knob of butter.
7. Bake in the centre of the oven for 10-15 minutes, until just golden brown. Serve immediately

Replace the Cheddar cheese with 2 oz/50 g parmesan cheese.
CHO: 16 g Calories: 270

No change necessary.

Replace the grated cheese with cottage cheese flavoured with chives.

Cook and mash 1 lb/450 g potatoes to replace the instant mashed potato.

No change necessary.

Use vegetarian cheese.

Butter Bean and Leek Mornay

Serves 4: 470 calories per portion

6 small leeks
3 hard-boiled eggs
3 oz/75 g mature Cheddar cheese, grated
15-oz/415-g can butter beans
milk
2 oz/50 g polyunsaturated margarine
1 oz/25 g plain flour
1 teaspoon sage and onion mustard

Topping:

1 oz/25 g rolled oats
1 oz/25 g mature Cheddar cheese, grated
½ teaspoon paprika

1. Trim the leeks, wash and cut through to the centre. Open out and wash out any soil. Cut in slices, place in a saucepan and simmer in salted water for 5 minutes; drain and place in a shallow ovenproof dish.
2. Shell the eggs and cut in halves. Place in the dish with the leeks. Drain the butter beans, reserving the stock in a measuring jug. Add the beans to the dish.
3. Make the butter-bean stock up to ½ pint/250 ml with milk, pour into a saucepan and add the margarine and flour. Whisk or stir over a low heat until the sauce boils. Add the mustard, cheese and salt and pepper to taste.
4. Pour the sauce over the vegetables, mix the topping ingredients and sprinkle over. Cool and chill if not required immediately.
5. To serve, heat in a moderate oven (375°F/190°C/Gas 4) for 30-40 minutes.

Use low-fat margarine, low-fat cheese and skimmed milk. Replace the plain flour with wholemeal.
CHO: 35 g Calories: 380 calories

Thicken the sauce with ground rice instead of flour, and cook for 10 minutes. Check that the mustard does not contain wheat flour.

Use polyunsaturated margarine. Replace the Cheddar cheese in the sauce with skimmed-milk soft cheese and 1 tablespoon chopped fresh herbs. Use skimmed milk. Replace the cheese in the topping with chopped dry roast peanuts.

No change necessary.

Use wholemeal flour.

No change necessary.

Cheese Omelette

Serves 1: 628 calories per portion

> 2 eggs
> salt and pepper
> small knob of butter
> 2 teaspoons groundnut oil

Filling:

> 2 oz/50 g grated Cheddar cheese
> 1 oz/25 g watercress

1. Beat the eggs with 2 tablespoons water, a shake of salt and a generous grind of black pepper.

2. Heat the butter and oil in an omelette pan until the butter foams. Before the butter browns, add the eggs and cook over a high heat, stirring with a fork in a figure of eight and gradually tilting the pan away from the handle (grip the pan underneath the handle).

3. Remove from the heat while still soft in the centre, spread the cheese over, then flip the part nearest the handle over to enclose the cheese; invert on to a warm plate. Garnish with watercress and serve immediately with wholemeal rolls.

Special Diets

Reduce the cheese to 1 oz/25 g and serve with a crisp green salad.
CHO: – Calories: 513

No change necessary. Serve with a jacket potato or crisp green salad.

Do not serve more than once a week. Replace the butter with polyunsaturated margarine. Replace the cheese with a low-fat variety.

No change necessary.

Serve with baked beans in tomato sauce.

Not suitable for a vegan diet; if eggs are acceptable, replace the butter with vegetable margarine and use rennet-free cheese. Alternatively, fill with beanshoots mixed with chopped fresh herbs.

Spinach Cannelloni

Serves 4: 510 calories per portion

> 1 lb/500 g frozen chopped spinach, thawed
> 6 oz/175 g matured Cheddar cheese, grated
> 2 oz/50 g fresh breadcrumbs
> salt and pepper
> grated nutmeg
> 8 sheets of lasagne
> 1 oz/25 g polyunsaturated margarine
> 1 oz/25 g plain flour
> ½ pint/250 ml semi-skimmed milk
> 1 teaspoon made mustard

1. Place the lasagne in plenty of boiling salted water, adding one sheet at a time to avoid sticking. Cook for 15 minutes or until just tender. Drain and rinse in cold water. Cut each piece in half and lay on a clean tea-towel.
2. Drain the spinach well and mix with 2 oz/50 g cheese and 1½ oz/40 g of the breadcrumbs.
3. Divide the spinach mixture between the sheets of lasagne and roll up. Place in a greased shallow ovenproof dish with the join downwards.
4. Place the butter, flour and milk in a saucepan and heat, whisking or stirring, until the sauce thickens. Add 3 oz/75 g cheese, the mustard, salt and pepper. Pour over the cannelloni.
5. Mix the remaining breadcrumbs and cheese and sprinkle over the sauce.
6. Bake in a moderately hot oven (375°F/190°C/Gas 5) for 20-30 minutes or until the topping is golden.

Special Diets

Use wholemeal breadcrumbs, lasagne and flour, and skimmed milk. Replace half the cheese with cottage cheese.
CHO: 50 g Calories: 435

Use gluten-free pasta (see recipe, page 216). Replace the breadcrumbs with gluten-free breadcrumbs or cottage cheese. Use maize flour instead of wheat flour for thickening the sauce. Check that the mustard does not contain wheat flour.

Replace the Cheddar cheese with cottage cheese and flavour with 1 tablespoon anchovy purée. Use skimmed milk.

No change necessary.

Use wholemeal breadcrumbs, lasagne and flour.

No change necessary.

Macaroni Cheese Flan

Serves 8: 355 calories per portion

Shortcrust pastry:

    8 oz/225 g plain flour
    4 oz/100 g polyunsaturated margarine
    cold water to mix

    4 oz/100 g short-cut macaroni
    6½-oz/186-g can sweet red peppers
    3 oz/75 g strong Cheddar cheese
    4 eggs
    ¾ pint/375 ml semi-skimmed milk
    ¼ level teaspoon mustard
    salt and pepper
    parsley

1. Pre-heat a moderately hot oven (375°F/190°C/Gas 5).
2. Place the flour in a bowl, add the margarine, cut up with a knife, then rub in by hand or machine. Add about 2 tablespoons water and mix to a firm dough. Roll out the pastry and line a deep swiss-roll tin 11 × 7 × 1½ inches/28 × 18 × 4 cm. Trim off the surplus pastry and flute the edges. Prick the base and chill.
3. Cook the macaroni in boiling salted water for 10-12 minutes, or until tender. Drain and rinse under cold water.
4. Drain the peppers and chop finely; grate the cheese coarsely. Mix the macaroni, peppers and cheese; spread in the pastry case.
5. Beat the eggs, milk, mustard, salt and pepper together. Pour into the pastry case.
6. Bake in the centre of the oven for 45-50 minutes until the filling feels firm and the pastry is golden brown. Leave to cool. Cut into squares. Garnish with parsley.

Use wholemeal flour and macaroni. Use low-fat Cheddar cheese and skimmed milk.
CHO: 33 g Calories: 332

Use special gluten-free pastry (see recipe, page 217). Make gluten-free pasta (see recipe, page 216). Use Dijon mustard and check that it contains no starch.

Replace the Cheddar cheese with cottage cheese and add 1 heaped tablespoon each of chopped fresh herbs and sesame seeds. Use skimmed milk.

No change necessary.

Use wholemeal flour and macaroni. Replace the peppers with 8 oz/225 g spinach, cooked, drained and chopped.

Use vegetable margarine and cooking fat; use vegetarian cheese.

Cauliflower Cheese

Serves 4: 190 calories per portion

    1 medium-sized cauliflower
    salt
Sauce:
    1 oz/25 g polyunsaturated margarine
    1 oz/25 g plain flour
    ½ pint/250 ml semi-skimmed milk
    4 oz/100 g Cheddar cheese
    pepper

1. Trim the tough outside leaves from the cauliflower. Hollow out the thick lower part of the stalk. Place the cauliflower in a large saucepan with 2 inches/5 cm depth of boiling salted water. Return to the boil. Cover and simmer for 15-20 minutes, until the stalk and small leaves are tender. Lift out of the saucepan and drain carefully. Place in a warmed serving dish and keep warm. Pre-heat a hot grill.

2. Place the margarine, flour and milk in a saucepan and stir or whisk over a low heat until thickened. Cook for 3 minutes.

3. Grate the cheese and stir 3 oz/75 g into the sauce. Taste and season with salt and pepper; pour over the cauliflower. Sprinkle the remaining cheese on top and brown under the grill.

Use wholemeal flour and skimmed milk. Use low-fat cheese, replace half with low-fat soft cheese and chives and sprinkle with 1 oz/25 g dry roast peanuts.
CHO: 5.5 g Calories: 170

Replace the flour with rice or potato flour and beat an egg into the sauce with the cheese to thicken.

Omit the margarine and flour. Thicken the milk with 1 oz/25 g cornflour. Use low-fat cheese replacement as for diabetic.

No change necessary.

Use wholemeal flour. Place the cauliflower on a layer of cooked chopped spinach and top the sauce with chopped salted peanuts.

No change necessary.

Cheesy Bread Pudding

Special Diets

Serves 4: 385 calories per portion

4 oz/100 g Cheddar cheese, grated
6 slices bread from a large loaf
1½ oz/40 g polyunsaturated margarine
mustard, made up
yeast extract
2 eggs
½ pint/250 ml semi-skimmed milk
1 level teaspoon salt
pepper
8 tomatoes

1. Butter the bread and spread half with mustard and half with yeast extract. Cut into strips.
2. Butter a 1¾-pint/1-litre shallow ovenproof dish. Layer in the dish one-third of the cheese, the mustard-spread bread, another third of cheese then the yeast extract-spread bread and the remaining cheese.
3. Beat the eggs, milk, salt and a generous shake of pepper together. Pour over the bread then leave to soak for ½ hour.
4. Pre-heat a moderate oven (375°F/190°C/Gas 5). Cut a cross in the top of each tomato; place in an ovenproof dish.
5. Place the dish with the bread on a baking sheet and bake in the centre of the oven for 35-40 minutes. Cook the tomatoes for the last 10 minutes.

Use wholemeal bread; use low-fat spread instead of butter; reduce cheese to 3 oz/75 g.
CHO: 25 g Calories: 315

Use special gluten-free bread (see recipe, page 214). Use Dijon mustard and check that it does not contain wheat-based thickener.

Use cottage cheese with chives, low-fat polyunsaturated spread and skimmed milk.

No change necessary.

Use wholemeal bread.

Use vegetarian cheese and margarine.

Wholefood Vegetable Pizza

Serves 6: 310 calories per portion

    10 oz/275 g packet brown bread mix
    1 medium-sized onion
    1 clove garlic
    1 lb/450 g tomatoes
    1 medium-sized green pepper
    2 small carrots
    8 oz/225 g courgettes
    2 tablespoons sunflower oil
    1 level teaspoon dried oregano or marjoram
    salt and pepper

Topping:

    2 oz/50 g Cheddar cheese
    1 oz/25 g sesame seeds
    1 oz/25 g wheatgerm
    1 level teaspoon dried oregano or marjoram
    1 oz/25 g parmesan cheese

1. Grease a swiss-roll tin, 11 × 7 inches/28 × 18 cm. Make up the bread mix as directed on the packet. Roll out and line the base and sides of the tin. Cover with clingfilm and leave to rise whilst preparing the filling.

2. Pre-heat a moderately hot oven (400°F/200°C/Gas 6). Peel and slice the onion; crush the garlic. Place the tomatoes in a bowl and cover with boiling water; leave for 1 minute, drain and peel, then chop roughly. De-seed and slice the pepper. Trim the carrots and grate coarsely. Trim the courgettes and slice.

3. Heat the oil in a saucepan. Add the onion and garlic and cook gently until softened but not browned (about 5 minutes). Add the carrots and pepper; cook for 1 minute.

4. Add the tomatoes, oregano or marjoram, 1 level teaspoon salt and a good shake of pepper. Bring to the boil, reduce the heat and cook gently for about 10 minutes until thickened. Add the courgettes and cook for 5 minutes. Remove from the heat and cool slightly.

5. Grate the Cheddar cheese. Place in a bowl with the sesame seeds, wheatgerm, oregano or marjoram and parmesan cheese. Mix well.

6. Spread the filling over the bread base. Sprinkle the wheatgerm mixture over the top. Bake in the centre of the oven for 40 minutes. Serve hot or cold.

No change necessary.
CHO: 40 g Calories: 310

Replace the brown bread mix with bread dough made from gluten-free flour (see recipe, page 214). Omit the wheatgerm and replace with chopped almonds.

Omit the Cheddar cheese.

Replace the brown bread mix with bread dough made from 8 oz/225 g plain wholemeal flour, ½ oz/15 g fresh yeast and mixed with ¼ pint/150 ml water.

No change necessary.

Use rennet-free cheese.

Makes 2 large pizzas, each dividing into 8: 245 calories per portion

Filling:

>2 medium-sized onions
>2 oz/50 g polyunsaturated margarine
>¼ level teaspoon mixed dried herbs
>2 oz/50 g plain flour
>15-oz/425-g can tomatoes
>1 level teaspoon sugar
>salt and pepper

Scone base:

>1 lb/450 g self-raising flour
>1 level teaspoon salt
>4 oz/100 g polyunsaturated margarine
>6 fl oz/175 ml semi-skimmed milk

Topping:

>5 cheese slices
>1 pickled dill cucumber
>4 oz/100 g garlic sausage, sliced
>parsley

1. Peel and finely chop the onions; place in a saucepan with the margarine and herbs and cook over a low heat until tender. Remove the saucepan from the heat and stir in the flour, canned tomatoes, sugar, some salt and pepper.

2. Bring to the boil, stirring; cook for 2 minutes. Leave to cool.

3. Pre-heat a hot oven (400°F/200°C/Gas 6). Lightly grease two baking sheets.

4. To make the scone base, place the flour and salt in a bowl, add the margarine, cut into small pieces, and rub in with the fingertips until the mixture resembles fine breadcrumbs. Add the milk all at once and mix with a fork to form a soft dough.

5. Turn out on to a floured board and knead lightly. Cut the dough in half and roll out each half to an oblong 10 × 8 inches/25 × 20 cm. Place each on a baking sheet and pinch up the edges by fluting with the fingers.

6. Divide the filling between the two scone bases and spread evenly.

Use wholemeal flour. Omit the sugar from the tomato sauce. Reduce the cheese slices to two and the garlic sausage to 2 oz/50 g.
CHO: 7 g Calories: 200

In the filling, replace the wheat flour with maize flour. Make the scone base using Trufree or Jubilee no.4 white flour (see recipe, page 215).

In the topping, replace the garlic sausage with flaked tuna or sweetcorn.

Use skimmed milk. Replace the cheese slices with sliced olives and garlic sausage with flaked tuna.

Replace the garlic sausage with flaked tuna and the cheese slices with Cheddar cheese.

Use wholemeal flour.

Use vegetable margarine. Replace the garlic sausage with flaked tuna or sweetcorn.

Bake on the second and third shelves from the top of the oven for 20-25 minutes, until golden brown at the edges. Leave to cool on a wire rack.

7. Cut each of the cheese slices into four triangles, thinly slice the dill cucumber and remove the skin from the garlic sausage.

8. Arrange at both ends of each pizza five triangles of cheese with a cucumber slice between each. Place 12 slices of folded garlic sausage in two rows down each pizza; garnish with parsley.

9. Place the pizza under a moderate grill for 10 minutes to heat before serving.

Note Wrap and freeze the cooked pizzas.

Welsh Rarebit

Serves 4: 300 calories per portion

> 2 tablespoons semi-skimmed milk
> 2 teaspoons Worcestershire sauce
> 1 oz/25 g butter
> 1 teaspoon dry mustard
> ¼ teaspoon salt
> ¼ teaspoon pepper
> 6 oz/150 g Cheddar cheese, grated
> 4 slices bread from a large loaf

1. Pre-heat a hot grill.
2. Place the milk, Worcestershire sauce, butter, mustard, salt and pepper in a small saucepan; heat, but do not boil. Leave to cool slightly.
3. Stir in the grated cheese; beat until smooth.
4. Toast each side of the bread on one side; spread the untoasted side thickly with the cheese mixture. Grill for 2-3 minutes until golden brown. Serve immediately.
Note Alternatively, substitute beer for 1-2 tablespoons milk, and omit the Worcestershire sauce.

Omit the butter; use wholemeal bread and low-fat Cheddar cheese. CHO: 12.5 g Calories: 185

Omit the mustard and add a few drops of tabasco instead. Use special gluten/wheat-free bread.

Use skimmed milk, omit the butter and use low-fat Cheddar cheese.

No change necessary.

Add a small can of haricot or borlotti beans before spreading on toast.

Use margarine and vegetarian cheese.

Potato Griddle Cakes

Makes 12: 135 calories each

> 1 (2-3 serving) packet instant mashed potato
> 8 oz/225 g self-raising flour
> 2 level teaspoons baking powder
> 2 level teaspoons salt
> 3 oz/75 g polyunsaturated margarine
> 1 tablespoon semi-skimmed milk

1. Make up the instant mashed potato as directed on the packet; leave until cold.

2. Sift the flour, baking powder and salt into a bowl; add the margarine, cut into small pieces, and rub in with fingertips until the mixture resembles fine breadcrumbs. Add the cold potato and milk; mix with a fork to form a dough.

3. Lightly grease a griddle or thick-based frying-pan and place over a moderate heat.

4. Turn out the dough on to a floured board and knead lightly. Roll out to ½-inch/1.25-cm thickness. Cut into rounds with a 2½-inch/7.25-cm plain cutter. Arrange half the 'cakes' on the griddle or in the frying-pan and cook for 3-4 minutes until golden brown. Turn and cook on the other side, remove from the pan and keep warm. Repeat with the remaining cakes. Serve the cakes hot, split and buttered.

Use wholemeal self-raising flour.
CHO: 17 g Calories: 132

Use gluten-free baking powder (see recipe, page 223) and Trufree or Jubilee self-raising flour.

Use skimmed milk. Flour the griddle instead of greasing it.

Cook and mash 8 oz/225 g potato; omit the baking powder and use **a** small egg instead of the milk.

Add 2 rounded tablespoons natural bran and 3 tablespoons extra milk.

No change necessary. Serve with sunflower margarine.

141

Vegetable Samosas

Makes 12: 180 calories each

    1 small onion
    8-oz/227-g packet frozen mixed vegetables
      (cauliflower, peas, carrots)
    1 teaspoon Madras curry powder
    1 teaspoon salt
    1 oz/25 g sultanas
    2 tablespoons tomato ketchup
    14-oz/395-g packet frozen puff pastry, just thawed
    oil for deep frying

1. Peel and finely chop the onion. Fry in a little oil until softened. Add the frozen vegetables, curry powder, salt and sultanas. Cook, stirring occasionally, for about 5 minutes. Stir in the tomato ketchup. Cool.

2. Roll out the pastry and trim to an oblong 9 × 12 inches/21 × 28 cm. Cut into 3-inch/7-cm squares. Divide the filling between the squares. Brush the edges with water; fold to form triangles. Press the edges to seal firmly.

3. Fill a deep-fat pan one-third full with oil. Heat the oil to 350°F, 180°C. Fry about 3 samosas at a time, for 2-3 minutes until puffed up and golden. Drain on kitchen paper. Serve the samosas hot or cold.

Omit the sultanas, include some baked beans in tomato sauce with the mixed vegetables and omit the tomato ketchup. Bake the samosas in a hot oven for 15 minutes instead of frying them.
CHO: 13 g Calories: 150

Replace the puff pastry with gluten-free pasta (see recipe, page 216) and shallow-fry. Check that the curry powder does not contain starch.

Use home-made puff pastry, made with polyunsaturated fat. Bake instead of frying.

Check that the vegetables have no additives.

Include some baked beans in tomato sauce with the vegetables and omit the tomato ketchup.

Use vegetable-fat puff pastry.

Houmus

This Middle-Eastern dip ideally contains tahini (sesame paste). This may be hard to find, so in this recipe sesame oil is used to ensure a good flavour (failing this, use corn oil). Serve with plenty of pitta bread or crackers.

Serves 6: 269 calories with tahini, 184 calories without, per portion

 4 oz/100 g dried chick peas
 2 cloves garlic
 ¼ teaspoon salt
 6 tablespoons sesame or corn oil
 4 tablespoons tahini (optional)
 2 tablespoons lemon juice

1. Soak the chick peas in cold water overnight. Drain and place in a saucepan. Cover with cold water, bring to the boil, cover and simmer for 4 hours until tender. Alternatively, cook in a pressure cooker at high pressure for 45 minutes. Drain and remove the skins. Press the peas through a sieve with a wooden spoon.
2. Peel and crush the garlic; add to the pea purée. Gradually beat in the oil, tahini (if using) and lemon juice. Taste and add more salt or lemon juice as necessary. Beat in enough water (about 4 tablespoons) to give a soft dipping consistency. Alternatively, put the skinned chick peas, peeled garlic, oil and lemon juice in a food processor and blend until smooth. Gradually pour water through the lid until the mixture is of a soft consistency. Store, covered, in the refrigerator for up to 2 days.

No change necessary.
CHO: 10 g Calories: 260 with tahini, 184 without

No change necessary.

No change necessary.

No change necessary.

No change necessary.

No change necessary.

Tzatziki

Cool and refreshing, this Greek cucumber dip is best made with fresh mint, but dried mint also gives a good flavour. Serve with fresh warmed pittas or crusty bread for a snack lunch or as a starter.

Serves 6: 9 calories per portion

>   15.9-oz/450-g carton natural yoghurt
>   ½ cucumber
>   ¼ teaspoon salt
>   1 teaspoon chopped fresh mint
>   or ½ teaspoon dried mint

1. Place a piece of kitchen paper in a sieve and drain the yoghurt through it for 1 hour.
2. Finely chop the cucumber and stir into the drained yoghurt with the salt and mint. Leave the flavours to mix for 1 hour before serving. Store, covered, in the refrigerator for up to 2 days. Stir before serving.

Use low-fat yoghurt.
CHO: 1.5 g Calories: 9

No change necessary.

Use low-fat yoghurt.

Use fresh mint.

No change necessary.

No change necessary.

Puddings

Serve fresh fruit for dessert most days, but for treats and entertaining make one of these traditional puddings. Diabetics and slimmers should avoid those with a high calorie rating.

Vanilla Ice Cream

Serves 6: 335 calories per portion

> 2 eggs separated
> 2 oz/50 g granulated sugar
> ½ oz/15 g custard powder
> ½ pint/275 ml semi-skimmed milk
> 1 teaspoon real vanilla essence
> ½ pint/275 ml double cream, chilled
> 2 oz/50 g icing sugar

1. Blend the egg yolks, sugar, custard powder and milk in a saucepan. Bring just to the boil, stirring. Place the saucepan in a bowl of cold water and stir until cool. Beat in the vanilla essence, then chill.
2. Whisk the cream until thick. Whisk the egg whites until stiff; whisk in the icing sugar, then fold into the cream. Fold in the custard a tablespoonful at a time. Pour into an oblong container, cover and freeze until mushy. Turn into a chilled bowl or food processor and whisk or process until smooth; re-freeze until firm.
3. Before serving, leave to soften in the refrigerator for 1 hour. Serve with wafers and fruit or chocolate sauce (see recipe, page 169).

Special Diets

Replace the granulated sugar with liquid sweetener, and the icing sugar with 1 oz/25 g fructose. Replace the double cream with 5 oz/100 g poly-unsaturated margarine melted in 5 fl oz/25 ml skimmed milk, to which has been added ½ teaspoon gelatine softened in 1 teaspoon water. Liquidize, cool, then chill and whip.
CHO: 26 g Calories: 270 per portion

No change necessary, but make sure that the custard powder is gluten-free.

As for diabetic but sugar may be used.

Replace the custard powder with cornflour. Omit the vanilla essence and flavour the milk with a vanilla pod, by cutting up the pod and infusing in warmed milk for 1 hour. Strain, wash the vanilla pod and store in sugar to flavour.

Serve with a topping of muesli.

No change necessary.

Chocolate Ice Cream

Make as for vanilla ice cream, adding 1 oz/15 g cocoa to the egg yolk mixture and 3 oz/75 g grated plain dessert chocolate to the cooked custard.

Make as for diabetic vanilla ice cream, adding cocoa as for basic recipe. Use diabetic chocolate. Serve small portions (8 from this quantity). CHO: 30 g Calories: 466 per portion

Check that the cocoa and chocolate are starch-free.

Make as for vanilla ice cream, adding cocoa and chocolate as for basic recipe.

Make as for vanilla ice cream, adding cocoa and chocolate as for basic recipe.

Serve with a topping of chopped nuts.

No change necessary.

Coffee Ice Cream

Make as for vanilla ice cream, adding 1 tablespoon instant coffee dissolved in 2 tablespoons boiling water. For the special diets follow the recipe adaptations for the vanilla ice cream adding coffee as above.

CHO: 27 g Calories: 275

Omit the instant coffee and infuse 1 oz/25 g ground coffee in the boiling milk. Strain before adding to the custard.

Strawberry Ice Cream

Make as for vanilla ice cream, replacing the custard powder, milk and vanilla essence with ½ pint/250 ml strawberry purée made from 8 oz/250 g strawberries and 2 tablespoons lemon juice sweetened with the 2 oz/50 g sugar. Whisk the egg yolks into the cream. Add a few drops of red food colouring if desired.

As for diabetic vanilla ice cream, replacing the custard as above.
CHO: 12 g Calories: 190

No change necessary.

As for diabetic recipe but sugar may be used.

No change necessary but do not use red food colouring.

Serve with a sprinkling of nuts.

No change necessary.

Fresh Strawberry Mouse

Serves 6: 120 calories per portion

        8 oz/225 g strawberries
        1 tablespoon lemon juice
        1 level tablespoon gelatine
        2 oz/50 g caster sugar
        1 1.6-oz/44-g packet dessert topping mix
        milk

1. Wash and hull the strawberries, reserve 6 for decoration. Press the strawberries through a sieve into a basin, or liquidize; add the lemon juice.
2. Place ¼ pint/125 ml water in a basin; add the gelatine. Leave to melt over a saucepan of hot water or in a microwave oven. Add the sugar and stir until dissolved; stir into the strawberry purée.
3. Make up the dessert topping mix as directed on the packet, using milk. Reserve 1 tablespoon of topping for decoration.
4. Add the strawberry mixture to the dessert topping a little at a time, whisking well after each addition. Leave in a cool place, stirring occasionally, until just on the point of setting.
5. Turn the mixture into 6 individual moulds; chill until set. Turn out and decorate each with a teaspoonful of reserved topping and a whole reserved strawberry.

Replace the sugar with a few drops of liquid sweetener.
CHO: 17 g Calories: 85

Check that the dessert topping mix does not contain starch.

Replace the dessert topping mix and milk with ½ pint/275 ml low-fat strawberry yoghurt; whisk when partially set. Decorate with skimmed-milk soft cheese mixed with 1 teaspoon orange rind and juice or Cointreau liqueur.

Replace the dessert topping mix with ¼ pint/142 ml whipping cream (or for lower fat use half whipping cream and half strawberry yoghurt).

Replace the strawberries with raspberries or apricots.

Replace the gelatine with agar-agar.

Apple Crumble

Serves 4: 305 calories per portion

> 1 lb/500 g cooking apples
> 1 tablespoon sugar
> 4 oz/100 g plain white or wholemeal flour
> 2 oz/50 g butter or margarine
> 2 oz/50 g demerara sugar

1. Pre-heat a moderately hot oven (400°F/200°C/Gas 6). Peel, core and slice the apples into a 1½-pint/1-litre pie dish and add the sugar.
2. Place the flour in a bowl, rub in the butter, then add the demerara sugar. Sprinkle over the apples, place the dish on a baking sheet and bake in the centre of the oven for 25-35 minutes, until the crumble is golden brown.

Special Diets

Use wholemeal flour and polyunsaturated margarine. Reduce the demerara sugar to 1 oz/25 g and omit the sugar for sweetening the apples. Add ½ oz/15 g toasted chopped almonds to the crumble.
CHO: 37 g Calories: 280

Replace the flour with ground rice, add 1 heaped tablespoon each of sunflower seeds, sesame seeds and chopped walnuts and 1 oz/25 g ground almonds. Bake in a hot oven (450°F/230°C/Gas 8) for 10-15 minutes.

Use polyunsaturated margarine.

No change necessary.

Use wholemeal flour and add 1 heaped tablespoon bran cereal. Leave the skins on the apples and grate them into the dish. Add 2 oz/50 g dried apricots to the apple.

Replace the butter with polyunsaturated margarine.

Rice Pudding

Serves 4: 130 calories per portion

½ oz/15 g butter
2 oz/50 g short-grain (pudding) rice
1 oz/25 g granulated sugar
½ teaspoon grated nutmeg
1 pint/550 ml semi-skimmed milk
strip of lemon peel

1. Butter a 1½-pint/750-ml ovenproof dish. Wash the rice in a sieve under running water, drain well and place in the dish with the sugar, nutmeg, milk and lemon peel. Leave to soften the rice for ½ hour.
2. Place the dish on a baking sheet and bake in a cool oven (300°F/150°C/Gas 2) for 2-2½ hours. Remove from the oven and stir gently after ½ hour.
Note To shorten the cooking time to 1½ hours, use boiling milk. Alternatively, use flaked rice, barley, tapioca or macaroni.

Use brown rice and a non-sugar sweetener instead of sugar. Use low-fat margarine instead of butter. Cook for 2½ hours.
CHO: 19 g Calories: 120

No change necessary, but use only white or brown rice or ground rice.

Use skimmed milk and replace the butter with polyunsaturated margarine.

No change necessary.

Use brown rice and cook for 2½ hours.

No change necessary.

Custard

Serves 4: 110 calories per portion

    1 oz/25 g custard powder
    1 oz/25 g sugar
    1 pint/550 ml semi-skimmed milk

1. Mix the custard powder and sugar to a smooth paste with a little of the milk. Boil the remainder, pour on to the blended powder and stir until smooth.
2. Return to the saucepan and stir over heat until the sauce boils, pour into a jug and serve with puddings and pies.

Omit the sugar and sweeten when cooked with liquid sweetener.
CHO: 7 g Calories: 80

Replace the custard powder with maize or cornflour and add ½ teaspoon vanilla essence after cooking.

Alternatively, replace the custard powder with 3 beaten eggs. Add the boiling milk gradually, and cook over a very low heat, stirring occasionally, until the custard coats the back of the spoon. Do not boil. Add ½ teaspoon vanilla essence to the cooked custard.

Use skimmed milk.

Replace the custard powder with cornflour and infuse a vanilla pod in the milk as it slowly comes to the boil. Remove the vanilla pod, wash and store in a jar of sugar, then use again.

Alternatively, replace the custard powder with 3 eggs as for gluten/wheat-free.

It is not practical to add fibre. Serve with high-fibre foods.

No change necessary.

Pancakes

Special Diets

Serves 8: 120 calories each portion

Batter:

> 4 oz/100 g plain flour
> ¼ level teaspoon salt
> 1 egg
> ½ pint/250 ml semi-skimmed milk
> lard for frying
> lemon juice
> sugar

1. Place the flour and salt in a bowl. Make a well in the centre of the flour; add the egg. Stir in half the milk gradually. Mix well, using a wooden spoon; beat until smooth. Add the remainder of the milk; pour the batter into a jug.
2. Heat a little lard in a medium-sized (8-inch/20-cm) frying-pan. Pour off any excess lard into a small bowl, leaving the pan lightly greased. Pour sufficient batter into pan, swirling quickly to coat the pan thinly. Cook until the underside is golden brown.
3. Hold the pan over a sheet of greaseproof paper (sugared for sweet pancakes): slip the pancake to the side of the pan opposite the handle. Quickly toss (or flip over with a palette knife). Cook over a moderate heat until brown.
4. Invert the pancake on to the greaseproof paper; sprinkle with lemon juice and sugar, then roll up, using 2 forks. Place on a warmed serving dish; keep warm in a cool oven. Use the remaining batter to make 7 more pancakes.

Note To make the batter in a mixer, place half the milk, the egg, flour and salt in a mixer bowl. Mix at medium speed until the batter is smooth; mix in the remaining milk at low speed. Alternatively, place all the batter ingredients in a liquidizer goblet and run the machine until well mixed.

Serve with either sweet or savoury fillings. To store, stack between greaseproof paper and wrap in foil. Store in the refrigerator for up to 4 days or in a freezer for up to 3 months.

Use wholemeal or buckwheat flour, add a second egg and replace the milk with skimmed milk, reducing to 8 fl oz/200 ml. Use a non-stick pan and the smallest possible amount of fat for greasing: just rub over with an oiled piece of kitchen paper. Use low-calorie powdered sweetener.
CHO: 12 g Calories: 95

Use Trufree or Jubilee no.7 self-raising flour and an extra egg.

Use polyunsaturated oil for cooking. Use a non-stick pan but keep the heat low. Use skimmed milk.

No change necessary.

Use wholemeal or buckwheat flour as for diabetic.

Use groundnut oil for frying.

Summer Pudding

Special Diets

Serves 4: 215 calories per portion

    7 thin slices white bread from a large loaf
    8 oz/250 g redcurrants
    1 lb/500 g raspberries
    6 oz/175 g caster sugar

1. Remove the crusts from the bread and line the side and base of a 1½-pint/750-ml pudding basin with 5 slices of bread, trimming to fit where necessary.
2. Wash the redcurrants; strip from the stalks with a fork. Place the fruits and 1 tablespoon water in a saucepan; stew the fruit for 5 minutes or until soft. Remove from the heat; stir in the sugar.
3. Pour the mixture into a lined pudding basin; cover with the remaining slices of bread, trimming to fit where necessary. Cover with a saucer, small plate or foil and place a weight on top. Leave overnight. Invert on to a serving plate and serve with cream.

Use wholemeal bread. Sweeten the fruit with low-calorie liquid sweetener when cold.
CHO: 20 g Calories: 100

Use bread made with Jubilee or Tru-free no.1 or no.4 flour.

No change necessary.

No change necessary.

Use wholemeal bread or malted wheatmeal bread.

No change necessary.

Swedish Chocolate Pudding

Serves 6: 240 calories per portion

2 eggs
3 oz/75 g caster sugar
1 teaspoon vanilla essence
4 level tablespoons cocoa
1 level teaspoon instant coffee
½ pint/275 ml semi-skimmed milk
½ oz/15 g (1 envelope) gelatine
1 5-fl-oz/142-ml carton double cream
1 tablepoon flaked almonds

1. Separate the eggs; place the whites in a clean, grease-free basin, and the yolks, caster sugar and vanilla essence in a bowl. Beat the egg-yolk mixture until light and creamy.
2. Blend the cocoa and coffee with a little of the measured milk in a saucepan. Add the remaining milk and bring to the boil. Stir into the egg-yolk mixture. Return to the saucepan; bring to the boil, stirring, and cook for 1 minute, stirring continuously. Remove from the heat; return to the bowl.
3. Measure 3 tablespoons cold water into a small basin; add the gelatine and leave for 5 minutes. Stir the gelatine into the chocolate mixture. Leave in a cool place until just setting.
4. Place the cream in a basin; whisk until just thick. Reserve 2 rounded tablespoons cream for decoration. Whisk the egg whites until stiff but not dry.
5. Carefully fold the cream and egg whites into the chocolate mixture. Place in a 1½-pint/825-ml fluted mould. Leave to set in the refrigerator.
6. Dip the mould in a bowl of hand-hot water and turn out on to a serving plate. Place the reserved cream in a nylon piping bag fitted with a star tube. Pipe stars round the top and bottom of the pudding; arrange flaked almonds round the side. Chill until ready to serve.

Omit the sugar. Sweeten to taste at step 3 after adding the gelatine with liquid sweetener. Replace the cream with thick natural unwhipped Greek yoghurt.
CHO: 5 g Calories: 100

Check that the cocoa used is gluten/wheat-free, or use carob powder instead.

Use skimmed milk and replace the cream with low-fat fromage frais.

Omit the vanilla essence and use 1 oz/25 g vanilla sugar plus 2 oz/50 g caster sugar.

🍬
Double the amount of almonds.

✋
Replace the gelatine with agar-agar.

Serves 8: 350 calories per portion

    4 oz/100 g self-raising flour
    1 level teaspoon baking powder
    ½ level teaspoon ground cinnamon
    a pinch each of ground cloves and nutmeg
    1 oz/25 g ground almonds
    4 oz/100 g polyunsaturated margarine
    4 oz/100 g caster sugar
    2 eggs
    3 tablespoons semi-skimmed milk
    1 1 lb 12-oz/822-g can apricot halves in natural juice

Topping:
    1 oz/25 g flaked almonds
    2 oz/50 g plain flour
    1 oz/25 g margarine
    1 level tablespoon caster sugar

Apricot sauce:
    apricot juice from can
    1 level teaspoon cornflour

1. Pre-heat a moderate oven (375°F/190°C/Gas 5).
2. Brush an oblong 11 × 7 × 1½-inch/28 × 18 × 4-cm cake-tin or oven-proof dish with melted fat.
3. Sift the self-raising flour, baking powder, cinnamon, cloves and nutmeg into a bowl. Add the ground almonds, soft margarine, 4 oz/100 g sugar, 1 whole egg plus 1 egg yolk (reserve the white in a grease-free bowl) and milk. Mix together with a wooden spoon and beat for 1-2 minutes until well blended. Whisk the egg white until stiff but not dry. Fold into the mixture, using a metal spoon.
4. Place the mixture in the tin or dish; level the top with the back of a metal spoon. Drain the apricots, reserving the syrup. Arrange about three-quarters of the apricots, cut side downwards, on top of the mixture; reserve the remaining halves.
5. To make the topping, toast the flaked almonds; place the plain flour in a bowl; add the margarine and rub in; stir in the sugar; sprinkle over the apricots and top with flaked almonds. Bake in the

Use fine wholemeal flour and reduce the sugar in the pudding by half. Serve small portions.
CHO: 24 g Calories: 253

Replace the self-raising flour with 2 oz/50 g potato flour, 2 oz/50 g rice flour and 2 teaspoons gluten-free baking powder (see recipe, page 223).

    In the topping, replace the flour with crushed cornflakes. Use maize flour for thickening the sauce.

Use polyunsaturated margarine and skimmed milk.

No change necessary.

Use fine wholemeal flour. Add ½ oz/15 g bran to the topping.

No change necessary.

centre of the oven for 20-40 minutes until golden brown.

6. To make the apricot sauce, place the reserved apricots and syrup from the can in a measuring jug. Make up to ½ pint/250 ml with water, if necessary. Place in a pan, bring to the boil, cover and simmer for 5 minutes, until the apricots are soft. Remove from the heat and liquidize. Blend the cornflour with a little cold water in the pan; add the apricot purée. Bring to the boil, stirring, and cook for 2 minutes. Serve with the pudding.

Crème Caramel

Special Diets

Serves 4: 150 calories per portion

Caramel:

    2 oz/50 g granulated sugar
    2 tablespoons water

Custard:

    3 large eggs, size 2
    ¾ pint/425 ml semi-skimmed milk
    1 oz/25 g caster sugar
    ½ teaspoon vanilla essence

1. Pre-heat a very cool oven (275°F/170°C/Gas 1). Half-fill a roasting tin with warm water and warm a 1¼-pint/650-ml soufflé dish. To prepare the caramel, place the sugar and water in a thick saucepan and heat slowly until the sugar has dissolved; boil steadily, without stirring, until the sugar turns a deep golden brown. Pour into the warmed dish and leave for 2 minutes to set, then place the dish in the water bath.

2. Beat the eggs in a bowl. Place the milk and caster sugar in a saucepan and heat just enough to dissolve the sugar. Add to the eggs, with the vanilla essence, and beat lightly.

3. Strain the egg and milk mixture on to the caramel. Place the tin containing the dish in water in the centre of the oven; cook for about 1 hour or until set and lightly brown on top. Remove the dish from the baking tin and leave until the custard is quite cold (about 3 hours). Loosen the edge by pulling towards the centre gently with the fingers and turn out on to a serving plate.

Reduce the sugar in the caramel by half. Replace the caster sugar in the custard with an acesulfame sweetener such as Diamin.
CHO: 12 g Calories: 95

No change necessary.

Use skimmed milk.

No change necessary.

Serve with a high-fibre fruit such as apricots.

No change necessary.

Banana Trifle

Serves 6: 420 calories per portion

    3 bananas
    4-6 tablespoons sweet sherry
    1 large packet (8) trifle sponge cakes
    strawberry jam
Custard:
    4 egg yolks
    1 rounded tablespoon caster sugar
    ½ level teaspoon vanilla essence
    1 pint/550 ml semi-skimmed milk
Decoration:
    about 8 blanched almonds
    5-fl-oz/142-ml carton double cream
    2 tablespoons semi-skimmed milk
    1 tablespoon lemon juice

1. Slice 2 bananas into a bowl, add the sherry and turn to coat.
2. Split the trifle sponge cakes in halves; sandwich together with strawberry jam. Cut up into small pieces; place in a 3-pint/1½-litre glass bowl. Add the bananas and sherry; mix together lightly.
3. Place the egg yolks and caster sugar together in a large basin; add the vanilla essence and beat with a wooden spoon. Bring the milk to the boil in a small saucepan; gradually stir into the egg mixture. Place the basin over a saucepan of boiling water over a moderate heat (or pour the custard mixture into the inner pan of a double boiler). Stir frequently, until the custard thickens and coats the back of a spoon. Remove the custard from the boiling water.
4. Leave the custard to cool slightly, stirring occasionally. Pour into the glass bowl and leave in a cool place until the custard has set.
5. Pre-heat a moderate grill, shred the almonds, spread out in the grill pan and brown under the grill.
6. Place the cream and milk in a bowl and whisk until thick.
7. Pile 12 dessertspoonsful of cream round the edge of the bowl. Slice the remaining banana, turn in the lemon juice and arrange on the cream with the shredded almonds. Keep cool until ready to serve.

Omit the trifle sponges. Make a jelly with 1 pint/550 ml slimline dry ginger ale set with 1 envelope gelatine. When on the point of setting, stir in 2 eating apples, grated with their skin, bananas and sherry (use dry). Pour into the trifle bowl and leave to set. Sweeten the custard with liquid sweetener. Spread over the jelly when cool. Replace the cream with low-fat thick natural yoghurt.
CHO: 17 g Calories: 160

Use gluten-free Victoria sponge cake (see recipe, page 222) instead of trifle sponges.

Use skimmed milk. Replace the cream with low-fat thick natural yoghurt.

No change necessary.

Mix 2 rounded tablespoons muesli and 2 oz/50 g high-fibre dried fruit such as apricots, prunes or figs with the banana.

No change necessary. Replace the cream with low-fat thick natural yoghurt, if preferred.

English Apple Tart

Serves 8: 300 calories per portion

Filling:

    1½ lb/750 g cooking apples
    3 oz/75 g sugar
    4 cloves

Shortcrust pastry:

    8 oz/225 g plain flour
    ½ level teaspoon salt
    2 oz/50 g cooking fat
    2 oz/50 g polyunsaturated margarine
    cold water to mix
    granulated sugar

1. Pre-heat a moderately hot oven (400°F/200°C/Gas 6).

2. Peel, core and slice the apples, sprinkle with the sugar and mix in the cloves.

3. Sift the flour and salt into a bowl. Add the fats, cut in small pieces, and rub in with the fingertips until the mixture resembles fine breadcrumbs.

4. Add about 2 tablespoons water and mix with a fork to a firm dough.

5. Divide the dough in half and roll out one piece to line an 8-inch/20-cm ovenproof plate. Brush the edge with water.

6. Arrange the apples on the pastry, making sure the cloves are evenly distributed.

7. Roll out the remaining pastry, and lift it over the rolling-pin on to the apples. Seal the edges well, trim, cut with the back of a knife to thicken, then pinch the edges to decorate. Make a small hole in the centre of the pie to enable the steam to escape.

8. Brush the top of the tart with a little cold water and sprinkle with granulated sugar.

9. Bake for 35-45 minutes until the apple is soft and the pastry lightly browned.

For the filling, wash the apples and grate without peeling. Mix with 2 oz/50 g fructose. For the pastry, replace 4 oz/100 g plain flour with wholemeal flour.

CHO: 22.5 g Calories: 270

Use gluten-free shortcrust pastry (see recipe, page 217). Divide the dough in two and roll out each piece between sheets of non-stick baking parchment.

Use polyunsaturated margarine for the pastry.

No change necessary.

As for diabetic but sugar may be used.

Use vegetable fats.

Swiss Apple Tart

Serves 8: 405 calories per portion

Pastry:
>8 oz/225 g plain flour
>5 oz/125 g polyunsaturated margarine
>cold water to mix

Filling:
>2 oz/50 g shelled hazelnuts, toasted
>1 lb/500 g cooking apples
>5 oz/125 g caster sugar
>1 level tablespoon cornflour
>2 fl oz/50 ml semi-skimmed milk
>2 eggs
>5 fl oz/142 ml soured cream

1. Pre-heat a moderate oven (375°F/190°C/Gas 5). Place a 10-inch/25-cm loose-based fluted flan-tin on a baking sheet.

2. Place the flour in a bowl. Add the margarine, cut into small pieces, and rub in with the fingertips until the mixture resembles fine breadcrumbs. Add about 1 tablespoon water and mix with a fork to form a firm dough.

3. Turn out on to a floured board and knead lightly. Roll out the pastry to a circle 1½ inches/4 cm larger all round than the flan-tin. Roll the pastry round the rolling-pin and lift on to the flan-tin. Gently ease the pastry into the flan-tin and into the base and flutes of the tin with the fingers. Roll off the surplus pastry with the rolling-pin, across the top of the flan-tin. Press the pastry into the flutes again with the fingers.

4. Rub off the skins of the hazelnuts, then chop the nuts.

5. Sprinkle the nuts over the pastry base. Peel, core and slice the apples. Place slices of apple, overlapping, in 2 circles over the nuts. Sprinkle with 2 rounded tablespoons of the measured sugar.

6. Place in the centre of the oven and cook for 15 minutes; remove from the oven.

7. Meanwhile, blend the cornflour with milk in a basin. Add the remaining sugar and eggs; whisk together. Whisk in the soured cream; pour the cream mixture over the apples.

8. Return the tart to the centre of the oven and cook for 20 minutes, until the mixture has set. Serve warm or cold.

Use wholemeal flour for the pastry; leave the skins on the apples and omit the sugar (replace with a sprinkle of Diamin if sweetness is necessary). Replace the soured cream with low-fat yoghurt.

CHO: 30 g Calories: 305

Use gluten-free shortcrust pastry (see recipe, page 217). No change necessary to filling but make sure the cornflour is maize flour.

Use skimmed milk. Replace the soured cream with low-fat yoghurt.

No change necessary.

Use fine wholemeal flour for the pastry and unpeeled apples for the filling.

No change necessary.

Treacle Tart

Serves 6: 270 calories per portion

Shortcrust pastry:

    4 oz/100 g plain flour
    ¼ level teaspoon salt
    1 oz/25 g margarine
    1 oz/25 g lard
    cold water to mix

Filling:

    2 oz/50 g fresh white breadcrumbs
    2 teaspoons lemon juice
    3 rounded tablespoons golden syrup

1. Pre-heat a hot oven (425°F/210°C/Gas 7).
2. Place the flour and salt in a bowl. Add the fats, cut into small pieces, and rub in with the fingertips until mixture resembles fine breadcrumbs. Add about 1 tablespoon cold water and mix with a fork to form a firm dough. Turn out on to a floured board and knead lightly.
3. Roll out and line an 8-inch/20-cm pie-plate, allowing the pastry edge to overlap the rim of the plate by ½ inch/2 cm. Turn the overlapping pastry under, to give a double thickness of pastry on the rim. Cut up the edge with the back of a knife and flute the edge.
4. Spread the breadcrumbs over the pastry. Sprinkle the lemon juice over and trickle the syrup on top.
5. Place in the centre of the oven and cook for 20-25 minutes until golden brown. Serve hot or cold.

For the pastry, replace 2 oz/50 g plain flour with wholemeal flour and increase the water by half.

In the filling, use 1 oz/25 g wholemeal breadcrumbs, 1 eating apple, grated with its skin, and only 1 rounded tablespoon golden syrup. CHO: 210 g Calories 170

Use gluten-free shortcrust pastry (see recipe, page 217). Make the crumbs from special gluten-free bread or use cornflakes.

Use polyunsaturated margarine instead of lard.

No change necessary.

As for diabetic but more syrup may be used.

Use vegetable margarine instead of lard.

Mincemeat Apple Oatie

Makes 20 bars: 180 calories each

Shortcrust pastry:
- 6 oz/175 g plain flour
- 3 oz/75 g lard and margarine mixed
- 1 tablespoon cold water

- 1 lb cooking apples
- 4 rounded tablespoons mincemeat

Topping:
- 4 oz/100 g self-raising flour
- 4 oz/100 g (porridge) oats
- 2 oz/50 g dark moist brown sugar
- 4 oz/100 g polyunsaturated margarine
- 2 level tablespoons golden syrup
- icing sugar

1. Pre-heat a moderately hot oven (375°F/190°C/Gas 5).
2. Place the flour in a bowl or food processor and rub in the fats (by hand or machine). Roll out the pastry and line an 11 × 7-inch/27 × 18-cm swiss-roll tin. Trim off the surplus pastry. Prick the base and chill.
3. Peel and coarsely grate the cooking apples into a bowl; mix in the mincemeat. Spread in the pastry case.
4. Place the self-raising flour, oats and sugar in a bowl; add the margarine, cut into small pieces, and rub in with the fingertips or by machine until the mixture resembles breadcrumbs.
5. Measure the golden syrup carefully, levelling off the spoon with a knife and making sure there is none on the underside of the spoon. Add to the oat mixture and mix together with a fork to form a soft dough.
6. Turn out on to a floured board and knead lightly. Roll out to an oblong 11 × 7 inches/27 × 18 cm; place the oat topping over the mincemeat filling; press the edges to seal. Prick all over the top to allow steam to escape.
7. Bake in the centre of the oven for 35-40 minutes until golden brown. Leave to cool in the tin, then cut into 20 bars. Dredge with icing sugar.

Special Diets

Make the pastry with half wholemeal flour and half plain.

For the topping, replace 2 oz/50 g of the flour with 2 oz/50 g wholemeal self-raising flour. Omit the sugar from the topping. Omit the dredging with icing sugar; sprinkle with low-calorie sweetener (powder) instead. CHO: 19 g Calories: 170

Make half the quantity of gluten-free shortcrust pastry (see recipe, page 217). Top the apple and mincemeat with a crumble mixture: Rub 3 oz/75 g margarine into 6 oz/150 g ground rice. Stir in 2 oz/50 g chopped browned hazelnuts, 1 heaped tablespoon toasted sesame seeds and 2 oz/50 g demerara sugar.

Use polyunsaturated margarine. Use mincemeat made with polyunsaturated margarine instead of suet. Use 3 oz/75 g polyunsaturated margarine in the pastry.

No change necessary.

Make the pastry with half wholemeal flour and half plain. In the topping, replace the flour with 2 oz/50 g wholemeal self-raising flour and 2 oz/50 g chopped nuts.

Use vegetable margarine. Use mincemeat made with vegetable suet.

Hazelnut Meringue Gâteau

Serves 8: 290 calories per portion

Cake:

> 4 oz/100 g shelled hazelnuts
> 4 egg whites
> 9 oz/250 g caster sugar
> ½ teaspoon vinegar
> ¼ teaspoon vanilla essence

Filling:

> 15-oz/425-g can apricots in juice
> 5 fl oz/142 ml double cream
> 1 small lemon

1. Pre-heat a moderate oven (375°F/190°C/Gas 5). Brush two 8-inch/20-cm sandwich tins with melted fat. Line the bases and sides with non-stick baking parchment.
2. Place the hazelnuts on a baking sheet; bake in the centre of the oven for 15-20 minutes or until deep golden brown. Rub off the skins; reserve 8 nuts for decoration. Chop the remaining nuts finely.
3. Place the egg whites in a clean, grease-free bowl; whisk until stiff but not dry. Whisk in the sugar gradually. When the mixture is very stiff, whisk in the vinegar and vanilla essence.
4. Fold in the chopped nuts, cutting through the mixture with a metal spoon until all the nuts have been incorporated. Divide the mixture between the prepared tins; level the tops with the back of a metal spoon. Bake in the centre of the oven for 35-40 minutes or until firm to the touch.
5. Leave in the tins to cool completely. Turn out on to a wire rack; remove the paper.
6. Drain the apricots, reserving the juice for the sauce. Press the apricots through a nylon sieve with a wooden spoon (or liquidize) to make a purée.
7. Pour the cream in a basin; whisk until just stiff. Place 2 rounded tablespoons cream in a nylon piping bag fitted with a medium-sized star tube. Carefully fold 3 rounded tablespoons apricot purée into the remaining cream for the filling.
8. Sandwich the cakes together with filling. Pipe 8 whirls of cream on

Reduce the sugar to 7 oz/200 g. Replace half the cream with low-fat natural yoghurt and whisk the yoghurt into the whipped cream.
CHO: 32 g Calories: 230

No change necessary.

Replace the cream with skimmed-milk soft cheese.

Replace 1 oz/25 g of the sugar with vanilla sugar and omit the vanilla essence.

No change necessary.

No change necessary.

Mincemeat Apple Oatie

the top edge of the gâteau; place a reserved hazelnut on each whirl. Place the gâteau on a serving dish.

9. To make the sauce, add the reserved juice to the remaining apricot purée. Scrub the lemon; grate the rind and squeeze the juice. Add to the sauce and stir well; pour into a serving jug.

Note This gâteau improves if kept overnight in the refrigerator before serving.

Mandarin Fudge Puffs

Serves 4: 515 calories per portion

  1 oz/25 g butter or polyunsaturated margarine
  2 oz/50 g plain flour
  1 egg
Orange fudge filling:
  1 small orange
  3 oz/75 g light soft brown sugar
  1 oz/25 g butter
  1 small can evaporated milk
  11-oz/300-g can mandarin oranges in juice
  5 fl oz/142 ml double cream
  1 tablespoon semi-skimmed milk

1. Pre-heat a moderately hot oven (400°F/200°C/Gas 6). Grease a baking sheet. Place ¼ pint/150 ml water and 1 oz/25 g butter or margarine in a small saucepan and bring to the boil. Remove from the heat and stir in the flour; beat well.
2. Return the saucepan to a low heat; cook for a further 2-3 minutes, beating continuously with a wooden spoon until the mixture leaves the side of the saucepan.
3. Remove from the heat and allow to cool slightly. Whisk the egg and beat into the mixture, a little at a time.
4. Place 14 separate spoonsful of the mixture on a baking sheet. Bake just above the centre of the oven for 25-30 minutes until golden brown, well risen and crisp. Remove from the oven; make a slit in the side of each puff and leave to cool on a wire rack.
5. Scrub the orange; grate the rind and squeeze the juice. Place the orange juice, soft brown sugar, butter and evaporated milk in a saucepan. Bring to the boil and cook, stirring continuously, for 4-5 minutes, until the mixture thickens (the filling may have a slightly curdled appearance before thickening). Remove from the heat and leave to cool, stirring occasionally.
6. Drain the mandarin oranges. Fill each puff with a heaped teaspoonful of filling and a mandarin orange. Arrange the puffs and remaining mandarins in a pile in a glass bowl.
7. Place the cream and milk in a basin; lightly whisk until the cream

d
Use wheatmeal (81%) flour in the puffs. For the filling, sweeten with liquid sweetener and make sure you use unsweetened milk. Replace half of the cream with natural yoghurt, whisk the cream then whisk in the yoghurt (omit the milk).
CHO: 22 g Calories: 370

Make gluten-free choux pastry (see recipe, page 218). No change necessary for filling.

Use 4 fl oz/100 ml skimmed milk instead of canned milk and thicken with 1 teaspoon cornflour blended with orange juice. Replace the cream with thick low-fat yoghurt, stirred into the cold sauce.

No change necessary.

Use wheatmeal (81%) flour instead of plain white. Replace the can of oranges with a higher-fibre fruit such as apricots or banana.

Replace the butter with margarine.

coats the back of a spoon. Spoon some cream over the puffs; sprinkle with orange rind. Serve the remaining cream separately.

Note Puffs can be made in advance and stored in an airtight tin. Crisp in a moderate oven and leave to cool before filling. Orange fudge filling can be made in advance and stored in a jar in a refrigerator for up to 1 week.

Chocolate Ring Pavlova

Serves 8: 240 calories per portion

- 3 egg whites
- 1 level teaspoon cornflour
- 1 teaspoon vinegar
- 1 teaspoon vanilla essence
- 7 oz/200 g caster sugar
- ¼ pint/142 ml whipping cream
- 2 tablespoons Tia Maria or dark rum (optional)
- 2 small bars chocolate flake, crushed

1. Pre-heat a cool oven (300°C/150°C/Gas 2). Wet a baking sheet and cover with greaseproof or non-stick baking parchment.
2. Place the egg whites in a clean, grease-free bowl; whisk until stiff but not dry.
3. Mix the cornflour, vinegar and vanilla essence together and whisk into the egg whites, with the sugar, a little at a time, until very stiff.
4. Spread on the greaseproof paper to an even circle, about 1 inch/2.5 cm thick.
5. Place in the oven and immediately turn the heat down to 275°F/140°C/Gas 1. Cook for 1 hour. Turn the oven off; leave to cool in the oven without opening the door.
6. Carefully peel the paper off the pavlova and place on a serving dish. Whisk the cream until stiff, then whisk in the liqueur, if using. Spread the cream in the centre and sprinkle a border of chocolate flake round the edge of the cream.
Note The pavlova will keep for about a week in a closed tin. Decorate just before serving.

Not very suitable. Serve tiny portions (half normal size) and use 2 oz/50 g diabetic chocolate, grated, instead of flakes. Omit the liqueur and decorate with apricots canned in natural juice. Use half the amount of cream and replace with yoghurt.
CHO: 14 g Calories: 82

Replace the cornflour with rice flour if it is not gluten-free. Use cider or wine vinegar.

Replace the cream with thick low-fat hazelnut yoghurt and decorate with apricots.

No change necessary.

Fold toasted chopped hazelnuts into the meringue just before shaping. Decorate with apricots.

No change necessary.

Profiteroles

Serves 8: 290 calories per portion

Choux pastry:
    2 oz/50 g polyunsaturated margarine
    2½ oz/75 g plain flour
    2 eggs
Chocolate sauce:
    2 oz/50 g plain dessert chocolate
    4 level tablespoons golden syrup
    1 oz/25 g butter

    10 fl oz/284 ml double cream
    2 tablespoons semi-skimmed milk

1. Pre-heat a moderately hot oven (400°F/200°C/Gas 6). Brush a baking sheet with melted fat or oil.
2. Place ¼ pint/125 ml water and margarine in a medium-sized saucepan; bring to the boil. Remove the pan from the heat; add the flour all at once and beat until the mixture leaves the sides of the saucepan. If the mixture does not leave the side of the saucepan, return it to a low heat and cook, beating continuously with a wooden spoon, until it does so. Leave to cool slightly.
3. Beat the eggs; add to the mixture by stages. Beat well each time.
4. Place the mixture in a nylon piping bag fitted with a ½-inch/1-cm plain tube. Pipe about 50 small balls of mixture on to a baking sheet.
5. Bake in the centre of the oven for 30-35 minutes, until the balls are crisp and golden brown. Remove from the oven, slit each ball to allow the steam to escape; leave to cool on a wire rack.
6. Break up the chocolate, place in a small, dry basin over a saucepan of hot, but not boiling, water. Measure the golden syrup carefully, levelling off the spoon with a knife and making sure there is none on the underside of the spoon; add to the chocolate, with the butter. Stir occasionally, until the chocolate and butter have melted; remove the saucepan from the heat.
7. Place the cream and milk in a basin; whisk until the cream just holds its shape. Place the cream in a piping bag, fitted with a ½-inch/1-cm plain tube; pipe some cream into each choux ball.
8. Pile the profiteroles into a glass serving dish; pour some of the warm chocolate sauce over and serve the remainder in a jug.

Use diabetic chocolate and diabetic syrup. Replace the cream with skimmed-milk soft cheese or fromage frais.
CHO: 18 g Calories: 200

Use gluten-free choux pastry (see recipe, page 218).

Replace the cream with skimmed-milk soft cheese or fromage frais.

No change necessary.

Sprinkle generously with chopped hazelnuts.

No change necessary.

Orange and Lemon Cheesecake Bar

Serves 6: 360 calories per portion

1 large packet (8) trifle sponge cakes
11-oz/312-g can mandarin oranges
1 small lemon
1 packet lemon jelly
8 oz/250 g quark or skimmed-milk soft cheese
4 fl oz/125 ml double cream

1. Split the sponge cakes in halves horizontally. Line the base and sides of a 2½-pint/1¼-litre loaf-tin, 7½ × 3½ inches/19 × 9 cm base measurement, with the sponge halves, cut sides inwards, trimming them to fit the sides of the tin.
2. Drain the mandarin oranges in a sieve over a measuring jug; make up the syrup to ¼ pint/125 ml with water.
3. Scrub the lemon, grate the rind and squeeze the juice, then place together in a basin. Place the jelly and measured syrup in a small saucepan. Heat gently until the jelly has melted; do not boil. Pour into the basin with the lemon rind and juice.
4. Gradually whisk the soft cheese into the jelly with two-thirds of the cream. Whisk for about half a minute; chill until almost set. Pour into the sponge-lined tin; chill until completely set.
5. Trim the sponge cakes level with the filling. Invert the cheesecake on to an oblong serving dish. Place a line of mandarin oranges down each side at the top and bottom of the cheesecake.
6. Whisk the remaining cream until just stiff and pile teaspoonsful along the top of the cheesecake between the rows of mandarin oranges.

Use diabetic jelly. Omit the sponge cakes and pour the cheesecake mixture straight into a greased mould that has the crumbs of 1 digestive biscuit pressed round the sides. Replace 2 fl oz/50 ml double cream with orange yoghurt.
CHO: 20 g Calories 170

Line the tin with gluten-free cake (see recipe, page 222).

Omit the cream; replace with low-fat thick yoghurt.

Replace the jelly with gelatine, dissolve 1 envelope (½ oz/15 g) in the fruit juice and add 2 oz/50 g sugar.

Decorate with chopped walnuts.

No change necessary.

Raspberry Summer Cloud

Serves 6: 168 calories per portion

2 eggs
5 oz/150 g caster sugar
1 oz/25 g cornflour
¾ pint/425 ml semi-skimmed milk
4 oz/100 g raspberries

Decoration:
a few extra whole raspberries

1. Pre-heat a cool oven (325°F/170°C/Gas 3).
2. Separate the eggs; place the whites in a clean, grease-free bowl and put the yolks in a basin. Add 1 rounded tablespoon of the measured sugar to the egg yolks and mix well with a wooden spoon.
3. Place the cornflour in a saucepan and gradually blend in the milk. Bring to the boil, stirring, and cook for 1 minute. Add to the egg yolk mixture, stirring. Pour into a round, shallow, 1-pint/½-litre oven-proof dish and bake, just below the centre of the oven, for 45 minutes. Remove from the oven and leave to cool for about 20 minutes.
4. Press the raspberries through a sieve and add to the egg whites with the remaining sugar. Bring a large saucepan of water to the boil; remove from the heat. Place the bowl over the saucepan and whisk the mixture with a rotary whisk or electric mixer until the mixture stands in soft peaks (about 10 minutes). Remove the bowl from the saucepan and continue whisking until the mixture stands in stiff peaks.
5. Pile the raspberry mixture on to the custard. Decorate with a few whole raspberries and serve warm or, if preferred, leave to cool, then chill in the refrigerator for 1-2 hours.
Note Use other fruits when in season or sieved apricots from a can or stewed dried apricots.

Special Diets

Increase the eggs to 3 and omit the cornflour. Omit the caster sugar and sweeten the custard with 1 level teaspoon fructose and a few drops of liquid sweetener. Whisk the fruit purée with 1 oz/25 g fructose. Serve with 1 oz/25 g raspberries per portion.
CHO: 5 g Calories: 90

Make sure the cornflour is gluten-free. If in doubt, use maize flour or an extra egg and omit the cornflour.

No change necessary.

No change necessary.

Serve with a generous quantity of fresh raspberries or use apricots.

No change necessary.

Cider Fruit Tansy

Serves 4: 240 calories per serving

>1 lb/500 g mixed red fruits (raspberries, loganberries,
>   redcurrants, strawberries)
>½ pint/275 ml sweet cider
>1 rounded tablespoon cornflour
>caster sugar
>¼ pint/142 ml double cream
>2 tablespoons milk

1. Reserving a few raspberries or loganberries for decoration, place the fruit in a pan with the cider.
2. Bring gently to the boil, cover and simmer for 5 minutes. Press the fruit through a nylon sieve or place in a liquidizer goblet and blend until the mixture is smooth, then strain. Rinse the saucepan, then add the cornflour and blend to a smooth paste with 2 tablespoons water. Add the fruit and a rounded tablespoon sugar. Bring to the boil, stirring. Cook for 1 minute. Taste and add more sugar if necessary.
3. Cool slightly, then pour into 4 individual serving dishes and sprinkle each with sugar. Chill for at least 3 hours.
4. Whisk the cream and milk until it stands in soft peaks. Divide between the dishes and decorate each with the reserved fruit.

Use dry cider and sweeten to taste after cooling with low-calorie liquid sweetener. Use low-calorie powdered sweetener to sprinkle on the surface. Omit the cream and use half low-fat 'cream' with an equal amount of yoghurt whisked in.
CHO: 20 g Calories: 160

Replace the cornflour with potato flour.

Replace the cream with thick low-fat natural yoghurt.

No change necessary.

No change necessary.

If dairy products are not tolerated, top the dessert with whisked dessert topping mix.

Pineapple Cheese Dessert

Serves 4: 200 calories per portion

    1 small ripe pineapple
    8 oz/225 g strawberries
    8 oz/225 g cottage cheese
    icing sugar

1. Wash the pineapple and strawberries; dry on kitchen paper. Hull the strawberries and cut into halves.
2. Cut the pineapple into quarters lengthwise, scoop out the flesh and chop.
3. Place the cottage cheese in the bowl; stir in the pineapple. Sweeten with icing sugar to taste, about 2 oz/50 g.
4. Pile into the pineapple 'shells'. Decorate each with strawberry halves. Place on a serving dish and keep cool until ready to serve.

Special Diets

d
Omit the icing sugar.
CHO: 22 g Calories: 150

Check that the cottage cheese does not contain starch.

No change necessary.

No change necessary.

No change necessary.

No change necessary.

Strawberry Rice Flan

Serves 8: 325 calories per portion

Base:

      6 oz/175 g digestive biscuits
      1 level tablespoon golden syrup
      2 level teaspoons cocoa
      3 oz/75 g polyunsaturated margarine

Filling:

      ½ lemon
      1 lb/500 g strawberries
      1 15-oz/425-g can rice milk pudding
      1 envelope dessert topping mix
      ½ pint/375 ml semi-skimmed milk
      2 oz/50 g caster sugar
      pink food colouring
      ½ oz/50 g (1 envelope) gelatine

1. Butter an 8-inch/20-cm loose-bottomed cake-tin.
2. Place the biscuits in a bag and crush finely with a rolling-pin.
3. Measure the syrup carefully; place in a saucepan and add the cocoa and margarine; heat gently until the margarine has melted. Stir in the crushed biscuits.
4. Press the mixture over the base of the prepared tin. Chill until firm.
5. Pare the rind from the lemon with a sharp knife. Cut into thin strips and reserve; squeeze the juice. Halve 12 strawberries and reserve for decoration. Chop the remainder and place in a bowl with the rice and lemon juice. Whisk the dessert topping mix into the milk until thickened and smooth. Add to the rice mixture with sugar and a few drops of pink food colouring. Stir well.
6. Measure 2 tablespoons cold water into a small basin, add the gelatine and stir. Place the basin in a pan of water over a moderate heat; stir until the gelatine has dissolved. Add to the rice mixture. Stir well.
7. Pour the mixture into the tin and chill until set. Loosen the edges with a palette knife. Place the tin on top of a 1-lb can and gently push the cake-tin down from the dessert. Ease the dessert on to a plate.
8. Decorate with halved strawberries round the edge and lemon peel in the centre.

Halve the base ingredients and make a thinner layer. Replace the dessert topping mix and milk with 2 cartons (300 ml) thick low-fat yoghurt. Replace the sugar with some sugar-free sprinkle product.
CHO: 24 g Calories: 190

Use crumbled wholemeal crunchie biscuits (see recipe, page 204) and omit the cocoa. Replace the dessert topping mix and milk with ½ pint/ 275 ml whipping cream or thick, creamy yoghurt.

Replace the dessert topping mix and milk with 2 cartons (300 ml) thick low-fat yoghurt.

Replace the dessert topping mix and milk with 2 cartons (300 ml) thick, creamy yoghurt (or use a carton of Greek yoghurt). Omit the pink colouring.

Replace 2 oz/50 g biscuits with crushed All-bran.

If gelatine is not tolerated, replace with unflavoured agar-agar.

Serves 6: 195 calories per portion

Shortcrust pastry:
    4 oz/100 g plain flour
    ¼ level teaspoon salt
    1 oz/25 g polyunsaturated margarine
    1 oz/25 g lard or cooking fat
    cold water

Filling:
    16-oz/449-g can sliced peaches in juice
    1 level tablespoon cornflour
    ¼ pint/125 ml peach juice (from the can)
    2 tablespoons lemon juice
    ½ level teaspoon cinnamon
    flaked almonds

1. Pre-heat a hot oven (425°F/220°C/Gas 7). Place the flour and salt in a bowl and add the fats. Cut the fats into small pieces and rub in with the fingertips or with a mixer until the mixture resembles fine breadcrumbs.
2. Add water (about a teaspoon to each 1 oz/25 g flour) and mix with a fork. Press together to form a firm dough.
3. Roll the pastry out into a 10-inch/25-cm circle. Roll the pastry round the rolling-pin and lift on to an 8-inch/20-cm flan ring. Place on a baking sheet.
4. Gently ease the pastry into the flan ring and press into the flutes of the ring. Roll off the surplus pastry with a rolling-pin across the top of flan ring. Press the pastry into the flutes again with the finger. Prick all over with a fork.
5. To bake blind, line the flan case with a circle of greaseproof paper and fill with baking beans or rice. Place in the centre of the oven. Bake for 15 minutes to set the pastry, then remove from the oven and lift out the paper and beans. Bake for a further 5 minutes, then cool on a wire rack. When cold, arrange the drained peaches in the flan case. Place the cornflour in a small saucepan and blend in ¼ pint/ 125 ml juice from the can, the lemon juice and cinnamon. Bring to the boil, stirring, and boil for 3 minutes. Pour over the fruit and leave to cool. Sprinkle with the flaked almonds.

Replace half of the flour with wholemeal flour and add the cinnamon. Omit the cornflour and thicken the juice with 1 teaspoon gelatine. Spoon over the fruit when almost set. CHO: 20 g Calories: 175

Use gluten-free shortcrust pastry (see recipe, page 217), adding cinnamon; make sure that the cornflour is gluten/wheat-free.

Use polyunsaturated margarine instead of lard or cooking fat.

No change necessary.

Replace half of the flour with wholemeal flour and the peaches with apricots.

Use polyunsaturated margarine and omit the lard from the pastry.

Lemon Meringue Pie

Special Diets

Serves 6: 260 calories per portion

Shortcrust pastry:

    4 oz/100 g plain flour
    ¼ level teaspoon salt
    1 oz/25 g cooking fat
    1 oz/25 g polyunsaturated margarine
    cold water to mix

Filling:

    2 oz/50 g cornflour
    4 oz/100 g caster sugar
    ½ pint/250 ml cold water
    2 medium lemons
    2 eggs

1. Pre-heat a moderately hot oven (425°F/220°C/Gas 7).

2. Sift the flour and salt into a basin.

3. Add the fats, cut into small pieces, and rub in with the fingertips until the mixture resembles fine breadcrumbs.

4. Mix to a firm dough with water.

5. Roll out the pastry to line a 7-inch/18-cm fluted flan ring; prick well. Place a circle of greaseproof paper in the flan and fill with baking beans. Bake for 15 minutes. Remove the beans and greaseproof paper and return to the oven for a further 5 minutes. Leave to cool.

6. Turn the oven temperature to very cool (200°F, 100°C/Gas ¼).

7. Place the cornflour, 2 oz/50 g sugar and the water in a small pan and bring slowly to the boil, stirring. Cook until the cornflour has cleared and thickened.

8. Add the grated rind of 1 lemon and the juice of both lemons to the saucepan.

9. Separate the eggs and beat the yolks into the lemon mixture; pour into the flan case.

10. Whisk the egg whites until stiff, then whisk in the remaining 2 oz/50 g sugar. Pile the meringue on top of the lemon mixture and bake for 20 minutes until golden brown.

Replace 2 oz/50 g plain flour with wholemeal flour. Replace the cornflour, caster sugar and water with 1 lb/500 g eating apples, grated with their skins. Add the yolks, lemon rind and juice and a few drops low-calorie liquid sweetener. Bake in the raw pastry flan case for 20 minutes, then continue from step 10, replacing the sugar with 1 oz/15 g fructose and browning in a very cool oven.
CHO: 17 g Calories: 145

Use gluten-free shortcrust pastry (see recipe, page 217). Make sure that the cornflour is gluten-free.

Use 2 oz/50 g polyunsaturated margarine for the pastry.

No change necessary.

Replace 2 oz/50 g plain flour with wholemeal flour. Add 1 large cooking apple, grated with its skin, to the cornflour mixture and reduce the water by 4 tablespoons.

Use vegetable fats for the pastry.

Jamaican Delight

Serves 6: 494 calories per portion

16-oz/454-g can pineapple pieces
1 miniature bottle Tia Maria
¼ pint/125 ml double cream
1 rounded teaspoon caster sugar
1 rounded teaspoon instant coffee
1 family-size brick coffee ice cream
6 walnuts

1. Place the pineapple with a little syrup from the can in six glasses. Add 2 teaspoons Tia Maria to the pineapple in each glass.
2. Place the cream in a basin; add the sugar and instant coffee. Stir gently until dissolved; whisk until thick.
3. Just before serving, spoon or scoop the ice cream into each glass; quickly top each with coffee-flavoured cream and decorate each with a walnut. Serve immediately.

Use pineapple pieces in natural juice. Replace the Tia Maria with a sprinkling of grated orange rind in each glass. Replace half the cream with yoghurt, whisked in when the cream is thick. Omit the sugar from the cream. Use home-made ice cream (see recipe, page 146).
CHO: 31 g Calories: 236

No change necessary.

Replace the cream with skimmed-milk soft cheese. Use home-made ice cream (see recipe, page 146).

Use home-made ice cream.

Increase the quantity of walnuts.

No change necessary.

Christmas Pudding

Special Diets

Serves 14: 465 calories per portion

8 oz/225 g fresh white breadcrumbs
2 oz/50 g plain flour
8 oz/225 g shredded suet
8 oz/225 g brown sugar
8 oz/225 g large raisins, stoned
6 oz/175 g sultanas
6 oz/175 g currants
2 oz/50 g mixed peel
2 oz/50 g shelled almonds
1 rounded teaspoon mixed spice
1 lemon
1 apple or carrot
4 eggs
3 tablespoons sherry, rum or brandy

1. Prepare a saucepan or steamer for cooking. Grease a 2-pint/1-litre basin and a ½-pint/275-ml basin (or a 1½-pint/825-ml basin and a 1-pint/550-ml basin). Fit a circle of greaseproof paper in the bottom of each basin; grease the paper. Grease a double thickness of greaseproof paper for covering the basins.

2. Place the breadcrumbs in a large bowl; add the flour, suet, sugar and dried fruit (if bought unwashed, wash the previous day and spread out to dry on baking sheets). Chop the mixed peel and add to the bowl.

3. Place the almonds in a small saucepan, cover with water and bring to the boil; strain off the water and slip off the skins. Shred the almonds finely with a knife and add, with the mixed spice, to the bowl. Scrub the lemon and grate the rind into the bowl; squeeze the juice and add. Peel and grate the apple or carrot and add. Beat the eggs and add to the bowl, together with the sherry, rum or brandy. Mix all the ingredients together thoroughly.

4. Fill the basins with the mixture and level the tops with the back of a spoon. Make a pleat in the greaseproof paper, to allow the puddings to rise. Cover the puddings and tie down securely with string, making a loop over the top of each basin to form a handle.

Replace the white breadcrumbs with wholemeal ones and the white flour with wholemeal. Replace the suet with melted polyunsaturated margarine. Replace the brown sugar with 4 oz/100 g fructose. Reduce the sultanas and currants to 6 oz/175 g each. Add both an apple and a carrot, washed and grated but not peeled. CHO: 42 g Calories: 360

Use breadcrumbs from gluten-free bread and 2 oz/50 g Trufree no.4 gluten-free flour instead of plain flour. Use both an apple and a carrot, washed and grated but not peeled. Replace the suet with melted margarine.

Replace the suet with melted polyunsaturated margarine.

Replace the suet with melted margarine.

Replace the white breadcrumbs and flour with wholemeal. Leave the skin on the apple and carrot and use both. Replace 4 oz/100 g sultanas and 4 oz/100 g currants with dried apricots.

Use vegetable suet or melted margarine.

Steam each pudding for 6 hours, keeping the pan of water filled with boiling water. (Alternatively, cook in a pressure cooker: place 2 pints water in the cooker and bring to the boil; place the pudding on a rack and close the lid; steam for 1 hour; place the pressure weights on the cooker and bring up to 15 lb pressure; cook for 1 hour.) Replace the paper covers with clean sheets of greaseproof paper. Tie down securely as before.

5. On Christmas Day, steam the pudding for a further 3-4 hours (or ½ hour in a pressure cooker, followed by ½ hour at 15 lb pressure; or 10 minutes in a microwave oven on medium setting).

6. Invert the pudding on to a warmed serving dish, remove the circle of greaseproof paper and decorate the top of the pudding with a sprig of holly. Serve with brandy or rum butter (see recipe) or custard (see recipe).

Note Silver charms can be inserted in the pudding just before serving. Scrub and boil them before use.

Brandy (or Rum) Butter

Serves 4: 100 calories per portion

> 4 oz/100 g butter
> 4 oz/100 g caster sugar (or brown sugar with rum)
> 4 tablespoons brandy or rum (or to taste)

1. Cream the butter and sugar until soft and fluffy.
2. Beat in the brandy, a little at a time.
3. Place the mixture in a piping bag fitted with a large star tube; pipe into small dishes. Chill.

Replace the butter with 2 oz/50 g polyunsaturated margarine and add 2 oz/50 g skimmed-milk soft cheese. Replace the 4 oz/100 g caster sugar with 1 oz/25 g soft brown sugar and 1 oz/25 g fructose.
CHO: 5 g Calories: 85

No change necessary.

As for diabetic.

No change necessary.

Add 2 oz/50 g ground walnuts or almonds.

Replace the butter with vegetable margarine.

Mince Pies

Special Diets

Makes 12: 215 calories each

> 8 oz/225 g plain flour
> ½ level teaspoon salt
> 2 oz/50 g polyunsaturated margarine
> 2 oz/50 g lard
> 2 level teaspoons caster sugar
> cold water to mix

Filling:

> 12 oz/300 g mincemeat
> icing sugar

1. Pre-heat a moderately hot oven (400°F/200°C/Gas 6).
2. Place the flour and salt in a bowl. Add the fats, cut into small pieces, and rub in with the fingertips until the mixture resembles fine breadcrumbs. Dissolve the caster sugar in 1 tablespoon cold water and add, then add about 1 scant tablespoon more of water and mix with a fork to form a firm dough.
3. Turn out on to a floured board and knead lightly. Roll out the pastry to ⅛-inch/6-mm thickness. Cut out 12 rounds, using a 3¼-inch/8-cm fluted cutter; press one of each into 12 deep tartlet tins. Knead the trimmings together, re-roll and cut out 12 more rounds, using a 2¼-inch/6-cm fluted cutter, for lids. Place heaped teaspoonsful of mincemeat in each pastry case. Dampen the edges of the lids, press into position and seal well. Snip the tops of the pies twice with scissors.
4. Place in the centre of the oven and bake for 20-25 minutes, until pale golden brown. Remove from the tins and leave to cool on a wire rack. Dredge the tops of the pies with icing sugar before serving. Re-heat before serving if desired.

d
Use diabetic mincemeat or replace half the mincemeat with 6 oz/175 g grated eating apple. Replace half the flour with wholemeal and omit the sugar and icing sugar.
CHO: 24 g Calories: 180

Use home-made mincemeat and omit the suet (use melted margarine instead). Replace the pastry with gluten-free shortcrust (see recipe, page 217).

Use home-made mincemeat and replace the suet with polyunsaturated margarine. Replace the lard with polyunsaturated margarine.

Use home-made mincemeat.

Replace half the flour with wholemeal.

Use mincemeat made with vegetable suet or use home-made mincemeat and replace the suet with melted vegetable fat.

Serves 6: 350 calories per portion

      11-oz/312-g can mandarin oranges
      1 orange jelly
      6 level tablespoons golden syrup
      3 oz/75 g butter
      2 level tablespoons cocoa
      3 oz/75 g cornflakes
      1 small can evaporated milk

1. Drain the mandarin oranges, reserving the syrup in a measuring jug. Reserve 18 segments for decoration: chop the remainder and divide between six individual glasses. Make up the syrup to ½ pint/250 ml with water.
2. Place the jelly cubes and ¼ pint/125 ml of the diluted syrup in a small saucepan. Heat gently, stirring, until dissolved; do not boil. Pour into a measuring jug with the remaining diluted syrup. Cool quickly by placing the jug in a bowl of cold water and ice cubes. Leave until the jelly is almost set, stirring occasionally.
3. Measure the golden syrup carefully, levelling off the spoon with a knife and making sure that there is none on the underside of the spoon. Place in a medium-sized saucepan with the butter and cocoa Melt over a low heat, stirring; remove from the heat. Lightly crush the cornflakes; add to the pan and stir with a wooden spoon until well coated. Leave to cool.
4. Place the evaporated milk in a bowl and whisk until thick and creamy. Gradually whisk in the partially set jelly. Divide the mixture between six glasses; leave in a cool place until set.
5. Divide the cornflake mixture between the glasses. Decorate the top of each glass with three orange segments. Leave in the refrigerator until ready to serve.

Use oranges in natural juice. Replace the jelly cubes with 1 packet gelatine softened in some of the diluted juice, then heat until dissolved and added to the rest. Replace the golden syrup and cocoa with 2 oz/50 g diabetic chocolate. Replace the butter with 1 oz/25 g polyunsaturated margarine.
CHO: 31 g Calories: 230

Replace the cornflakes with rice krispies and cocoa with 3 oz/75 g dessert chocolate (reduce the syrup to 2 tablespoons).

Replace the butter with polyunsaturated margarine. Replace the evaporated milk with 8 oz/225 g skimmed-milk soft cheese.

Use gelatine instead of orange jelly (see diabetic section).

Use bran flakes instead of cornflakes.

Use vegetable margarine.

Cakes and Bakes

These recipes show how to adapt traditional favourites to special diets. Note that gluten-free flour is essential for the gluten/wheat-free modifications, and that diabetics should try to confine their consumption of sweet biscuits and cakes to special occasions.

Hot Cross Buns

Special Diets

Makes 16: 155 calories each bun

Yeast batter:
> 5 oz/150 g plain flour
> 1 level teaspoon caster sugar
> 2 level teaspoons dried yeast
> 8 fl oz/200 ml hand-hot semi-skimmed milk (110°F/44°C)

Dough:
> 11 oz/300 g plain flour
> 1 level teaspoon mixed spice
> 2 oz/50 g polyunsaturated margarine
> 1 egg
> 1 level teaspoon salt
> 1 oz/25 g caster sugar
> 2 oz/50 g currants
> 1 oz/25 g cut mixed peel

Glaze:
> 1 level tablespoon caster sugar
> 2 tablespoons milk

1. Place the batter ingredients in a large bowl. Beat with a wooden spoon until smooth; leave in a warm place until frothy (about 20 minutes).

2. Place 11 oz/300 g plain flour and the mixed spice in a bowl. Add the margarine, cut into small pieces, and rub in with the fingertips until the mixture resembles fine breadcrumbs. Beat the egg and salt together in a small basin.

3. Add the rubbed-in mixture, egg, 1 oz/25 g caster sugar, currants and peel to the batter. Mix well with a wooden spoon or with the hands. Turn out on to a lightly floured board. Knead and stretch the dough by folding towards you, then pushing away with the palm of the hand. Give the dough a quarter turn and repeat, developing a rocking motion. Knead for about 10 minutes, until the dough feels firm and elastic and no longer sticky.

4. Place the dough in a lightly floured bowl or saucepan. Cover with greased polythene, foil or a lid. Leave to rise for about 1 hour, or until the dough has doubled in size and will spring back when pressed

Use wheatmeal (81% extraction) flour. Use only 1 oz/25 g polyunsaturated margarine. Spread the cooked buns with low-fat margarine.
CHO: 25 g Calories: 125

Use the sweet bread dough (see recipe, page 219), adding 1 level teaspoon each of cinnamon and mixed spice (check the label to ensure it is wheat-free), 2 oz/50 g currants and 1 oz/25 g mixed peel. Glaze and shape as for above recipe.

No change necessary.

No change necessary.

Use wheatmeal (81% extraction) flour.

No change necessary.

with a floured finger. Grease two baking sheets.

5. Turn out the dough on to a lightly floured board; cut into 16 pieces. Shape each piece into a round with the fingertips. Place on the baking sheets and flatten slightly. Brush with glaze (made by dissolving 1 level tablespoon caster sugar in 2 tablespoons warmed milk). Mark crosses with a sharp knife. Cover loosely with greased polythene and leave in a warm place for 30 minutes, or until the buns have doubled in size.

6. Meanwhile, pre-heat a hot oven (425°F/220°C/Gas 7). Remove the polythene and bake the buns in the centre of the oven for 10-12 minutes. Place on a wire rack and brush with glaze.

7. Before serving, warm the buns in a cool oven (300°F/150°C/Gas 2) for 15 minutes, or in a grill pan under a low heat, turning once.

Note Alternatively, use ½ oz/12 g fresh yeast in place of 2 teaspoons dried yeast; use warm milk in place of hand-hot.

Farmhouse Fruit Cake

48 servings: 127 calories each

> 1 lb/450 g self-raising wheatmeal (81% extraction) flour
> 1½ level teaspoons mixed spice
> 8 oz/225 g polyunsaturated margarine
> 8 oz/225 g moist brown sugar
> 1 lb/450 g mixed dried fruit
> 3 eggs
> 4 tablespoons semi-skimmed milk
> 2 rounded tablespoons thick-cut marmalade
> 4 level tablespoons golden syrup
> 1 rounded tablespoon granulated sugar

1. Pre-heat a cool oven (325°F/160°C/Gas 3). Brush a 12 × 10 inch/ 30½ × 26 cm roasting tin with melted fat and line the base and sides with greaseproof paper; grease the paper.
2. Place the flour and spice in a bowl. Rub in the margarine. Add the brown sugar and fruit.
3. Place the eggs, milk and marmalade in a basin. Measure the golden syrup into a basin and beat well. Stir into the dry mixture; mix well.
4. Turn out into a tin and level the top with the back of a spoon; sprinkle with granulated sugar and bake in the centre of the oven for 1 hour. Reduce the heat to cool (300°F/150°C/Gas 2) and continue cooking for a further 20-30 minutes. Test by pressing with the fingers. If cooked, the cake should spring back, have stopped bubbling and have begun to shrink from the sides of the tin.
5. Leave to cool in the tin for 30 minutes; turn out, remove the paper and leave to cool completely on a wire rack.
6. Just before serving, cut across into 1-inch/2½-cm bars; cut each bar into 4 pieces.

Special Diets

Increase the milk to 6 tablespoons. Replace the brown sugar with 5 oz/ 125 g fructose and use reduced-sugar marmalade. Omit the syrup and the granulated sugar. Cut the cake into 42 bars.
CHO: 15 g Calories: 125 per bar

Follow the gluten-free Victoria sponge recipe (page 222), adding 4 oz/100 g mixed chopped nuts and sesame seeds instead of the maize flour or cornflour. Bake in a 11 × 7 inch/28 × 18 cm shallow tin.

No change necessary.

Use home-made marmalade or 'extra fruit' grade.

No change necessary.

Use vegetable margarine.

Victoria Sandwich Cake

Special Diets

Serves 8: 285 calories per slice

4 oz/100 g butter or polyunsaturated margarine
4 oz/100 g caster sugar
2 eggs
4 oz/100 g self-raising flour
  (or 4 oz/100 g plain flour
  and 1 level teaspoon baking powder)
6 oz/175 g jam

1. Pre-heat a moderate oven (375°F/180°C/Gas 5). Cut two circles of greaseproof paper the exact size of two 7-inch/18-cm tins. Grease the tins, place the paper in the tins and grease the paper.
2. Cream the butter and sugar together until light and fluffy. Beat the eggs together and add gradually, beating after each addition.
3. Sift the flour and baking powder (if using) together and fold into the creamed mixture to make a soft dropping consistency.
4. Spread the mixture evenly in the tins and smooth with a spoon. Bake for 20-25 minutes.
5. Test by pressing with the fingers. The cake should spring back and should have shrunk from the sides of the tin. Turn out on to a folded tea-towel, remove the paper carefully and place on a wire rack. When cool, sandwich with jam and dredge the top with icing or caster sugar.
Note Alternatively, place all the ingredients in a bowl or food processor and beat or whisk together until smooth and glossy (about 1 minute).

The basic recipe can be adapted to make the following cakes:
Chocolate Replace 1 oz/25 g flour with 1 oz/25 g cocoa.
Coffee Dissolve 1 heaped teaspoon instant coffee in the beaten eggs before adding.
Cherry Add 2 oz/50 g halved glacé cherries before adding the flour.
Coconut Add 2 oz/50 g desiccated coconut and 1 tablespoon milk with the flour.
Orange or lemon Add the grated rind of 1 orange or lemon to the creamed mixture. Use the juice in the cake icing.
Queen cakes Add 2 oz/50 g dried fruit and a few drops vanilla essence. Bake in small tins or paper cake cases for 15-20 minutes.

Replace 2 oz/50 g flour with 2 oz/50 g self-raising wholemeal flour. Use 3 oz/75 g each of polyunsaturated margarine and fructose (instead of sugar). Cut smaller slices (to serve 10) and sandwich with sugar-reduced jam.
CHO: 23 g Calories: 170

Replace the self-raising flour with 4 oz/100 g Trufree or Jubilee no.7 self-raising flour and 1 oz/25 g maize flour. When adding the flavouring, check that the cocoa, instant coffee and coconut are wheat-free.

Use polyunsaturated margarine.

Use 'extra' quality jam.

Replace 2 oz/50 g flour with 2 oz/50 g self-raising wholemeal flour.

Use polyunsaturated margarine.

Moist Gingerbread

Special Diets

Serves 24: 115 calories per portion

    1 egg
    8 oz/225 g plain flour
    1 level teaspoon mixed spice
    2 level teaspoons ground ginger
    3 oz/75 g sultanas
    2 oz/50 g dark soft brown sugar
    ¼ pint/125 ml semi-skimmed milk
    4 oz/100 g lard
    4 oz/100 g black treacle
    4 oz/100 g golden syrup
    1 level teaspoon bicarbonate of soda

1. Pre-heat a moderate oven (350°F/180°C/Gas 4). Line a shallow 7 × 10 inch/18 × 25 cm tin with greaseproof paper and grease lightly. Beat the egg. Sift the flour and spices into a bowl; add the sultanas and sugar.
2. Warm the milk in a small saucepan and place in a jug. Place the lard, treacle and syrup in the same pan and heat until the lard has melted.
3. Add the soda to the milk and stir until dissolved. Pour the lard and syrup mixture into the centre of the dry ingredients, followed by the milk, soda and egg. Beat until smooth.
4. Pour into the prepared tin. Place just below the centre of the oven and bake for 40-45 minutes.
5. Press the cake in the centre with the fingertips. If cooked, it should spring back, have shrunk from sides and stopped bubbling. Leave in the tin until almost cold, then remove the paper and finish cooling on a wire rack. Store in an airtight tin and, when required, cut into 24 squares.

Not recommended. Replace the flour with wholemeal flour, the sugar with 1 oz/50 g fructose. Omit the sultanas. Use skimmed milk. Replace the lard with low-fat spread.
CHO: 15 g Calories: 84

Use 3½ oz/90 g Trufree or Jubilee no.7 self-raising flour, 1 level teaspoon ground ginger, 2½ oz/70 g brown sugar, 1 tablespoon black treacle, 1 egg and 2½ tablespoons each of vegetable oil and milk. Bake in a base-lined 7-inch/18-cm tin for 45-50 minutes.

Replace the lard with polyunsaturated margarine.

No change necessary.

Replace the flour with wholemeal flour.

Replace the lard with polyunsaturated margarine.

Wholemeal Apple Gingerbread

Makes 16 squares: 170 calories each

- 8 oz/225 g cooking apples
- milk
- 8 oz/225 g golden syrup and black treacle, mixed
- 7 tablespoons sunflower oil
- 4 oz/100 g light soft brown sugar
- 8 oz/225 g wholemeal flour
- ½ level teaspoon bicarbonate of soda
- ½ level teaspoon salt
- 3 level teaspoons ground ginger
- 1 egg

1. Pre-heat a cool oven (300°F/150°C/Gas 2). Grease a deep 7-inch/18-cm-square cake-tin. Line the base of the tin with greaseproof paper, then grease the paper.

2. Peel, core and slice the apples. Place in a medium-sized saucepan with 1 tablespoon water. Cook over a medium heat until the apples are soft and pulpy (about 8 minutes).

3. Place the apple purée in a measuring jug, to measure ¼ pint/150 ml; make up with milk if necessary.

4. Weigh the golden syrup and treacle carefully. Pour into a medium-sized saucepan and scrape off the scale pan with a spatula. Add the oil and brown sugar.

5. Heat gently for about 5 minutes until the sugar has dissolved; remove from the heat and leave to cool.

6. Sift the flour, bicarbonate of soda, salt and ginger into a bowl. Add the bran flakes that remain in the sieve. Make a well in the centre of the flour; add the melted ingredients, apple purée and egg. Mix with a wooden spoon for 1-2 minutes.

7. Pour the mixture into the tin. Bake in the centre of the oven for 70-75 minutes. Test by pressing with the fingers. If cooked, the cake should spring back and have begun to shrink from the sides of the tin. Leave to cool in the tin for 15 minutes. Loosen the edges with a round-ended knife, turn out the gingerbread and remove the paper; leave to cool completely on a wire rack.

Note Gingerbread improves with keeping. Store in a tin for up to one week.

Use unpeeled apples: just grate down to the cores. Replace the soft brown sugar with 2 oz/50 g fructose and add 6 tablespoons skimmed milk with the egg. Reduce the golden syrup mixture by 2 oz/50 g.
CHO: 22 g Calories: 150

Leave the skins on the apples and replace the flour with 4 oz/100 g potato flour and 4 oz/100 g ground rice.

No change necessary.

No change necessary.

Leave the skins on the apples and grate down to the cores. Add 3 oz/75 g dried figs, chopped.

No change necessary.

Cider Apple Cake

Makes about 30 slices: 280 calories per slice

1¼ lb/550 g sultanas
½ pint/275 ml sweet cider
1½ lb/675 g cooking apples
1 lb/450 g caster sugar
12 oz/350 g butter
4 eggs
1¼ lb/550 g plain flour
3 level teaspoons baking powder
2 level teaspoons ground coriander or mixed spice

1. Place the sultanas and cider in a basin, then cover with a plate and leave in a cool place overnight.
2. Pre-heat a moderate oven (350°F/180°C/Gas 4). Brush a large 5-pint/2.75-litre (12 × 10 inch/30 × 25 cm) roasting tin with a little melted fat. Line the base with greaseproof paper, then grease the paper.
3. Peel and core the apples; weigh 1 lb/450 g of the prepared apples and chop finely.
4. Cream the sugar and butter together in a bowl until light and fluffy. Beat the eggs and add them gradually, beating well after each addition.
5. Sift the flour, baking powder and coriander or mixed spice together on to a plate; add to the creamed mixture with the chopped apples, sultanas and any remaining cider. Mix well with a metal spoon. Turn the mixture into the prepared tin; level the top with the back of a metal spoon.
6. Bake in the centre of the oven for 1½-1¾ hours. Test by pressing with the fingers. If cooked, the cake should spring back and have begun to shrink from the sides of the tin. Leave to cool in the tin; turn out and remove the paper.

Replace ingredients as follows: 8 oz/225 g sultanas; 4 oz/100 g dried apricots, snipped; 2 oz/50 g natural bran; ¾ pint/425 ml dry cider; 1 lb/450 g prepared cooking apples; 4 oz/100 g fruit sugar; 2 oz/50 g soft brown sugar; 12 oz/350 g polyunsaturated margarine; 4 size 3 eggs; 8 oz/225 g fine wholemeal self-raising flour; 8 oz/225 g self-raising white flour; 2 teaspoons ground coriander or mixed spice; 4 oz/100 g ground almonds; 2 oz/50 g chopped walnuts. Prepare the recipe as above, adding the bran with the sultanas, apricots and cider.
CHO: 16 g Calories: 140

See the recipe for wholefood Dundee cake (page 220). Replace the unsweetened orange juice with cider.

Replace the butter with polyunsaturated margarine.

No change necessary.

Use wholemeal flour and add 4 tablespoons milk. Replace 4 oz/100 g sultanas with dried apricots, snipped into strips.

Replace the butter with vegetable margarine.

Ground Rice Cake

Makes 12 slices: 145 calories each

       4 oz/100 g polyunsaturated margarine
       4 oz/100 g caster sugar
       2 eggs
       ½ teaspoon vanilla essence
       3 oz/75 g ground rice
       1 oz/25 g self-raising flour
       large pinch of salt

1. Pre-heat a moderate oven (375°F/190°C/Gas 5). Brush a 7-inch/18-cm sandwich tin with melted fat and line the base and side with greaseproof paper; grease the paper.

2. Cream the butter or margarine and sugar together in a bowl until light and fluffy. Beat the eggs, 1 tablespoon water and vanilla essence together and add gradually, beating well after each addition. Fold in the ground rice, flour and salt with a metal spoon.

3. Spread the mixture evenly in the tin and level the top with the back of a spoon. Bake in the centre of the oven for 30 minutes.

4. Test by pressing with the fingers. If cooked, the cake should spring back, have begun to shrink from the side of the tin, and be golden brown. Leave in the tin until cold, then loosen the edges with a knife, turn out and remove the paper; store in an airtight container.

Note This cake will improve in flavour if stored for up to 4 weeks in an airtight container.

Use wholegrain ground rice and reduce the sugar to 3 oz/75 g.
CHO: 14 g Calories: 128

Replace the self-raising flour with Trufree no.7 self-raising flour.

No change necessary.

No change necessary.

Use wholegrain ground rice.

No change necessary.

Walnut and Cherry Loaf

Makes 10 slices: 205 calories each

    8 oz/225 g self-raising flour
    ½ level teaspoon salt
    2 oz/50 g walnuts
    2 oz/50 g glacé cherries
    1 oz/25 g light moist brown sugar
    1 oz/25 g polyunsaturated margarine
    1 rounded tablespoon pure malt extract
    1 egg
    6 tablespoons semi-skimmed milk

Topping:
    1 oz/25 g walnuts
    1 oz/25 g glacé cherries
    1 oz/25 g sugar
    1 tablespoon water

1. Pre-heat a cool oven (325°F/160°C/Gas 3). Grease a 1-lb/500-g loaf-tin.
2. Sift the flour and salt together. Roughly chop the walnuts and cherries.
3. Place the sugar, butter and malt in a saucepan and heat until the butter has melted.
4. Stir the dry ingredients into the pan with the cherries and walnuts, egg and milk; beat until well blended. Pour the mixture in to the tin.
5. Bake in the centre of the oven for 1 hour or until firm and well risen.
6. Remove from the tin and leave to cool on a wire rack.
7. To prepare the topping, halve the walnuts and cherries; place the sugar and water in a small saucepan and heat until the sugar has dissolved; boil quickly for 1 minute. Stir in the fruit and spread the topping over the centre of the loaf; leave to set. Serve with low-fat spread.

Replace the flour with self-raising wholemeal flour and add an extra 1 tablespoon milk. Omit the sugar and water from the topping. Sprinkle walnuts and cherries over the top before baking.
CHO: 26 g Calories: 195

Use 4 oz/100 g Trufree or Jubilee no.7 self-raising flour, 2 oz/50 g caster sugar, 2 oz/50 g soft margarine, 1 heaped teaspoon honey, 1 egg, 2 oz/50 g each of walnuts and glacé cherries and beat together. Bake in a moderate oven (375°F/190°C/Gas 5) for ½ hour, then lower the heat to 350°F/180°C/Gas 4 and cook for a further ½ hour.

Replace the butter with polyunsaturated margarine. Use skimmed milk.

No change necessary.

Replace the flour with self-raising wholemeal flour; add 2 oz/50 g each of chopped dried figs and apricots and an extra 2 tablespoons milk.

No change necessary.

Serves 12: 246 calories per slice

4 oz/100 g polyunsaturated margarine
2 oz/50 g soft dark brown sugar
1 level tablespoon black treacle
3 level tablespoons golden syrup
3 oz/75 g stoned dates
3 oz/75 g shelled almonds
5 fl oz/150 ml natural yoghurt
2 eggs
8 oz/225 g plain flour
1 level teaspoon mixed spice
½ level teaspoon bicarbonate of soda
icing sugar

1. Pre-heat a cool oven (300°F/150°C/Gas 2). Brush a 2-pint plain ring mould with soft margarine.
2. Place the margarine and brown sugar in a small saucepan. Measure the black treacle and golden syrup carefully, levelling off the spoon with a knife, and add to the saucepan. Stir over a moderate heat until the margarine has melted. Remove from the heat and allow to cool.
3. Coarsely chop the dates and almonds. Beat the yoghurt and eggs together. Sift the flour, spice and bicarbonate of soda into a bowl. Add the dates, almonds, melted mixture and yoghurt mixture; mix well with a wooden spoon.
4. Pour the mixture into the prepared mould and bake in the centre of the oven for 60-70 minutes. Test by pressing with the fingers. If cooked, the cake should spring back and have begun to shrink from the sides of the mould.
5. Allow to cool in the mould for 10 minutes. Invert on to a wire rack, remove the mould and leave to cool. Dust with icing sugar before serving.
Note This cake improves in flavour if kept for 2-3 days in a tin.

Replace the margarine with low-fat spread. Replace the sugar with 1 oz/25 g fructose; reduce the syrup to 1 tablespoon and the dates to 2 oz/50 g. Use low-fat yoghurt; replace half the flour (4 oz/100 g) with wholemeal flour and add 4 tablespoons skimmed milk. Omit the icing sugar for serving.
CHO: 2 g Calories: 127

Replace with gluten-free wholefood Dundee cake (see recipe, page 220), substituting yoghurt for 2½ fl oz/75 ml orange juice and dates for the mixed fruit.

No change necessary.

Use an additive-free brand of yoghurt or home-made yoghurt.

Replace half the flour with wholemeal flour and add 1 tablespoon milk. Leave the skins on the almonds.

No change necessary.

Queen Cakes

Makes 9 small cakes: 113 calories each

> 2 oz/50 g polyunsaturated margarine
> 2 oz/50 g caster sugar
> 1 egg
> 2 oz/50 g currants
> 3 oz/75 g self-raising flour
> 1 tablespoon milk

1. Pre-heat a moderately hot oven (400°F/200°C/Gas 6). Place 9 paper cases in tartlet tins (the deeper the tins, the better shaped the cakes will be).
2. Cream the margarine and sugar together until light and fluffy. Beat the egg and add, a little at a time, beating well after each addition. Mix in the currants.
3. Fold in the flour alternately with the milk.
4. Divide the mixture between the paper cases, taking care not to touch the edges of the cases with the mixture.
5. Bake just above the centre of the oven for 15-20 minutes, until risen and golden brown. Test by pressing with the fingers. If cooked, the cakes should spring back, and have begun to shrink from the sides of the paper cases. Remove from the tins and leave to cool on a wire rack.

Special Diets

Use wheatmeal (81% extraction) self-raising flour. Replace the caster sugar with 1 oz/25 g fructose. Replace the currants with walnuts.
CHO: 10 g Calories: 112

Follow the gluten-free Victoria sandwich recipe (see page 222), using a 4 oz/100 g quantity.

No change necessary.

No change necessary.

Use fine wholemeal self-raising flour.

No change necessary.

Yorkshire Cheese Tart

Special Diets

Serves 6: 276 calories per portion

Shortcrust pastry:
- 4 oz/100 g plain flour
- 1 oz/25 g cooking fat
- 1 oz/25 g polyunsaturated margarine
- cold water to mix

Filling:
- 8 oz/225 g cottage cheese
- 1 oz/25 g butter
- 2 oz/50 g caster sugar
- 1 egg
- grated rind of 1 lemon
- 1 oz/25 g currants
- grated nutmeg

1. Pre-heat a moderate oven (375°F/190°C/Gas 5).
2. Place the flour in a bowl. Add the fats, cut into small pieces, and rub in with the fingertips until the mixture resembles fine bread-crumbs. Add about 1 tablespoon cold water and mix with a fork to form a firm dough.
3. Turn out on to a floured board and knead lightly. Roll out the pastry and line a 7½-inch/19-cm pie-tin, turning the edge of the pastry under itself to make a double thickness; flute the edge.
4. Press the cottage cheese through a sieve on to a plate. Melt the butter in a small saucepan. Remove from the heat and stir in the sugar, egg, lemon rind, currants and cottage cheese. Mix well; turn into the pastry case. Sprinkle the mixture with a little grated nutmeg.
5. Bake in the centre of the oven for about 40 minutes, until the mixture is set. Serve warm or cold.

[d] Use wheatmeal (81% extraction) flour for the pastry. Replace the cooking fat and butter with polyunsaturated margarine. Omit the currants. Reduce the caster sugar to 1 oz/25 g. CHO: 19 g Calories: 235

[🔥] Use gluten-free shortcrust pastry (see recipe, page 217).

[💧] Use polyunsaturated margarine instead of cooking fat and butter.

[✏] No change necessary.

[🌰] Use wholemeal flour.

[🥄] Use vegetable margarine and cooking fat.

Date Teabread

Makes 2 loaves (15 slices each): 125 calories per slice

> 1 lb/500 g stoned dates
> 8 oz/225 g moist brown sugar
> ¾ pint/425 ml pint warm tea
> 1 egg
> 2 rounded tablespoons thick-cut marmalade
> 1 lb/450 g self-raising flour

1. Cut the dates into small pieces; place in a bowl. Add the sugar and ½ pint/275 ml warm tea; mix together. Leave to soak overnight.
2. Pre-heat a cool oven (325°F/160°C/Gas 3). Grease two 1-lb/450-g loaf-tins.
3. Stir the remaining ¼-pint/150 ml tea, the egg and marmalade into the date mixture; beat well. Add the flour: mix until well blended.
4. Divide the mixture between the tins; level the tops with the back of a spoon.
5. Bake in the centre of the oven for 1¼ hours, until well risen. Test by pressing with the fingers. If cooked, the loaves should spring back. Leave in the tins for 10 minutes; turn out and leave to cool on a wire rack. Serve thinly sliced and buttered.
Note The loaves will improve in flavour if stored for 2-3 weeks in an airtight tin.

Replace half the dates with chopped walnuts; use 3 oz/175 g fructose instead of sugar. Use reduced-sugar marmalade; use fine wholemeal self-raising flour and increase the tea by 2 tablespoons. Store for up to 1 week only.
CHO: 20 g Calories: 100

Replace the flour with Trufree no.7 self-raising flour.

No change necessary.

No change necessary.

Use fine wholemeal self-raising flour.

No change necessary.

 # Banana Butterfly Cakes

 ## Special Diets

Makes 9: 185 calories each

    2 oz/50 g polyunsaturated margarine
    2 oz/50 g caster sugar
    1 egg
    2 oz/50 g self-raising flour

Filling:

    1½ level tablespoons cornflour
    2 level tablespoons drinking chocolate
    ¼ pint/150 ml milk
    1 oz/25 g caster sugar
    1 ripe banana
    icing sugar

1. Pre-heat a moderate oven (350°F/180°C/Gas 4). Place 9 paper baking cases on a baking sheet.
2. Place all the cake ingredients in a mixing bowl; beat together with a wooden spoon for 1-2 minutes, until well blended.
3. Divide the mixture between the baking cases. Bake just above the centre of the oven for 10-15 minutes. Test by pressing with the fingers; if cooked, the cakes should spring back. Leave to cool on a wire rack.
4. To make the filling, place the cornflour and drinking chocolate in a small saucepan; gradually blend in the milk. Stir over a moderate heat until the mixture boils. Cook, stirring, for 2 minutes. Remove from the heat and beat until cool.
5. Cream the butter and sugar together until light and fluffy. Peel the banana and mash with a fork. Mix the banana into chocolate mixture.
6. Gradually add the chocolate mixture to the creamed butter and sugar, beating well after each addition. Leave in a cool place for 30 minutes.
7. Cut a thin slice from the top of each cake; pile the banana filling on each cake. Dust the cut slices of cake with icing sugar, cut each slice in half and place on each cake as 'wings'.

Not very suitable. Replace the sugar with 1 oz/25 g fructose and white flour with wheatmeal (81% extraction) self-raising flour. For the filling, replace the drinking chocolate with 1 tablespoon cocoa and replace the sugar with ½ oz/15 g fructose. Omit the icing sugar for dusting.
CHO: 17 g Calories: 155

Replace the self-raising flour with 2 oz/50 g Trufree or Jubilee no.7 and 1 tablespoon maize flour or gluten/wheat-free cornflour.

No change necessary.

No change necessary.

Replace the white self-raising flour with wheatmeal (81% extraction) self-raising flour.

No change necessary.

Christmas Cake

Special Diets

Makes 50 1-inch/2.5-cm pieces: 110 calories each

14 oz/400 g currants
7 oz/200 g sultanas
7 oz/200 g raisins
1½ oz/50 g shelled almonds
1½ oz/50 g citrus peel
3 oz/75 g glacé cherries
7 oz/200 g plain flour
½ level teaspoon mixed spice
3 large eggs
7 oz/200 g butter or margarine
7 oz/200 g soft brown sugar
grated rind and juice of 1 lemon
2 tablespoons sherry, rum or brandy (optional)

1. Pre-heat a moderately hot oven (400°F/200°C/Gas 6). Brush a deep, round 8-inch/20-cm cake-tin with melted fat and line the base and side with a double thickness of greaseproof paper; grease the paper. Cut a double strip of brown paper or newspaper, 1 inch/2.5 cm higher than the depth of the tin; wrap round the outside of the tin and secure with string.
2. Prepare the fruit (if not bought ready-cleaned, wash and spread out on a baking sheet to dry overnight); stone the raisins, if necessary. Place the almonds in a small saucepan, cover with water and bring to the boil; strain off the water and slip off the skins. Shred finely with a knife. Chop the citrus peel. Cut the cherries in halves. Sift the flour and mixed spice together. Beat the eggs together in a small basin. Cream the butter or margarine and sugar together in a large bowl, until light and fluffy.
3. Add the eggs, a little at a time, beating well after each addition; stir in the lemon rind.
4. Add the fruit, almonds and citrus peel and mix thoroughly. Stir in the flour and mixed spice; add the lemon juice. Mix well, then place in the tin, pressing the mixture down the side. Level the top with the back of a spoon.
5. Place the cake on a double sheet of brown paper on a baking sheet.

Replace the sugar with 4 oz/100 g fructose. Replace 8 oz/225 g currants with dried apricots. Reduce the sultanas and raisins by half. Use wholemeal flour. Use polyunsaturated margarine.
CHO: 12 g Calories: 87

See recipe for gluten-free Christmas cake, page 221.

Use polyunsaturated margarine.

Use cherries without added colouring.

Use wholemeal flour.

Use polyunsaturated margarine.

Reduce the oven heat to cool (325°F/170°C/Gas 3). Place the cake one shelf below the centre of the oven and bake for: (1st hour) 325°F/170°C/Gas 3; (2nd hour) 300°F/150°C/Gas 2; (3rd hour) 275°F/140°C/Gas 1; (4th hour) 250°F/130°C/Gas ½. If not sufficiently brown after 3 hours' cooking time, cook the cake for a 4th hour at 275°F/140°C/Gas 1. If the cake is sufficiently brown at the end of 3 hours' cooking time, place a sheet of brown paper over the top. Test to see if the cake is cooked at half-hourly intervals after 3 hours, by pressing with the fingers. If cooked, the cake should spring back, have stopped bubbling and have begun to shrink slightly from the side of the tin.

6. When cooked, remove the cake from the oven and leave to cool in the tin.

7. When quite cold, remove the cake from the tin and peel off the paper. To increase the keeping time of the cake and to ensure moistness, prick the cake on top with a skewer and spoon a little sherry, rum or brandy into the cake. Invert the cake and treat the base similarly. Wrap in foil; store the cake in a tin. Repeat the pricking and adding of spirits twice, at weekly intervals.

8. Decorate the cake, if desired.

Brazilian Biscuit Cake

Serves 16: 270 calories per slice

    3 level tablespoons golden syrup
    4 oz/100 g margarine
    6 oz/175 g unsalted butter
    7 oz/200 g plain chocolate
    6 oz/175 g glacé cherries, halved
    4 oz/100 g sultanas
    3 tablespoons dark rum, sherry or strong black coffee
    3 tablespoons hot water
    5 oz/125 g rich tea or Marie biscuits

1. Line a 7-inch/18-cm or 8-inch/20-cm round tin with foil.
2. Measure the syrup carefully, levelling the spoon with a knife and making sure there is none on the underside of the spoon; place in a saucepan with the margarine and butter. Break up the chocolate and add to the pan. Place the pan over a very low heat until the contents are melted.
3. Add the cherries to the pan with the sultanas.
4. Place the rum and water in a bowl. Break the biscuits into small pieces and add to the bowl; keep turning the biscuits over until the liquid has been absorbed. Stir the biscuits into the pan, then pour the mixture into the tin. When cool, chill until set.
5. Remove the cake from the tin; remove the foil. Keep the cake in the refrigerator until ready to serve.

Not suitable.

Replace the biscuits with home-made gluten/wheat-free biscuits (page 201).

Use 10 oz/275 g polyunsaturated margarine and home-made biscuits made with polyunsaturated margarine.

Use uncoloured cherries.

Use digestive biscuits (marginal increase).

Replace the butter with vegetable margarine.

Shortbread

Makes 16 pieces: 153 calories each

    3 oz/75 g caster sugar
    6 oz/175 g butter
    9 oz/250 g plain flour

1. Pre-heat a moderate oven (325°F/170°C/Gas 3).
2. Cream the sugar and butter and mix in the flour, or mix all the ingredients in a food processor or mixer.
3. Divide the mixture in two, roll out each to a 7-inch/18-cm circle, place on baking sheets and flute the edges with the fingers. Mark the centre with a 3-inch/7.5-cm cutter and prick towards the edge with a fork.
4. Bake in the centre of the oven until pale golden brown for about 35 minutes. Cut each into 8 while warm; store in a tin.

Alternatively, press all the mixture into a 7-inch/18-cm square tin and bake for about 40 minutes. Sprinkle with sugar and cut into bars while still warm.

Replace the caster sugar with 2 oz/ 50 g fructose and the plain flour with wholemeal flour.
CHO: 14 g Calories: 153

Replace the flour with half Trufree no.6 or a gluten-free flour and half ground rice.

Replace the butter with polyunsaturated margarine.

No change necessary.

Replace the plain flour with wholemeal flour. For extra fibre add up to 2 oz/50 g chopped nuts.

Replace the butter with vegetable oil or margarine.

Makes 12: 160 calories each

> 2 oz/50 g shelled walnuts
> 3 oz/75 g polyunsaturated margarine
> 2 level tablespoons clear honey
> 2 level tablespoons golden syrup
> 3 oz/75 g soft brown sugar
> 5 oz/125 g rolled (porridge) oats

1. Pre-heat a moderate oven (350°F/180°C/Gas 4). Grease a shallow 7-inch/18-cm square tin. Chop the walnuts.
2. Melt the margarine, honey and syrup in a medium-sized saucepan, but do not boil. Stir in the sugar and rolled oats.
3. Spread evenly in the tin and sprinkle with chopped walnuts. Press in lightly.
4. Bake in the centre of the oven for 25-30 minutes, until golden brown and bubbling.
5. Remove from the oven; leave to cool for 5 minutes, then cut into 12 bars. Leave in the tin until cold.

Use 2 oz/50 g walnuts, 4 oz/100 g margarine, no honey, 1 level tablespoon golden syrup or black treacle, 2 oz/50 g fructose and 6 oz/175 g rolled oats.
CHO: 16 g Calories: 175

Replace the oats with 2 oz/50 g mixed chopped nuts, 2 oz/50 g desiccated coconut and 1 oz/25 g each of sunflower seeds and sesame seeds, 1 oz/25 g soya flour, 2 oz/50 g ground almonds, 2 oz/50 g ground rice.

Use polyunsaturated margarine.

No change necessary.

Add 1 oz/25 g oat bran.

No change necessary.

Iced Biscuit Gems

Makes about 35: 100 calories each

Basic biscuit mixture:

       6 oz/175 g polyunsaturated margarine
       6 oz/175 g caster sugar
       1 teaspoon vanilla essence
       2 tablespoons semi-skimmed milk
       10 oz/275 g plain flour
       2 oz/50 g cornflour
       1 level teaspoon baking powder

       For decoration, see method

1. Pre-heat a moderately hot oven (400°F/200°C/Gas 6). Grease two baking sheets.
2. Cream the margarine and sugar together. Stir in the remaining ingredients, then knead until the mixture is smooth.
3. Roll out thinly, cut into 2-inch/5-cm squares, 2 × 1 inch/5 × 2.5 cm oblongs and 2½-inch/6-cm diamonds, cut some 2½-inch/6-cm and 2-inch/5-cm rounds (cut ¾-inch/2-cm rounds from the centre of some of the 2-inch/5-cm rounds).
4. Place the biscuits on the baking sheets and bake in the centre of the oven until pale golden brown (about 8 minutes). Leave to cool on a wire rack.
5. To decorate, sandwich the oblongs and diamonds with chocolate spread or coffee butter icing; decorate with white glacé icing or coffee butter icing and walnuts or chocolate vermicelli. Ice 2½-inch/6-cm rounds with pink glacé icing; top with glacé cherries. Sandwich some whole 2-inch/5-cm rounds with jam, decorate with white glacé icing and glacé cherries. Spread other whole 2-inch/5-cm rounds with red or green jam or lemon curd; place the cut rings on top.

Special Diets

Use wheatmeal flour (81% extraction) and add 2 tablespoons extra milk. Reduce the sugar to 4 oz/100 g. Omit the sweet icings and jam. Before baking, brush some with egg or milk and dip in rolled oats or chopped nuts. May be flavoured with grated rind of an orange or lemon, 1 teaspoon ground cinnamon or 1 tablespoon instant coffee.
CHO: 10 Calories: 80

Replace the biscuit mixture with gluten-free biscuit mix (see recipe, page 201).

Use polyunsaturated margarine in both the biscuits and the icings.

Use uncoloured glacé cherries. Paint the pink colouring lightly on to the biscuits instead of adding it to the icing.

Use wheatmeal flour and add 2 tablespoons extra milk. Use chopped nuts for decoration.

No change necessary.

Wholemeal Crunchies

Makes about 14: 90 calories each

> 5 oz/150 g wholemeal flour
> ¼ level teaspoon salt
> ½ level teaspoon baking powder
> 1 oz/25 g caster sugar
> 3 oz/75 g butter
> 1 egg

1. Pre-heat a moderate oven (350°F/180°C/Gas 4). Lightly dust two baking sheets with flour.
2. Place all the dry ingredients in a bowl; add the butter, cut into small pieces, and rub in with the fingertips, or mix by machine until the mixture resembles fine breadcrumbs.
3. Add the egg and mix with a fork. When the mixture holds together place on a floured surface and knead lightly until smooth. Cover and leave for 10-15 minutes. Roll out the mixture thinly and cut out biscuits with a 2½-inch/6-cm plain cutter. Place on the prepared baking sheets. Gather up the trimmings, re-roll and cut out to make more biscuits.
4. Bake in the centre and just above the centre of the oven for 15-20 minutes until the biscuits are lightly browned and firm to the touch.
5. Using a palette knife, place the biscuits on a cooling rack. When cold, store in an airtight container.

Replace the butter with polyunsaturated margarine.
CHO: 9 g Calories: 90

Replace the wholemeal flour with 2 oz/50 g each of Trufree or Jubilee no.7 self-raising flour and no.6 plain flour. Add 1 level tablespoon rice bran, a pinch each of salt and powdered cinnamon and 1 oz/25 g soft brown sugar. Rub in 1 oz/25 g soft margarine and bind with half a beaten egg mixed with 6 drops lemon juice.

Replace the butter with polyunsaturated margarine.

No change necessary.

No change necessary.

Replace the butter with polyunsaturated margarine.

204

Coconut Squares

Makes about 36: 65 calories per square

4 oz/100 g polyunsaturated margarine
4 oz/100 g caster sugar
4 oz/100 g plain flour
1 level teaspoon baking powder
4 oz/100 g desiccated coconut
a few glacé cherries

1. Pre-heat a moderate oven (350°F/180°C/Gas 4). Grease three baking sheets.
2. Cream the margarine and sugar together until light and fluffy. Sift the flour and baking powder together and add, with the coconut, to the creamed mixture. Knead with the hands until well mixed. Turn out on to a floured board.
3. Roll out to ¼ inch/6 mm thickness. Cut into 1½-inch/4-cm squares and place on the baking sheets; prick well. Re-roll any trimmings.
4. Cut the glacé cherries into small pieces and place a small piece in the centre of each biscuit. Bake for 10-15 minutes, until light golden brown. Cool on a wire rack.

Special Diets

Use wholemeal flour. Replace the caster sugar with 3 oz/75 g fructose, add 2 tablespoons skimmed milk and decorate with 1 oz/25 g flaked almonds instead of cherries.
CHO: 5 g Calories: 65

Use Trufree or Jubilee no.7 self-raising flour, omit the baking powder and add an egg white or half an egg to bind. Check that the coconut is flour-free.

No change necessary.

Use chocolate buttons instead of cherries to decorate (place on biscuits on removal from oven).

Use wheatmeal (81% extraction) flour and add 2 tablespoons semi-skimmed milk.

No change necessary.

Honey Nut Cookies

Makes 18 cookies: 70 calories each

    1 oz/25 g plain chocolate
    1 oz/25 g polyunsaturated margarine
    1 level tablespoon thick honey
    1 egg, beaten
    2 oz/50 g caster sugar
    3 oz/75 g wheatmeal 81% extraction flour
    2 oz/50 g walnuts, finely chopped

1. Pre-heat a moderate oven (350°F/180°C/Gas 4). Grease three baking sheets.
2. Break the chocolate into small pieces and place in a large basin over a saucepan of hot water. Add the margarine and honey and leave until the chocolate has melted.
3. Remove from the heat and leave to cool slightly. Add the egg and stir into the mixture with the sugar, flour and nuts.
4. Drop the mixture in small spoonfuls on to baking sheets, leaving room for spreading.
5. Bake for 12-15 minutes until slightly risen and brown at the edges; leave for 1 minute on the baking sheets, then transfer to a cooling rack.

Use diabetic chocolate. Replace the caster sugar with 1 oz/25 g fructose and the flour with wholemeal.
CHO: 6 g Calories: 65

Replace the flour with 2 oz/50 g ground rice and 1 oz/25 g ground almonds.

No change necessary.

No change necessary.

Use wholemeal flour and increase the walnuts to 3 oz/75 g.

No change necessary.

Crunchy Choc Fingers

Makes 15: 150 calories each

4 oz/100 g plain chocolate
2 oz/50 g glacé cherries
2 oz/50 g sultanas
2 oz/50 g blanched almonds
2 oz/50 g polyunsaturated margarine
4 oz/100 g caster sugar
1 egg
2 oz/50 g high-protein cereal

1. Pre-heat a moderate oven (350°F/180°C/Gas 4). Lightly grease a shallow 7-inch/18/cm-square tin.
2. Break up the chocolate and place in a dry basin over a saucepan of hot, but not boiling, water; stir until the chocolate has melted. Remove the bowl from the pan and spread the chocolate evenly over the base of the tin. Leave in a cool place until the chocolate has hardened.
3. Wash the sugar off the cherries; dry on kitchen paper. Chop the cherries, sultanas and almonds.
4. Cream the margarine and sugar together until light and fluffy. Beat the egg and add gradually, beating well.
5. Stir in the cherries, sultanas, almonds and high-protein cereal. Spread the mixture over the chocolate in the tin.
6. Bake in the centre of the oven for 30-35 minutes until golden brown. Remove from oven and leave in the tin until completely cold.
7. Using a round-ended knife, loosen the mixture from the sides of the tin. Cut into 5 bars; cut each bar into three 'fingers'.

Not very suitable. Replace the chocolate with diabetic chocolate. Replace the cherries with sliced dried apricots; reduce the sugar to 3 oz/75 g and use bran flakes. Cut into 18 pieces.
CHO: 17 g Calories: 140

Use good-quality dessert chocolate and replace the high-protein cereal with rice krispies.

No change necessary.

No change necessary.

Use bran flakes instead of high-protein cereal.

No change necessary.

207

Caribbean Squares

Makes 24 squares: 110 calories each

Filling:

4 oz/100 g dried figs
4 oz/100 g dried apricots
2 oz/50 g caster sugar
2 oz/50 g plain cake crumbs
1 lemon
2 bananas

Cake:

7 oz/200 g wheatmeal (81% extraction) flour
1½ level teaspoons baking powder
1 oz/25 g cornflour
4 oz/100 g polyunsaturated margarine
2 oz/50 g caster sugar
1 egg
1 tablespoon semi-skimmed milk
a few flaked almonds
icing sugar

1. Place the figs, apricots and 1 pint (500 ml) cold water in a saucepan. Bring slowly to the boil; reduce the heat, cover and simmer for 20 minutes. Remove from the heat and leave the fruit in the water until cold. Drain the fruit and chop; mix with the sugar and cake crumbs.

2. Scrub the lemon; grate the rind and add to the fruit mixture. Squeeze the juice and place in a small basin. Peel the bananas, chop and add to the lemon juice; mash with a fork. Mix the bananas into the fruit.

3. Pre-heat a moderately hot oven (375°F/190°C/Gas 5). Draw round the base of a 7 × 10 × 1 inch/18 × 25 × 12.5 cm tin on greaseproof paper. Cut paper 1½ inches/4 cm out from the line; crease the paper on the line. Grease the tin, press the paper down into the tin and grease the paper.

4. Place the flour, baking powder and cornflour in a bowl. Add the margarine, cut into small pieces; rub in with the fingertips until the mixture resembles fine breadcrumbs. Add the sugar and mix to a soft

Omit the sugar from the fruit mixture and replace the cake crumbs with wholemeal breadcrumbs.
CHO: 15 g Calories: 110

Replace the plain cake crumbs with crumbs from a gluten-free cake or cooked brown rice. For the cake mixture, cream 4 oz/100 g soft margarine with 6 oz/150 g moist brown sugar. Beat in 1 egg and ½ teaspoon almond flavouring and 9 oz/250 g Trufree or Jubilee no.7 self-raising flour. Roll between two sheets of non-stick baking parchment.

No change necessary.

No change necessary.

No change necessary.

No change necessary.

dough with the egg and milk. Place the dough on a lightly floured surface and knead until smooth.

5. Divide the mixture in two, roll one half and fit the tin. Support the dough over a rolling-pin and lift on to the base of the prepared tin; ease the dough into corners where necessary. Spread the fruit mixture evenly over the dough.

6. Roll out the remaining dough to an oblong about 6 × 9 inches/ 15 × 23 cm. Using a 1½-inch/4-cm fluted cutter, cut out 24 circles, kneading and re-rolling scraps as necessary. Place the circles side by side over the fruit, fitting four widthwise and six lengthwise to cover the filling.

7. Crush the almonds in the hands and sprinkle a few in the centre of each circle, pressing in lightly. Bake just above the centre of the oven for 35-40 minutes until lightly browned. Leave to cool in the tin, then invert on to a cooling rack; peel off the paper. Turn the cake back on to a large plate or board and sprinkle lightly with icing sugar. Cut into squares to serve. Caribbean squares will keep for several days in the refrigerator. Keep whole or cut in half for freezing. They are particularly good if re-heated and served with custard or cream for dessert.

Gingernuts

Special Diets

Makes about 36: 58 calories each

>   8 oz/225 g self-raising flour
>   pinch of salt
>   2 level teaspoons ground ginger
>   1 level teaspoon bicarbonate of soda
>   4 oz/100 g caster sugar
>   1 egg
>   2 level tablespoons golden syrup
>   2 level tablespoons black treacle
>   3 oz/75 g polyunsaturated margarine

1. Pre-heat a cool oven (325°F/170°C/Gas 3). Lightly grease two baking sheets.
2. Sift the flour, salt, ginger and bicarbonate of soda into a bowl; add the sugar. Beat the egg.
3. Measure the golden syrup and black treacle carefully into a medium-sized pan, levelling off the spoon with a knife and making sure that there is none on the underside of the spoon. Add the margarine and heat until melted. Remove from the heat. Gradually stir in the flour mixture and the egg. Mix well.
4. Leave the mixture to cool slightly. Form 24 heaped teaspoonsful of the mixture into balls. Place 12, a little apart to allow for spreading, on each baking sheet.
5. Bake near the centre of the oven for 15-20 minutes, until golden brown. Leave to cool on baking sheets for a few minutes, then remove and leave to cool completely on a wire rack. Repeat with the remaining mixture. Store in a tin.
Note Add 1 oz/25 g chopped walnuts, 2 oz/50 g sultanas or 2 oz/50 g chopped glacé cherries with the flour and egg to the melted mixture, if desired.

Not very suitable. Use wholemeal self-raising flour, replace the sugar with 3 oz/75 g fructose. Make smaller biscuits – 48 from this quantity. CHO: 5 g Calories: 40

Replace the flour with Trufree no.7 self-raising flour.

No change necessary.

No change necessary.

Use wholemeal flour and add 2 oz/ 50 g chopped walnuts.

Use vegetable margarine.

Ice-box Cheese Biscuits

Makes about 24: 26 calories each

> 8 oz/225 g margarine
> 6 oz/175 g Cheddar cheese, finely grated
> 1 egg
> 10 oz/275 g plain flour
> 4 oz/100 g cornflour
> 1 level teaspoon dry mustard
> 1 level teaspoon salt
> ¼ level teaspoon pepper

1. Cream the margarine and cheese together until light. Beat the egg and add gradually, beating well after each addition. Mix in the remaining ingredients.
2. Divide the dough into 6 equal pieces. If desired, knead one of the following into each piece: 1 level teaspoon poppy seeds; 1 level teaspoon caraway seeds; 1 level teaspoon paprika; 1 level teaspoon curry powder; ½ level teaspoon celery salt; ½ level teaspoon onion salt.
3. Form each piece of flavoured dough into a roll 6 inches/15 cm long. Wrap each roll in plastic clingwrap film. Place the rolls in a freezer bag and leave in the freezer section of the refrigerator.
4. Pre-heat a moderately hot oven (400°F/200°C/Gas 6). Grease two baking sheets. Remove the rolls from the freezer, unwrap and leave to thaw at room temperature, until they can be sliced. Cut off the required number of ¼-inch/0.5-cm slices from each roll and place on the baking sheets. (Re-wrap the remainder of the rolls and return to the freezer.) Cook the biscuits in the centre and just above the centre of the oven until pale golden brown (about 10 minutes). Leave to cool on a wire rack.

Replace 6 oz/175 g plain flour with wholemeal flour. Use low-fat hard cheese and add 1-2 tablespoons water to bind.
CHO: 2.5 g Calories: 24

Replace the flour and cornflour with Trufree or Jubilee no.6 plain flour. Use 3 oz/75 g soft margarine and 3 oz/75 g finely grated Cheddar cheese. Flavour as above but check that the celery salt, mustard and curry powder do not contain starch.

Use polyunsaturated margarine and 4 oz/100 g low-fat hard cheese.

Omit the onion salt if it contains MSG and use mixed herbs instead.

Replace 6 oz/175 g plain flour with wholemeal flour. Sprinkle the work surface with wheat or oat bran instead of flour before rolling.

Use vegetable margarine and vegetarian cheese.

Gluten-free Basic Recipes

These recipes are only for the gluten/wheat-free diet. They demonstrate the different procedures necessary for the flour-based staples such as bread, pastry and pasta which anyone catering for someone on this particular diet will find invaluable. Also included are some basic cake recipes, for Victoria sponge, Dundee and Christmas cake.

Gluten-free Basic White Bread

10 oz/275 g Trufree or Jubilee no.4 white flour
¼ oz/7 g instant yeast
5 fl oz/150 ml warm water
1 oz/25 g margarine
3 pinches salt
1 heaped teaspoon sugar

1. Pre-heat a hot oven (425°F/220°C/Gas 7).
2. Put the flour, yeast, salt and sugar into a bowl. Mix well and add the margarine. Rub in with the fingers. Now pour in the warm water and mix to a sticky dough. Knead without adding any more flour. If the dough is too stiff add another tablespoon warm water. Take out of the bowl as soon as it makes one ball and knead on a cool worktop. You should have a smooth, shiny dough after a couple of minutes' kneading.
3. Shape as required; leave in a warm place to rise. Bake and remove from the trays as soon as the bread is taken out of the oven. Cool on a wire rack.
Note This dough can be used for rolls, croissants, breadsticks, plaits, French sticks, pizza bases, etc.

Pizza with a Gluten-free Scone Base

2 oz/50 g Trufree or Jubilee no.4 white flour
3 pinches salt
½ oz/15 g margarine
1½ tablespoons water

1. Pre-heat a hot oven (425°F/220°C/Gas 7). Grease a baking sheet.
2. Put the flour into a bowl with the salt and mix. Rub in the margarine and add the water. Mix and knead to a soft dough, using a little more flour.
3. Put on a baking sheet and roll or press out to a flat circle about ¼ inch/1 cm thick. Brush with oil and cover with slices of tomato and grated cheese. Season to taste with salt and freshly ground black pepper.
4. Bake and serve still warm from the oven.

Gluten-free Pasta

8 oz/225 g Trufree or Jubilee no.4 flour
2 tablespoons oil such as sunflower oil
3 tablespoons cold water
3 pinches salt
1 egg, beaten

1. Put the flour and salt into a bowl and mix. Add the 2 tablespoons oil and rub in.
2. Put in the egg and mix. Lastly, add the water and mix again to a sticky paste. Knead, adding a small quantity of extra flour if necessary. Take out of the bowl and knead on a cool worktop until smooth. Divide the dough into 4 portions. Roll out each portion as thin as possible on a floured surface.
3. Cut into strips about ¼ inch/4 mm across and drop into plenty of boiling salted water. Cook half the total quantity at a time steadily for about 12 minutes and taste: it should be '*al dente*', that is, tender but still firm.
4. Drain in a colander and serve with bolognese sauce.
Note Cooked pasta will keep overnight in the refrigerator and can be warmed up, in a sauce, the following day. Alternatively use the flat sheets of pasta to make cannelloni. Cut into 3 × 4-inch/7.5 × 10-cm pieces.

Gluten-free Shortcrust Pastry

8 oz/225 g Trufree or Jubilee no.6 plain flour
2 pinches salt
3 oz/75 g soft margarine
5 tablespoons cold water

1. Pre-heat a hot oven (425°F/220°C/Gas 7).
2. Mix the flour with the salt in a mixing bowl. Rub in the margarine until the mixture resembles breadcrumbs. Add the water and mix to a sticky paste. (The water releases the binder from the flour.)
3. Knead gradually, adding only a very small amount of extra flour, until one ball of dough has formed and the bowl is clean.
4. Roll out between sheets of greaseproof paper or silicone paper.
5. Peel off the top paper. To use as a piecrust, turn the pastry upside down over the dish, allowing the backing sheet to peel off. Trim off any excess with a knife and press together any breaks. Then roll out the pastry lid in the same way and drop on to the filled pie.
6. Bake for about 20 minutes.

Gluten-free Choux Pastry

4 oz/100 g Trufree or Jubilee no.7 self-raising flour
¼ pint/150 ml water
½ teaspoon sugar
1 oz/25 g margarine
4 teaspoons cooking oil
2 eggs, beaten

1. Pre-heat a moderately hot oven (400°F/200°C/Gas 6). Grease and flour a baking sheet.
2. Put the water, sugar, margarine and oil into a saucepan. Bring to the boil, remove from the heat and add the flour. Stir well over a medium heat until it forms one ball of dough.
3. Remove from the heat and gradually beat in the eggs to form a tough elastic dough.
4. Put the dough on to the baking sheet in small balls for profiteroles or oblong shapes for eclairs.
5. Bake to a golden colour. Remove from the baking sheets with a spatula and cool on a wire rack.
6. Cut open the pastries after a couple of minutes and remove any uncooked dough with a teaspoon.
7. Use only when absolutely cold. Eat on the day of baking.

Gluten-free Basic Sweet Buns

10 oz/275 g Trufree or Jubilee no.4 white flour
¼ oz instant yeast
2 oz/50 g sugar
3 pinches salt
fruit and flavouring of choice
2 oz/50 g margarine
5 fl oz warm water

1. Pre-heat a hot oven (425°F/220°C/Gas 7). Grease a baking sheet.
2. Put the flour, yeast, sugar and salt in a bowl. Add the spice (if using) and mix well.
3. Rub in the margarine. Add the appropriate fruit and the warm water. Mix with a wooden spoon to a sticky paste. Wet the hands and divide the dough into equal portions according to the recipe chosen.
4. Roll into balls, without using more flour; flatten slightly and place on a greased baking sheet.
5. Leave to rise in a warm place. When doubled in size bake until golden brown.
6. Cool on a wire rack. Serve warm, freshly baked, or split and toasted with butter.
Note This dough can be used for bath buns, currant buns, etc.

Gluten-free Wholefood Dundee Cake

¼ pint/150 ml unsweetened orange juice
2 tablespoons brown sugar
¼ oz/7 g dried active yeast
3 tablespoons sunflower oil
3 oz/75 g eating apple, washed and cut into pieces but not peeled or cored
1½ oz/40 g fresh carrot, scrubbed and sliced
8 oz/225 g dried mixed fruit
grated rind of 1 orange or lemon
1 oz/25 g soya flour
4½ oz/120 g ground rice, preferably brown
½ oz/15 g yellow split-pea flour
2 oz/50 g ground almonds
split almonds

1. Pre-heat a moderate oven (350°F/180°C/Gas 4). Grease a 7-inch/18-cm cake-tin.
2. Warm the fruit juice and pour into a liquidizer goblet. Sprinkle in the dried yeast and leave to soften for a few minutes.
3. Put the oil into a mixing bowl and add the dried ingredients. Add the rind.
4. Put the apple and carrot pieces into the liquidizer with the juice and yeast. Blend and pour over the mixture in the bowl.
5. Mix and then spoon into the tin, flatten and decorate neatly with split almonds.
6. Bake on the top shelf of the oven for about 1 hour. Leave to cool in the tin for ½ hour.
7. Take out of the tin and finish cooling on a wire rack.
Note Keep in an airtight container and consume within 8-10 days.

Although this may seem a strange recipe the end result is very like a traditional Dundee cake, rich and moist, with a high nutritional value.

Gluten-free Christmas Cake

8 oz/225 g Trufree or Jubilee no.7 self-raising flour
¼ level teaspoon salt
1 level teaspoon cinnamon
1 heaped teaspoon mixed spice (gluten/wheat-free)
2 oz/50 g ground almonds
4 oz/100 g brown sugar
6 oz/175 g soft margarine
2 generous teaspoons black treacle
3 eggs
2 tablespoons sherry
1 lb/450 g dried mixed fruit
2 oz/50 g raisins
2 oz/50 g glacé cherries
grated rind of 1 lemon

1. Pre-heat a moderate oven (325°F/160°C/Gas 3). Line a 8-9-inch/20-23-cm cake-tin with greased greaseproof paper.
2. Mix the flour, salt, spices and ground almonds together.
3. Cream the sugar, margarine and treacle.
4. Beat the eggs with the sherry and add, alternating with the flour, to the margarine mixture.
5. Stir in all the fruit and lemon rind.
6. Put the cake mixture into the tin and flatten with a knife.
7. Bake on the middle shelf of the oven for 1¼ hours and then lower the heat to 300°F/150°C/Gas 2 to cook the centre.
8. Cool in the tin for several hours.

Gluten-free Victoria Sponge

8 oz/225 g caster sugar
8 oz/225 g soft margarine
4 eggs
8 oz/225 g Trufree or Jubilee no.7 self-raising flour
2 oz/50 g gluten-free maize flour or gluten-free cornflour
jam
icing sugar

1. Pre-heat a moderate oven (375°F/190°C/Gas 5).
2. Grease and flour the edges of two 8-inch/20-cm sponge tins. Cut out two circles of greaseproof paper to fit the bottoms. Grease and fit into the tins.
3. Put all the ingredients into a mixing bowl. Mix and beat until soft and creamy.
4. Spread evenly into the two prepared tins and bake.
5. When ready the sponges should spring back when pressed lightly. Leave for a minute or two in the tins.
6. Turn out, upside down, on to a wire rack to cool.
7. Peel off the greaseproof paper and leave the cakes to get cold. Sandwich together with jam and dust the top with icing sugar.

Gluten-free Baking Powder

2 oz/50 g cream of tartar
2 oz/50 g tartaric acid
3½ oz/90 g bicarbonate of soda
3 oz/75 g maize flour or cornflour

1. Sift together thoroughly about three times.
2. Store in an airtight container.
3. Use as for ordinary baking powder, adding 1 teaspoon/5 ml to each 2 oz/50 g gluten-free flour; sift well together.

About the author

Pam Dotter, FIHEc, was the first cookery editor of the magazine *Family Circle*, a position she occupied for nineteen years. During that period she also edited ten *Family Circle* cookbooks and wrote two books, *Preserving Food* (1976) and *Freezing* (1977), in the Macdonald Guidelines series as well as *Cake Icing and Decorating* (1978) for the St Michael Cookery Library and, with Peter Seabrook as co-author, *Good Food Gardening* (1983) for Hamish Hamilton. Among her other publications is *Miniature Cakes, Pastries and Desserts* (1986, Pelham). She has served as a panellist at various conferences on nutrition and has a particular interest in the concept of treating illnesses with food instead of drugs. She lives in Bromley, Kent.